ıce Praise for *Peaceful and Violent Origins of Voting Rights*

ɛxcellent book, well written and researched, it will be the 'go to' book :ion reforms of 1832 for the next several decades. The authors depart sual histories of this period leading up to the reform, both by their ed historical accounts of voting methods and rights both inside and rliament, and by their use of statistical techniques to demonstrate :onclusions are more than historical intuitions."

–Roger Congleton, West Virginia University, and author of *Perfecting Parliament*

ıterdisciplinary research at its very best: economics, political science, ry analyzed by cliometric methods, and carefully explained. It deals :omplex political events in connection with the start of democratiza- ngland almost 200 years ago and shows how economic and political ıteracted. Each step in the process is demonstrated by carefully col- ıta analyzed by solid econometric methods, by two researchers who strong theorists. It should be of great interest to many."

in Paldam, Aarhus University, Denmark, and author of *The Grand Pattern of Development and the Transition of Institutions*

ıid pre-modern elites across Europe share their power? This hallmark ɔcuses on a canonical case—the UK's 1832 Great Reform Act. Aidt and highlight the role of revolutionary unrest. The book stands out for its ıt synthesis of historical analysis and rigorous, quantitative insight into lti-causal nature of democratisation."

–Hans-Joachim Voth, University of Zurich

Peaceful and Violent Origins of Voting Rights

Peaceful and Violent Origins of Voting Rights

A Political Economy Analysis of the Great Reform Act of 1832

TOKE S. AIDT
RAPHAËL FRANCK

OXFORD
UNIVERSITY PRESS

OXFORD
UNIVERSITY PRESS

Oxford University Press is a department of the University of Oxford.
It furthers the University's objective of excellence in research, scholarship,
and education by publishing worldwide. Oxford is a registered trade mark of
Oxford University Press in the UK and in certain other countries.

Published in the United States of America by Oxford University Press
198 Madison Avenue, New York, NY 10016, United States of America.

CIP data is on file at the Library of Congress

ISBN 9780197679715

DOI: 10.1093/9780197679746.001.0001

Printed by Marquis, Canada

MIX
Paper | Supporting responsible forestry
FSC® C103567
FSC www.fsc.org

To Sven, Kirsten, Freya, and Vania, from T.S.A.

To Ilana, Meirav, Nili, and Uriyah, from R.F.

Preface

This book is the outcome of a longstanding research agenda that we embarked upon in 2006. We did not set out to write a book but were driven by a general curiosity to better understand what caused nineteenth-century Western elites to democratise, often in small steps. The early 2000s were rich with new theoretical works on the question. Daron Acemoglu and James Robinson's seminal paper 'Why did the West extend the franchise?' (Acemoglu and Robinson 2000*b*) and their book *Economic Origins of Dictatorship and Democracy* (Acemoglu and Robinson 2006) placed the threat of revolution theory firmly at the centre of the stage. This theory was, however, quickly challenged by competing theories of franchise extension developed by Lizzeri and Persico (2004) and Llavador and Oxoby (2005), as well as by Roger Congleton's work on constitutional bargaining (Congleton 2007), that emphasised the economic and political benefits accruing to the ruling elite under more democratic institutions. The accompanying evidence for these theories were rich case studies of reforms in the United Kingdom, Germany, and elsewhere. However, both empirical tests of the competing theories and attempts at isolating causal mechanisms were missing. We wanted to engage with this gap and soon realised that the University Library in Cambridge had volumes upon volumes of detailed micro-political data related to the British Reform Bills, information that could be employed to make headway in distinguishing between the different theories and to isolate causal mechanisms. The material collected in this book is the result of this endeavour. Some of it has been published in academic journals in economics and political science (*British Journal of Political Science*, *Econometrica*, *Journal of Economic History*, *Journal of Politics*, and *Public Choice*) but has been substantially rewritten for the book, while other parts are new.

The empirical analysis at the core of the book is based on a large micro-political database what we have put together from a combination of primary and secondary sources over more than fifteen years. We are grateful to John Bohstedt and Andrew Reeves for sharing their data with us and to Chris Tilly who kindly helped us track down a copy of the complete database (constructed by Takeshi Wada) with all of Charles Tilly's data on contentious gatherings in Britain. We are also grateful to the Cambridge Group for the History of Population and Social Structure and the Economics and Social Research Council (Grant RES-000-23-1579) for helping us with shape files for the maps of the ancient counties and parishes as well as to Charlotte Ellis, Roni Lavi and Carles Vila Martinez who spent hours inputting and organising data. We thank Sarah Jones for letting us use the Geographic Information System (GIS) of Greenwood's 1830 map of London constructed by the Layers of London project. Readers interested in the underlying data material can access the datasets used in Chapter 5 and Chapter 7 from the Inter-university Consortium for Political and Social Research[1] and the data used in Chapter 6 from the Econometric Society.[2]

The research that underpins the book was supported by grants from the British Academy/Leverhulme (SG121870), the People Programme (Marie Curie Actions) of the European Union's Seventh Framework Programme (FP 2007-2013) under REA grant agreement PIOF-GA-2012-327760 (TCDOFT), the Adar Foundation of the Department of Economics at Bar Ilan University, and the Israel Science Foundation (grant No. 1128/22).

A large number of people have helped and advised us over the years. The preliminary work for Chapter 6 related to the Swing riots and 1831 General Election was conducted while Aidt visited the Institute for Quantitative Social Science at Harvard University and Franck visited the Department of Economics at Brown University, and we benefited immensely from advice and encouragement from Daron Acemoglu, Oded Galor, Stelios Michalopoulos, and James Robinson. In equal measure, we have over the years benefited from many discussions with Roger Congleton and Martin Paldam on the general topic of democratisation and from the invaluable support from Gabriel Leon-Ablan and Peter S. Jensen, with whom we have worked on related research. We are also grateful to Omar Al-Ubaydli, Gerda Asmus, Jordi Blanes i Vidal, Richard Bluhm, Dan Bogart, Ekaterina Borisova, Ann Carlos, Bruno Caprettini, Samuele Centorrino, Kenneth Chay, Michael Dorsch, Mark Gradstein, Noel D. Johnson, Pierre-Guillaume Méon, Marc Klemp, Esteban Klor, Masao Ogaki, Hans Pitlik, Mathias Thoenig, David Samuels, Max Satchell, and Hans-Joachim Voth for their constructive input to the project. We would also like to thank Todd Elder and Olmo Silva for sharing their computer code with us.

Finally, we have been fortunate to receive support from our Oxford University Press editor, James Cook, throughout the writing of the book.

[1] Chapter 5: https://doi.org/10.3886/E108281V2; Chapter 7: https://doi.org/10.3886/E193941V1.

[2] Chapter 6: https://www.econometricsociety.org/publications/econometrica/2015/03/01/democratization-under-threat-revolution-evidence-great-reform (accessed 20 September 2023).

Contents

List of Figures xiv
List of Tables xv

PART I. MAIN IDEAS

1. Introduction and overview 3
 1.1 The idea 3
 1.2 Setting the stage: dramatis personae, scene, and plot 7
  1.2.1 Dramatis personae 7
  1.2.2 Scene 8
  1.2.3 Plot 9
 1.3 Overview of the book 10

2. Democratisation and franchise extension: the literature 17
 2.1 Introduction 17
 2.2 Bottom-up theories of democratisation 18
  2.2.1 The threat of revolution hypothesis 18
  2.2.2 The social movement hypothesis 20
 2.3 Top-down theories of democratisation and the political expedience hypothesis 23
  2.3.1 Pareto-improving extension of the franchise 23
  2.3.2 The franchise and post-reform electoral politics 24
  2.3.3 Representation and taxation 26
  2.3.4 Constitutional bargaining and piecemeal suffrage reform 27
 2.4 Three hypotheses about the causes of suffrage reform 28
 2.5 Evidence on the three hypotheses 29
  2.5.1 The consequences of suffrage reform 29
  2.5.2 The causes of suffrage reform 31
 2.6 The micro-political process-focused approach 35

PART II. HISTORICAL BACKGROUND

3. Reform politics before 1830 39
 3.1 Introduction 39
 3.2 From the English Civil War to the restoration of the monarchy in 1660 40

3.3 From the restoration to the accession of George III in 1760 42
3.4 From George III to the French Revolution 44
3.5 The French Revolution and the Napoleonic Wars 47
3.6 Reform attempts after the Napoleonic Wars 50
3.7 The end of the Unreformed Parliament 54

4. From the Unreformed Parliament to the Great Reform Act 56
4.1 Introduction 56
4.2 The Unreformed Parliament 56
4.2.1 The legislative process 56
4.2.2 Peers and bishops in the House of Lords 58
4.2.3 The voting franchise and the social composition of the MPs 59
4.2.4 Patrons and nomination seats 63
4.2.5 Political parties 68
4.3 The legislative journey of the Great Reform Act 69
4.4 The consequences of the Reform Bill 75
4.4.1 The Reform Bill's main features 75
4.4.2 Short-term consequences 79
4.4.3 Medium- and long-term consequences 90

PART III. A MICRO-POLITICAL ANALYSIS OF THE GREAT REFORM ACT

5. The cliffhanger: the vote in the Commons on 22 March 1831 95
5.1 Introduction 95
5.2 Voting on The Great Reform Act: the data 97
5.2.1 Reform support in the House of Commons 97
5.2.2 Violent unrest and social movement agitation 97
5.2.3 Political expedience 105
5.2.4 Political and economic control variables 107
5.3 Empirical strategy 110
5.4 Results 111
5.4.1 Public protest versus political expedience 111
5.4.2 Violent unrest and peaceful agitation 115
5.4.3 Two counterfactual scenarios 119
5.4.4 Interpretation 125
5.4.5 Omitted factors and indirect channels 126
5.5 Conclusion 131

6. A referendum on reform: the 1831 General Election 133
6.1 Introduction 133
6.2 The 1831 General Election and the Swing riots 135

6.2.1 A barometer of reform support 135
6.2.2 The Swing riots 137
6.2.3 Fear of revolution in 1830 141
6.2.4 Data 142
6.3 Empirical framework 145
6.3.1 Matching approach 146
6.3.2 Instrumental variable approach 147
6.4 Results 150
6.4.1 Ordinary least squares results 150
6.4.2 Matching estimates 154
6.4.3 Reduced form and instrumental variable estimates 157
6.4.4 Further falsification tests 161
6.4.5 Heterogeneity and local average treatment effects 163
6.4.6 Alternative explanations of the Whig victory in 1831 167
6.5 Conclusion 170

7. The battle with the lords: voting on reform in the House of Lords 172
7.1 Introduction 172
7.2 The Reform Bill in the House of Lords 173
7.3 Data 175
7.4 Empirical strategy 183
7.5 Evidence on the three hypotheses 186
7.5.1 Voting on reform 186
7.5.2 Attendance and selection effects 192
7.5.3 Change in voting behaviour across votes 192
7.5.4 The final vote on 4 June 1832 196
7.6 William IV and the threat from above 196
7.7 Conclusion 199

8. Conclusion 201

Historical printed sources 205
Newspapers 206
A note on the book cover 207
Bibliography 208
Index 221

List of Figures

4.1. Parliamentary boroughs in Essex under the Unreformed Parliament 61
4.2. The occupations of the English and Welsh MPs elected to the House of Commons in 1830 and 1831 62
4.3. Number of contested general elections between 1802 and 1831 in the English borough constituencies 67
4.4. The change in the size of the electorate between 1831 and 1832 in the surviving borough constituencies in England and Wales 83
4.5. Contested elections and the turnout rate before and after 1832 86
4.6. The effect of the Reform Bill on the patronage index in the English and Welsh borough constituencies 88
5.1. The spatial distribution of the number of participants in violent unrest or in peaceful agitation in the English and Welsh counties between 1 January 1828 and 22 March 1831 104
5.2. Violent unrest and peaceful agitation over time, 1830–1831 105
6.1. The shift in the support for the Whigs and the Tories between 1830 and 1831 across the 244 English constituencies 136
6.2. The number of Swing riots by month and the timing of the 1830 and 1831 General Elections 139
6.3. The spatial distribution of the Swing riots 140
6.4. Heterogeneous treatment effects: the instrumental variable estimate of the effect of local Swing riots on Whig support in the 1831 election by quartile 166
7.1. The spatial distribution of the number of participants in violent unrest and peaceful agitation within a radius of 10 kilometres of the country homes of the lords between 1 January 1828 and 7 May 1832 181
7.2. The spatial distribution of the number of participants in violent unrest and peaceful agitation within a radius of 1 kilometre of the London homes of the lords between 1 January 1828 and 7 May 1832 182
7.3. Probit estimates of the effect of different types of peaceful agitation or violent unrest around a lord's country or London home on the probability that a lord voted against reform in the three votes 190
8.1. The Great Reform Act in perspective: democracy indices for Britain, 1800–1930 203

List of Tables

4.1. The franchise types in the borough constituencies in England and Wales in 1830 64

4.2. Aristocratic influence and patronage in England and Wales under the Unreformed Parliament 66

4.3. Patrons in the House of Lords and the number of British seats in the House of Commons they controlled in the 1826, 1830, or 1831 General Election 66

4.4. How the MPs and lords voted on the three versions of the Reform Bill 72

4.5. The effect of the Reform Bill on the geography of representation 78

4.6. The number of voters before and after the Reform Bill 80

4.7. The change in the size of the electorate and in electoral turnout before and after the Reform Bill in the surviving borough constituencies in England and Wales 82

5.1. The breakdown of the second reading vote in the House of Commons on 22 March 1831 98

5.2. The number of participants involved in violent unrest and peaceful agitation by major regions between 1 January 1828 and 22 March 1831 99

5.3. Descriptive statistics related to the second reading on 22 March 1831 109

5.4. The probability that an MP voted in favour of the Reform Bill on 22 March 1831: probit and Heckman-probit estimates 112

5.5. The effect of violent unrest and different types of peaceful agitation on an MP's probability of voting in favour of the Reform Bill: probit estimates 117

5.6. Counterfactual analysis of the determinants of the MPs' votes 120

5.7. MPs absence from the House of Commons on 22 March 1831 122

5.8. The effect of violent unrest and peaceful agitation on the share of Whigs and Radicals elected in the 1830 General Election: OLS estimates 128

5.9. Falsification tests. The effect of violent unrest and peaceful agitation in 1828–1831 on the MPs' votes on the failed reform bills in 1810 and 1822 130

6.1. Descriptive statistics related to the 1831 General Election 143

6.2. Local Swing riots and the outcome of the 1831 election: baseline results 151

6.3. Local Swing riots and the outcome of the 1831 and 1830 elections. Alternative measures of local Swing riots and spatial correlation 153

6.4. Local Swing riots and the outcome of the 1831 and 1830 elections: matching estimates 155

6.5. Distance to Sevenoaks and the outcome of the 1831 and 1830 elections: reduced form estimates 158
6.6. Local Swing riots and the outcome of the 1831 and 1830 elections: instrumental variable estimates 159
6.7. Local Swing riots and the outcome of the 1831 election: additional placebo tests 162
6.8. Local Swing riots and the outcome of the 1831 election. Specification tests with transformations of the instrument 164
6.9. Local Swing riots and the outcome of the 1831 election: alternative explanations for the Whig victory 168
7.1. The votes for and against the Reform Bill in the House of Lords on 7 October 1831 176
7.2. The votes for and against the Reform Bill in the House of Lords on 13 April 1832 177
7.3. The votes for and against the Reform Bill in the House of Lords on 7 May 1832 178
7.4. Test of means differences by party affiliation of the lords 183
7.5. Descriptive statistics: the House of Lords 184
7.6. The determinants of the probability that a lord voted against reform in the three votes: probit estimates 188
7.7. The impact of violent unrest and peaceful agitation on the probability that a lord would change his mind between 7 October 1831 and 7 May 1832: probit estimates 194
7.8. The twenty-two lords who voted against the Reform Bill on 4 June 1832 197

PART I

MAIN IDEAS

Chapter 1
Introduction and overview

At a time when populist politicians gain votes and win elections to then implement authoritarian policies that undermine many of the unwritten conventions enabling the existence of liberal democracy (e.g. Levitsky and Ziblatt 2018; Stasavage 2020; Guriev and Papaioannou 2022, and the references therein), it is worth reflecting on the fact that the democratic institutions that are now under threat took centuries to build. While democratic reversals into autocracy can happen in a few years, history shows that establishing (or rebuilding) democracy takes time.

The aim of this book is to enhance understanding of the forces that historically enabled democratic institutions to take root and consolidate. Theoretical work in political economy over the past decades has conceptualised democratisation as a process that either originated from below or from above. Theories of democratisation from below stress threats of revolution and social violence (e.g. Acemoglu and Robinson 2006) or peaceful agitation by social movements and groups outside the elite (e.g. Tilly 1988; Tarrow 2011) as the causal drivers of democratic reform. The elite decision makers are either threatened by the prospect of social violence to pre-emptively democratise, or they are convinced by agitation from movements outside the elite. Conversely, theories of democratisation from above stress that groups within the elite may benefit from democratisation and, thus, voluntarily pursue reform (e.g. Lizzeri and Persico 2004) or that constitutional compromises between elite groups can cause democratic reform (e.g. Congleton 2011).

1.1 The idea

The conceptual idea behind the book can best be understood by way of contrast with the two established approaches to the study of democratisation in the field of political economy. The first approach, exemplified by the books of Boix (2003), Scheve and Stasavage (2016), Przeworski et al. (2000), and Paldam (2021), is comparative. The contention is that important generalisations about the cause or causes of democratisation can be derived from comparing many instances of democratic reform across time and space. It cannot be doubted that

Peaceful and Violent Origins of Voting Rights. Toke S. Aidt and Raphaël Franck, Oxford University Press.
 DOI: 10.1093/9780197679746.003.0001

this approach has brought important insights to light and identified systematic patterns that can help establish the root causes of democracy. However, by taking a bird's eye view and treating each democratic reform as an *event* which is comparable to other events, it necessarily abstracts itself from all the details that make up each of these events—and these details can be an extremely valuable source of information about what actually caused the particular democratisation event to happen.[1]

The second approach, exemplified by the books by Acemoglu and Robinson (2006) and Congleton (2011), may be called the theory-grounded historical narrative approach. The approach is theory-grounded in the sense that it develops mathematical models of democratisation that highlight particular causal mechanisms—for example, a threat of revolution and distributional conflict (Acemoglu and Robinson 2000*b*, 2001) or constitutional bargaining inside the elite (Congleton 2007). The evidence to support the theory mainly comes from detailed historical narratives of particular reforms (although it does not rule out econometric tests similar to the ones often used in the comparative approach). This combination of theory and narrative has the advantage that the historical details are brought to bear on particular theoretical mechanisms in a systematic way: to put it the other way, the historical record is interpreted through the lens of a particular theory. The weakness, however, is that the historical record can be interpreted in different ways, and different aspects may be emphasised while others fade into the background. In fact, it is not uncommon for the same democratisation episodes to be used in support of different theories. For example, interpretations of Britain's Second Reform Act of 1867 range from democratisation from below in the form of a revolutionary threat (Acemoglu and Robinson 2000*b*) to democratisation from above in the form of intra-elite competition (Lizzeri and Persico 2004; Llavador and Oxoby 2005).

Our approach differs from these traditional approaches. Instead of taking a bird's eye view of many democratisation episodes, we focus on one reform, and instead of using the historical narrative to provide evidence of a particular theory, we use micro-political data generated by the reform to test competing theories. The advantages of this micro-political approach are many. First and foremost, while it can be a useful abstraction to treat a democratic reform as one event, it is more accurate to describe such reforms as a process consisting of many important events. A successful reform has, typically, avoided numerous roadblocks that could have stopped it in its track. These roadblocks, and the way they were overcome, shed light on the mechanisms of democratisation.

[1] Small N studies such as Rueschemeyer et al. (1992) or Collier (1999) avoid this problem to some extent.

Our approach is to leverage the process aspect and exploit the multiple events that occur within a particular reform process to learn about the mechanisms of democratisation.

Second, all reform processes generate a wealth of micro-political data related to who the main actors were and what they did. Examples include data on the politicians who supported or opposed reform, information on roll call votes or divisions in pre-existing parliaments, and data on the geography of protest, unrest, and agitation, and social-economic conditions. These data are generated at different points in the process and enable quantitative, statistical tests of potential mechanisms. Most importantly, perhaps, these quantitative footprints are well-suited for formal testing of competing democratisation theories. They allow for theory testing within a particular reform process rather than theory testing between aggregate reform events.

Third, the approach highlights the multi-causal nature of democratisation and explicitly allows for the possibility that different causal mechanisms may operate with different intensities around different roadblocks within the same reform process. Conceptually, this is important because this diversity is lost in the comparative approach where each process is treated as one successful democratisation event and because the narrative approach is not geared towards quantitative assessment of competing theories.

We are not arguing that this process-focused approach is the only worthwhile approach, nor that it does not suffer from shortcomings. A lot can be learned from both the historical narrative and the comparative approach. In fact, we also conducted research using the comparative approach (e.g. Franck and Rainer 2012; Aidt and Jensen 2014). Our focus on one reform process rather than on many reform events raises questions about external validity. What we argue is that the process-based approach that focuses on one reform is a complement to these other approaches. It opens up the opportunity to study mechanisms at the micro level with a high degree of internal validity.

We select the United Kingdom's Great Reform Act of 1832 as the venue for this. The Great Reform Act was the first of several reforms that over the course of a century transformed the British political system from one based on privilege, exclusion, and factional politics to one based on universal suffrage, secret ballot, programmatic policies, and stable political parties. The immediate consequences of the reform were to redistribute parliamentary seats from small and sometimes 'rotten' boroughs to the fast-growing industrial cities and to the counties while granting voting rights to resident householders with property valued at ten pounds or more per year in the boroughs and to fifty-pound renters in the counties. The political process that culminated in the Great Reform Act lasted two years, and the Act is considered as a watershed in British economic and political history (Butler 1914; Brock 1973; Cannon 1973).[2]

The Great Reform Act has several features that make it particularly suitable for the type of process-focused analysis we want to pursue. First, the reform faced significant opposition and could have been blocked at several points. To succeed, it had to overcome these roadblocks, which included gaining a majority in both the House of Commons and the House of Lords as well as winning popular support in a general election. These features enable analysis of multiple causal mechanisms and accommodates the possibility that different mechanisms could have operated at different points in the process. This is important because it moves the analysis away from the presumption that there is one cause and acknowledges that there could be many. Second, the votes on the Reform Bill in the two houses of the British Parliament and the 1831 General Election took place in the context of heightened social unrest and extra-parliamentary agitation and debate. This generated a large quantity of micro-political data related to the actions of the key players and to the social context in which these actions were taken. This feature enables quantification, statistical analysis, and testing of competing theories.

The contribution of the book can, therefore, be summarised as follows. First, it articulates a new process-based perspective on the study of democratisation that we view as a significant complement to existing approaches. Second, it applies this approach to the Great Reform Act of 1832. This involves three substantive empirical investigations that draw on rich micro-political data to understand how the reform succeeded in overcoming particular roadblocks placed in its path. In that way, we test competing theories of democratisation. This investigation will partly be based on output from a research program we have worked on for more than a decade (some of which are published in part in Aidt and Franck (2013, 2015, 2019, 2025), Aidt and Leon-Ablan (2022), and Aidt, Leon-Ablan, and Satchell (2022)) and partly on new ongoing research. The added value of collecting this in a book is clear: each of these articles focuses on one particular roadblock that the reform overcame during its journey through the political process as well as on one question about causality or theory testing. This means that the bigger picture and the connections between the events within the reform process can be lost or, at the least, are hard to fully appreciate. This book brings the individual pieces together and brings the synergies to the forefront.

The analysis shows that different causal mechanisms were involved at different points in the process: the reform was not caused by one factor. The threat

[2] This political process also serves as the background for George Eliot's novel *Middlemarch* (Eliot 1871–1872).

of revolution, social movement pressure and agitation (factors associated with bottom-up democratisation), as well as political expedience (associated with top-down democratisation) played a role, but around different roadblocks. At a time of increased populist agitation from both ends of the political spectrum, this book offers a political economy analysis of a canonical historical democratisation process that enables a deeper and more nuanced understanding of the root causes of democracy and serves as a reminder that it is a complex task to build democratic institutions.

1.2 Setting the stage: dramatis personae, scene, and plot

The constitutional drama that led to the Great Reform Act began on 16 November 1830, when Lord Charles Grey became Prime Minister, and ended on 7 June 1832, when the bill received royal assent. During this period, many different individuals and groups, both inside and outside Parliament, played crucial roles. For readers who are unfamiliar with the historical context, this subsection gives a succinct presentation of the main actors, the scene, and the plot. Chapters 3 and 4 provide more details.

1.2.1 Dramatis personae

The reformers inside Parliament

- The Whigs. The members of Parliament (MPs) elected to the House of Commons and peers in the House of Lords affiliated with the Whig faction. They viewed themselves as the defenders of the independence of Parliament against the excess of the King's prerogatives and were, generally, reform-friendly. Their leaders advocated for a moderate reform of Parliament that would grant voting rights to the 'respectable' sections of society and reform the geography of the constituencies.
- Lord Charles Grey, second Earl Grey (1764–1845). Prime Minister between 16 November 1830 and 9 July 1834. He led the Whigs from the House of Lords.
- Sir Henry Brougham (1878–1868). Lord Chancellor in Grey's government.
- Lord John Russell (1792–1878). Paymaster of the Forces in Grey's government. Because of his previous involvement with parliamentary reform, and in spite of his junior ministerial position, he was amongst the four ministers whom Grey entrusted with drafting the Reform Bill. Russell's leadership was instrumental in passing the bill in the House of Commons.

- The Radicals. These were the few MPs who advocated for universal (male) suffrage and secret ballot in the House of Commons. They supported the limited reform proposals of the Whigs, who regarded their radical ideas with suspicion.

The reform agitators outside Parliament

- Thomas Attwood (1783–1856). Leader of the Birmingham Political Union that advocated for parliamentary reform.
- William Cobbett (1763–1735). Radical pamphleteer who was elected to the House of Commons after the Great Reform Act.
- Francis Place (1771–1854). Radical activist who later led the working-class Chartist movement, which advocated for additional democratic reforms.

The opponents of reform inside Parliament

- The Tories. The MPs elected to the House of Commons and peers in the House of Lords affiliated with the Tory faction. They had governed uninterruptedly between 1807 and 1830 and were united in the defence of the King's prerogatives and of the Anglican Church. Most of them opposed parliamentary reform.
- Arthur Wellesley, first Duke of Wellington (1769–1852). The 'Iron Duke' had led the army that defeated Napoleon at Waterloo in 1815. He was the Tory Prime Minister between 22 January 1828 and 16 November 1830 and sat in the House of Lords. The internal split within the Tory faction between 'Liberals' and 'Ultras' over the Catholic Relief Act in 1829 ultimately forced him to resign in November 1830. This enabled Grey to become Prime Minister.
- Robert Peel (1788–1850). The leader of the Tories in the House of Commons.

The King

- William IV (1785–1837). King of the United Kingdom of Great Britain and Ireland and King of Hanover (r. 1830–1837). He succeeded his elder brother George IV (r. 1820–1830) in June 1830, a few months before the reform process started.

1.2.2 Scene

- The House of Commons. The lower house of Parliament originated as the representation of towns that paid taxes to the monarch. The geographical distribution of constituencies (seats) in the House of Commons had not been modified since the mid-seventeenth century, leading to an acute geographic imbalance in political representation. Some populated parts of the country did not have representatives, while other constituencies had lost many of their inhabitants but still elected MPs. Many MPs belonged to aristocratic families.

- Parliamentary constituencies and elections. The constituencies with the right to elect MPs had been established over centuries with various voting franchises that restricted the vote to specific categories of the (male) population. As a result, some constituencies had large electorates, while in others, the number of voters was very small. Moreover, voting was open (i.e. no secret ballot), and the polling period for general elections was spread over four to six weeks.
- Rotten boroughs and electoral corruption. In many depopulated constituencies, elections were uncontested. Aided by the lack of secret ballot, one or two rich individuals (known as 'patrons') or the Treasury (i.e. the current government) often controlled the outcome of these 'elections'. Moreover, vote buying and electoral violence were common features in constituencies with competitive elections.
- The House of Lords. The upper house of Parliament originated as the representation of large landowners. At the time of the Great Reform Act, only male members holding a peerage title, as well as a few bishops and archbishops of the Church of England and of the Church of Ireland, could sit in the House of Lords. The majority of the peers were Tories. Throughout the reform process, there was never any discussion pertaining to reform of the House of Lords and its prerogatives.
- Social unrest and reform agitation. The period 1830–1832 was associated with a high level of social tension and unrest, with unprecedented level of social movement mobilisation and agitation. This occurred in rural and urban areas and could be peaceful or violent. It was not necessarily related to political issues and parliamentary reform, although much of it was. For instance, the violent rural Swing riots, which began in the south-east of England in August 1830 and peaked in November of that year, were triggered by dire economic circumstances, yet played a pivotal role for the eventual success of the reform.

1.2.3 Plot

There were five crucial moments in the reform process that culminated in the Great Reform Act, which we refer to as roadblocks. Had reform proponents failed to overcome just one of these roadblocks, parliamentary reform would have failed in 1832.

- Roadblock 1. On 16 November 1830, Wellington resigned, following a defeat the day before on a vote in the House of Commons caused by a split amongst the Tories. King William IV appointed the same day Charles Grey as Prime Minister. He immediately announced his intention to reform Parliament.
- Roadblock 2. On 22 March 1831, the members of the House of Commons voted in favour of reform by 302 against 301. However, fearing a stalemate in the committee stage over the details of the bill, Grey convinced William IV to call a general election in April–June 1831.
- Roadblock 3. In the aftermath of the violent rural Swing riots, the 1831 General Election was, in effect, a referendum on parliamentary reform. Voters elected a decisive majority of reform-friendly Whigs, and the Reform Bill now had solid majority support in the House of Commons.
- Roadblock 4. From September 1831 onwards, the lords discussed, voted on, and amended the Reform Bill, but ultimately rejected it on 7 May 1832. The lords' opposition to reform triggered large-scale urban unrest, called the Days of May, and also Grey's resignation. At the request of William IV, Wellington tried, but ultimately failed, to find support amongst the Tories for a government that would reform Parliament.
- Roadblock 5. William IV recalled Grey as Prime Minister on 18 May 1832. In a meeting held in the presence of Brougham later that day, the King promised to appoint reform-friendly peers to the House of Lords, if needed. Faced with this threat, which implied the end of the Tory majority in the upper house if carried out, most anti-reform Tory lords chose not to attend the final vote on 4 June 1832. The bill received 106 votes in support and 22 against it, and obtained royal assent on 7 June 1832.

1.3 Overview of the book

The book is divided into three parts. In Part I, besides this introduction, Chapter 2 surveys the theoretical political economics literature on franchise extension and evaluates the empirical literature in economics and political science that have attempted to confront the competing theories with historical and contemporaneous data. It emphasises three different theoretical hypotheses that seek to resolve the democratisation puzzle—that is, why an elite with a monopoly on political power will agree to democratic reforms that involve giving voting rights (and/or other rights) to non-elite groups. The first hypothesis—the threat of revolution hypothesis—is related to the threat of violent political change. The incumbent elite fears that non-elite groups may revolt and overthrow the current regime in a revolution. As a pre-emptive strike, the elite may agree to share power to eliminate that threat (e.g. Acemoglu and Robinson 2000*b*; Boix 2003). The second hypothesis—the social movement hypothesis—is related to peaceful pressure from pro-reform social movements and groups that through agitation, lobbying, and mass mobilisation try to convince the elite of the need for reform. Both the threat of revolution hypothesis and the social movement hypothesis are related to pressures from below (either in the form of threats of violence or in the form of agitation and popular demand) and may be considered as bottom-up theories of democratisation. In contrast, the final hypothesis—the political expedience hypothesis—views democratisation as a top-down process. A number of different theories have been proposed to explain why it can be in the strict self-interest of the incumbent elite, or at least a subset thereof, to voluntarily share power with others (e.g. Lizzeri and Persico 2004; Congleton 2007; Aidt et al. 2010). The common theme is that it is expedient for some or maybe even for all members of the elite to reform because partial or full democratisation will change the policy mix, give them an electoral advantage, and/or enable them to gain concessions in other policy dimensions such as expanding the tax base.

Part II of the book deals with the historical background to the Great Reform Act and the institutional details related to its passage through the two houses of the British Parliament. Chapter 3 takes a long-term perspective on parliamentary reform in Great Britain. It shows that the Great Reform Act did not emerge all of a sudden. Many unsuccessful attempts had been made between the Second English Civil War in the 1640s and 1830 to reform the parliamentary franchise as well as to change the geography of representation in the House of Commons. Reform demands from inside the elite, sometimes in response to threats of unrest, and from social movements and groups outside had ebbed and flowed over the years. Moreover, while the Great Reform Act—the Reform Bill for short—did constitute a break with the politics of the so-called Unreformed Parliament, it is clear that there was a lot of continuity in British politics before and after 1832.

Chapter 4 serves two purposes. First, it provides a brief overview of the mechanics of the British political system in 1830 and of the main features of the Unreformed Parliament that the reformers aimed to reform. Second, it provides a narrative of the reform process between 1830 and 1832. The emphasis is on the complexity of the Reform Bill's journey through the House of Commons and the House of Lords and on the obstacles that had to be overcome for its ultimate success. We identify five 'roadblocks': these were stages where the reform process could have come to a stop and the attempt to reform the House of Commons could have failed as it had previously. The chapter also includes a brief evaluation of some short- and medium-run consequences of the Reform Bill. In comparison to the many excellent histories of the Great Reform Act (e.g. Butler 1914; Brock 1973; Cannon 1973) and of its consequences (e.g. Gash 1953; Salmon 2002), a unique feature of this narrative is that we bring a wealth of quantitative information to the discussion—much of which will be used in the empirical analysis in Part III—and use these data to shine light on salient features of the Unreformed Parliament and on some of the consequences of the Great Reform Act itself.

Part III contains three core chapters with the statistical analysis and a concluding chapter to the overall book. We study four of the roadblocks and use them to test the three hypotheses laid out in Part I to provide evidence on the causal mechanisms that enabled the Reform Bill to overcome them. The roadblocks are: the pivotal vote on the Reform Bill in the House of Commons in March 1831, where it passed with just one vote (roadblock 2); the subsequent 1831 General Election, which we interpret as a referendum on the reform question and which returned a solid pro-reform majority to the House of Commons (roadblock 3); and the battle to secure a majority for the Reform Bill in the House of Lords in the second half of 1831 and the first half of 1832 (roadblocks 4 and 5).

In Chapter 5, we study the second reading vote on 22 March 1831 in the House of Commons. This was the first time the Reform Bill, which had been drafted by Lord Grey's newly formed pro-reform Whig government, was subjected to a vote amongst the MPs who were elected to the House of Commons in 1830 under the rules of the Unreformed Parliament. It was a cliffhanger: the Reform Bill passed with a one-vote majority. Almost all Whig and Radical MPs voted yes. A majority of Tory MPs voted no, but a pivotal minority of Tories voted with the Whig government. From a theoretical perspective, the vote record of the MPs enables us to statistically test the three hypotheses—the threat of revolution hypothesis, the social movement hypothesis, and the political expedience hypothesis—about the causes of suffrage reform. The vote on 22 March 1831 is well-suited for this purpose. First, it offers a way to get around the fundamental difficulty that the threat of revolution is not directly observed. We use the degree of actual violent unrest preceding the second reading of the Reform Bill as a proxy for the perceived threat of revolution. Between November 1830 when Lord Grey took office as Prime Minister and announced his intention to reform and the vote in the House of Commons in March 1831, England experienced high levels of social unrest. This included a major violent rural uprising and violent confrontations between workers and law enforcement in many of the industrial cities in the north of England and in London. Geographical dispersion in the intensity of violent unrest enables us to directly evaluate the effect of fears of revolution by comparing the votes of MPs elected in areas with high levels of violent unrest to those elected in areas with low levels. Second, during the same period, Britain also experienced a surge in public demand for democratic reform from social movements (often organised by reform societies such as the Birmingham Political Union) and from civic society more generally. Data from Horn and Tilly (1988) allow us to quantify the effect of peaceful mass mobilisation through public meetings, petitions, and demonstrations related to reform demands in the areas where the MPs were elected on their vote on the Reform Bill. Third, we can directly evaluate the extent of self-interested voting. This is because the Reform Bill's two main features—redistribution of seats and reform of the suffrage rules—allow us, when combined with detailed bibliographic information, to predict whether an MP would personally benefit or lose from the Reform Bill. In that way, we can test for political expedience in their voting behaviour. The results of our statistical analysis show that conditional on party affiliation (Radical, Tory, or Whig), which is a very strong predictor of voting preferences, the MPs' votes were influenced by violent social unrest in urban (but not rural) areas and by peaceful agitation and expressions of mass support for reform from social movements. They were, however, also motivated by political expedience. A horse race between the competing theories suggests that petitions and public agitation related to the reform were more important than fears of revolution created by exposure to violent urban unrest. Since the Reform Bill passed with a one-vote majority, two additional nays were all that was needed to block it. Our estimates enable us to evaluate counterfactual experiments to see if violent urban unrest and reform agitation were substantial enough to switch at least two votes. We find that this was the case. We, therefore, conclude that multiple causal factors were at play and that a combination of social movement agitation and fears of revolution helped the Reform Bill overcome this roadblock, while political expedience pushed in the opposite direction.

Chapter 6 provides causal evidence on the link between democratisation and the threat of revolution by taking advantage of the geography of the Swing riots. The riots occurred between the election in August 1830, held before the reform process started, and the election in April–June 1831, which was called because a one-vote majority in the House of Commons was insufficient to avoid the Reform Bill being watered down later in the legislative process and which, effectively, was a referendum on the Reform Bill. These Swing riots were an uprising of agricultural labourers in the English countryside. They were not motivated by parliamentary reform but instead resulted from poor economic conditions that were blamed on agricultural mechanisation and, in particular, on the adoption of threshers (Tilly 1995; Caprettini and Voth 2020). This rural aspect of the riots (as well as their timing in between the two elections) matters because the typical parliamentary constituency before 1832 was a small market town or sometimes simply a village embedded in the local agricultural economy. The Swing riots, therefore, gave the voters and patrons of the constituencies located in the affected areas first-hand experience with an uprising of unprecedented scale. We quantify the scale of riots at the constituency level by geo-referencing the 2818 Swing riots recorded by Holland (2005) and assessing the number of riots within a ten-kilometres radius of each constituency. To overcome the problem that the geography of the riots may be related to the change in reform attitude of the voters living in the constituencies in the affected areas between 1830 and 1831, we exploit the social dynamics of the riots to construct an instrumental variable that isolates exogenous variation in threat perceptions at the constituency level. Charlesworth (1979) and Aidt, Leon-Ablan, and Satchell (2022) show that the riot dynamics were driven by local social interaction effects. Firstly, agricultural workers willing to revolt were encouraged to do so by observing others engaged in rioting, but with diminishing strength as the distance from the epicentre of the riots (in Kent) increased. Secondly, the riots spread systematically along a route that closely followed the pre-existing road network and were amplified by markets. As a consequence, we can use the travel-time distance between each constituency and Sevenoaks—the village in Kent where the first three Swing riots occurred on 3 August 1830—as an instrument for the number of riots that happened in the vicinity of each constituency. Conditional on support for the pro-reform Whig party in past elections, this distance isolates exogenous variation in first-hand experience with social violence, which can be used to estimate the causal effect of fears of revolution on reform support in 1831. We find that the Swing riots induced, in a causal sense, voters to vote for pro-reform Whig candidates after experiencing first-hand the violence of the riots. This is strong evidence for the threat of revolution mechanism of democratisation and suggests that fears of revolution induced by first-hand experience with social violence helped the Reform Bill overcome this roadblock. The pro-reform Whig party needed to win at least thirty-five seats to command a majority amongst the English MPs (they won sixty-six seats). A conservative interpretation of our instrumental variable estimate indicates that exposure to Swing riots around a constituency helped the Whigs win at least thirty-one of the thirty-five required seats.

Chapter 7 turns the attention to the House of Lords. After the Whigs had won the 1831 election, the Reform Bill had a solid majority in the House of Commons. The opposite was true in the House of Lords, which was dominated by anti-reform Tory peers. To become law, the Reform Bill had to get a majority of the lords on board. As in the lower house, the lords voted on the Reform Bill, and they rejected it several times between October 1831 and May 1832. For three of these votes, the complete records of who voted for and against are preserved. We use these to statistically investigate if the voting behaviour of the lords was influenced by fears of revolution, by social movement agitation and pressure, or by self-interest. We use an approach similar to that taken in Chapter 5 in the study of the pivotal vote in the House of Commons in March 1831. This allows us to engage with the democratisation puzzle in a novel way. The lords and the MPs were two sub-groups of the elite whose incentives with respect to constitutional reform were potentially different. The MPs were partly accountable to the pre-reform electors, and their power would be directly affected by the reform. In contrast, the lords were unaccountable to the pre- and post-reform electorate, and the constitutional status of the House of Lords was not directly threatened by the Reform Bill. As such, we can ask if any of the mechanisms highlighted by the three hypotheses (laid out in Chapter 2) influenced the way the unelected lords voted on the Reform Bill and, if so, whether their reactions were similar to or different from those of the elected MPs in the House of Commons. We find that they were, in fact, remarkably different. The lords were caught between two forces. On the one hand, they observed the increase in social unrest and reform agitation, including the spike in unrest in the first half of May 1832, during the so-called Days of May. On the other hand, the Whig government repeatedly tried to extract a credible promise from King William IV that he would create, if needed, enough new Whig (pro-reform) lords to engineer a majority in favour of reform in the House of Lords—a move which would undermine Tory control of the upper house. Our empirical analysis shows that the lords, unlike the MPs, were not influenced by fears of revolution or by pro-reform social movement agitation. On the contrary, they appear to have been hardened in their opposition to the Reform Bill by exposure to violence or agitation. What in the end broke the stalemate was not pressure from below but a credible threat from King William IV that he would allow the creation of a pro-reform majority in the House of Lords if the lords continued to block the Reform Bill. In one aspect, however, the two elite groups behaved in a similar fashion: expedience and personal interest are clearly reflected in the vote record in both houses of Parliament.

Our analysis of the Reform Bill's journey through the British Parliament between 1830 and 1832 emphasises the process aspect of democratic reform. We highlight instances in the process where the Reform Bill could have come to an unsuccessful end and use the ways in which these roadblocks were overcome to test competing theories of democratisation. This process-centred perspective provides important new insights into the specifics of what enabled the Great Reform Act to succeed and into the general theoretical mechanisms behind democratisation. The analysis shows that multiple causal forces were at play and that some came to the forefront at particular points in the process while fading into the background at others. Pressure from below, in particular in the form of social movement agitation, was important to get the Reform Bill through the House of Commons at the start of the process, while the perceived threat of revolution induced by direct exposure to rural riots made a significant contribution to the victory of the pro-reform Whigs in the 1831 General Election. In contrast, despite the extraordinary high level of social unrest and significant pro-reform social movement mobilisation in 1832, pressures from below did not make much of an impression on the lords and, if anything, hardened their opposition to the Reform Bill. The threat they reacted to came from above: opposition in the House of Lords dissipated in the face of the King's credible threat to eliminate the anti-reform Tory majority. The vote records of both the MPs and the lords, however, show clear evidence of expedience and self-interest. The three hypotheses, therefore, all have something to contribute to our understanding of democratisation in general and to the Great Reform Act in particular. Our process-focused approach helps us see this clearly. In contrast to the comparative approach, which overlooks all the details of particular reforms, we are able to demonstrate that multiple causal mechanisms play a role; in contrast to the historical narrative approach, which is rich on details, but struggles to establish the relative importance of different mechanisms, our statistical evidence enables systematic judgements be made about what matters the most and when.

Chapter 2
Democratisation and franchise extension: the literature

2.1 Introduction

Democratisation remains one of the major puzzles in political economy: why would a powerful elite controlling the state institutions ever want to share power with other groups whose policy objectives are fundamentally different? Why would an elite extend the voting franchise to a broad segment of the population whose policy goals it may oppose? The starting point for virtually all theories of democratisation (that does not involve decolonisation, civil war, or major geopolitical events such as the end of the Cold War) is that democracy originates from the decision of the ruling elites to share their monopoly on power (Tullock 1987, Chap. 4). Their explanations, however, differ.

This chapter provides a concise survey of theories that aim at explaining the logic of franchise extension during the long nineteenth century in what Huntington (1991) refers to as the first wave of democratisation. These reforms were often piecemeal and gradually enabled more and more men to participate in elections by relaxing income, wealth, or tax-payment requirements on the right to vote.[1]

We classify these theories into two broad categories and briefly evaluate various attempts at testing them statistically. Bottom-up theories of democratisation emphasise that the members of the incumbent elite share power with other sections of society to avoid losing power entirely or because they become persuaded of the merits of doing so. Conversely, top-down theories of democratisation emphasise that the ruling elite, or some part thereof, can directly benefit from democratisation. Specifically, we focus on top-down theories that emphasise political expedience and self-interest, and on bottom-up theories which

[1] In the second and third waves, women obtained the right to vote, age restrictions were relaxed, and voting rights were given to racial, ethnic, and/or religious minorities. While some of the theories which we survey in this chapter also apply to these reforms, other theories specific to these aspects of franchise extension have been proposed (e.g. the survey by Hanlon 2022). Moreover, the rule that governs who can vote in elections is one of many elements of democracy. Other elements include the secret ballot and electoral rules, competitive elections, checks and balances on the executive, and orderly transition of power after elections (e.g. the survey by Stasavage 2022).

Peaceful and Violent Origins of Voting Rights. Toke S. Aidt and Raphaël Franck, Oxford University Press.
 DOI: 10.1093/9780197679746.003.0002

emphasise either a threat of revolution or the role of social movements and popular agitation.

We use this survey to develop three hypotheses of suffrage reform—the threat of revolution hypothesis, the social movement hypothesis, and the political expedience hypothesis—which we test in the subsequent chapters in the context of the Great Reform Act of 1832 using our process-focused approach.

2.2 Bottom-up theories of democratisation

Bottom-up theories suggest that the elite only reluctantly agree to share power with groups whose goals they oppose. The theories differ with regard to whether the political demands made by those outsider groups are peaceful or accompanied by credible threats of violence and revolution.

2.2.1 The threat of revolution hypothesis

The threat of revolution hypothesis holds that the suffrage was granted because the members of the elite with monopoly on power feared a revolution if they did not share some of their power. It has a long pedigree: many 'Whig historians' (e.g. McCarthy (1852), Trevelyan (1920), and Trevelyan (1937, 635–636)) emphasise it in relation to the Great Reform Act of 1832 (see the discussion in Chapter 3), and it plays a role in most historical narratives of franchise extension in the nineteenth century.

In two seminal papers and their subsequent book, Acemoglu and Robinson (2000*b*, 2001, 2006) develop what has become the canonical theoretical formulation of the threat of revolution hypothesis.[2] Their model considers an economy with two groups: an elite well-endowed with capital and workers endowed with less. This inequality gives rise to a distributional conflict. The elite do not want to impose taxes to fund transfers as they would pay more than they would receive. Workers, however, support high taxes as they are net beneficiaries from the tax-transfer system. Initially, the elite rule, but their hold on power may be threatened by a revolution organised by the workers. Revolution requires collective action, and it is not always possible to successfully organise one. Revolutions are, therefore, not a permanent threat. If a revolution were to occur, some assets would be destroyed, and the rest would be expropriated and shared amongst

[2] See also Justman and Gradstein (1999), Falkinger (1999), Boix (2003, Chap. 1), Overland et al. (2005), and Ellis and Fender (2008).

the workers. Since the elite would lose everything in a revolution, they want to avoid revolution by taking pre-emptive measures when needed.

In the baseline model, the elite have two strategies to prevent a revolution. First, they can change the tax system and offer a net transfer to the workers. This would encourage the latter to accept the political status quo rather than starting a costly revolution. Second, the elite can decide to give voting rights to workers. Under democracy, the decisive median voter will be a worker who favours maximum redistribution. From the perspective of the elite, occasional fiscal redistribution controlled by them is preferable to the transition to democracy. This is because transfers only have to be offered when there is a real threat of revolution, whereas the suffrage extension and the associated high level of redistribution is permanent or, at least, hard to reverse.[3] Accordingly, the elite always prefer the transfer solution. However, transfers may not be sufficient to avoid revolution, and in that case the elite must resort to a franchise extension. When that happens, the theory predicts that we should observe an increase in public spending on redistribution.

The fundamental insight is that there is no political Coase theorem: transfers without institutional change are not fully credible; a change in the institutions is permanent and, thus, has commitment value. Suffrage reform then happens when the 'window of opportunity' is open—the threat of revolution is real—and the most generous transfer policy that the elite can credibly offer is insufficient to persuade workers not to revolt. In this framework, inequality has an ambiguous effect on the chance of a franchise extension. On the one hand, higher inequality makes workers keener on revolting because there is more to expropriate after a revolution. On the other hand, higher inequality makes it possible for the elite to credibly offer more transfers. This makes workers less willing to revolt. Income growth, in contrast, has no effect on the likelihood of a suffrage reform as long as all incomes are proportional to total factor productivity.

In the baseline model, revolutions never happen. This is because the elite know exactly when and how they need to act to prevent the threat becoming a reality. It is the *threat* of revolution that is the potential trigger of democratisation, not the revolution itself. Ellis and Fender (2011) extend Acemoglu and Robinson's model with a micro-foundation for how, when, and why a revolution happens. Revolutions may happen because the elite are unsure if the workers are

[3] The logic of the model does not require that the transition to democracy be literally permanent. Acemoglu and Robinson (2001) show that democracy continues to have commitment value in situations where the elite may take back power in a coup in the future. In that case, democracy may be unstable and unconsolidated, but it is still possible that it will persist. There are indeed many examples of franchise extensions during the first wave of democratisation in the nineteenth century that were subsequently reversed, such as in Spain, Portugal, and Serbia amongst many other countries (e.g. Tilly (2004), Aidt and Jensen (2014, Table 1)). Geopolitics and foreign interventions played a role in many of these reversals (Aidt et al. 2021).

really willing to revolt and then take the chance of offering transfers in the rational belief that this would be sufficient. The revolution process itself generates this uncertainty because the incentive to revolt from the perspective of an individual worker is a function of how many other workers are willing to revolt. Each worker receives an independent signal about how costly it is to revolt, and, as in Lohmann (1993), an information cascade can trigger a revolution (see also Kuran 1989). Aidt and Jensen (2014) also model the possibility of revolutions along the equilibrium path, but they focus on international spillover effects whereby the elite in one country may learn about the likelihood that a revolution could happen at home by observing revolutionary events in other countries. Dorsch and Maarek (2015) develop a theory of inefficient institutions where democratic consolidations may happen through a revolution while Gilli and Li (2015) show that a revolutionary threat can help hold autocrats accountable.

In addition to transfers or franchise reform, the elite can use repression to prevent a revolution (Acemoglu and Robinson 2000*a*; Boix 2003, Chap. 1). Repression requires investment in an army, in the police force, or in the secret services and a moral willingness to repress dissent. This makes repression costly to the elite. Whether they want to use this prevention strategy rather than giving workers voting rights depends on how costly it is for them to live under democracy. In a society with high inequality, it is relatively costly for the elite to democratise, making it more likely that the threat of revolution will be answered by force.

2.2.2 The social movement hypothesis

Like the threat of revolution hypothesis, the social movement hypothesis is a bottom-up theory of democratisation that sees democratisation as demand-driven. However, it does not view actual or threatened violence as necessary. Instead, franchise extension takes place because politicians are influenced by peaceful agitation, lobbying, and mass mobilisation in support of reform, originating from social movements and groups outside the elite.

The large and varied literature on social movements in sociology studies how groups with a shared interest may mobilise to promote collective action, which may, in turn, trigger democratic reform or other forms of social change (e.g. Tilly 1988; Tarrow 2011). The interests, their organisation, and the means these groups employ to seek their goals can be very different. John Stuart Mill viewed collective action as originating from the calculating pursuit of individual interest (Mill 1931), while Marxian scholars (e.g. Banks 1970) attributed shared interest to common positions in the organisation of production and focus on the conflict of interest between workers and capitalists. Olson (1965) explains how pro-democracy advocacy groups or movements (as well as other types of lobby groups) emerge. Democratic concessions are a group-specific public good for those who benefit from the concessions. Accordingly, even though all members of a group may share a common objective (e.g. they all want a broader suffrage that gives them the right to vote), each individual has an incentive to free ride on the effort needed to achieve the goal. Olson (1965) highlights selective incentives—that is, the offer of private benefits—as the main mechanism to overcome this problem in a mass organisation. To this, Frohlich et al. (1971) add the important role of the political entrepreneur who has the motivation and the skills to set up an organisation that can coordinate collective action and make it cheap and easy for others to join in. These political entrepreneurs organised reform societies, political unions, or women suffrage organisations which put pressure on incumbent elites to share voting rights through petitions, demonstrations, and public meetings, as well as newspaper articles, pamphlets, and books.

Mobilisation of pro-reform social movements will have little to no effect on democratisation if the elite with the power to extend the franchise are insulated from, or unresponsive to, the calls for reform. Reform movements, therefore, need to connect with those who have the power to change the institutions through their pro-reform agitation. This can happen via (at least) two channels.

First, the theoretical literature on informational lobbying (e.g. Austen-Smith 1994; Lohmann 1995; Grossman and Helpman 2001) shows how agitation and costly mass mobilisation can convey credible information about the intensity with which social movements care about an issue. This is because such mobilisation is costly. The game theoretical logic is that pro-reform social movements with private information about how much reform support really exists have an incentive to overstate the level of support. By investing resources in organising meetings or demonstrations or getting many people to sign a petition, they can credibility signal their private information to the elite who are watching. As such, the scale of reform agitation can be viewed as a barometer of public opinion. The scale of pro-reform mobilisation— the number of petitions, the number of signatures on them, the size of public meetings, and the scale of demonstrations—or the risks that pro-reform agitators are willing to run in the face of repression can, therefore, send credible signals to elite decision makers about how much support exists in the population for suffrage reform.[4] There is, therefore, a key difference between the violent unrest that fuels fears of a revolution (as we discussed above) and peaceful reform agitation orchestrated by pro-reform social movements (besides the fact that one is violent and the other

[4] Even 'cheap talk' can be influential as long as the sender and receiver have sufficiently overlapping interests (Crawford and Sobel 1982).

is peaceful): threat perceptions are governed by observations of violent unrest, whether directly related to democratic demands or not, while peaceful agitation must be directly and specifically related to democratic demands.[5]

Second, members of the incumbent elite who are in favour of suffrage reform for some reason (maybe because they see personal or party political advantage and/or because they are ideologically convinced of the merits of particular democratic principles) may use expressions of public support from pro-reform movements to convince others within the elite of the necessity for reform. For example, throughout the nineteenth century, it was common for reform-friendly politicians in the United Kingdom to refer to extra-parliamentary agitation or to petitions in favour of reform in debates in the two houses of Parliament (Leys 1955).[6]

Pro-reform movements rarely have a permanent organisation or presence. They are single-issue movements with a specific purpose expressed at a particular point in time. Tilly (1988, Chap. 3) offers a powerful theoretical framework for the study of public contention that embeds this feature. His framework combines five elements: common interest (e.g. democratic reform), organisation (e.g. a political entrepreneur), mobilisation of resources (e.g. manpower and money), *and* opportunity (e.g. an elite group that will listen). Together, these elements determine how and when a group may take collection action. Pro-reform movements often emerge when an opening for reform appears for exogenous reasons. Such openings can be created by a rise in discontent caused by economic recessions, by economic conditions that fall below what is expected (Gurr 1970), or by political institutions that fail to keep up with rapid social change (Huntington 1977). The 'window of opportunity' can also be opened by a leader from within the elite with the willingness to reform. As with a revolutionary threat, the window of opportunity has to be open, and once a reform movement begins, positive self-reinforcing social dynamics of the type described by Granovetter (1978) sets in, helping the movement grow and become more powerful.

[5] In practice, the demarcation line between public contention instilling fears of revolution and peaceful mass meetings and demonstrations signaling public opinion is not always sharp. For example, a peaceful meeting can turn violent or the elite may fear that if a revolution were to start, then many of those who have publicly expressed support for reform may be willing to join an uprising. Moreover, Hamburger (1963) argues that pro-reform groups that are essentially peaceful may use the rhetoric of revolution to give the impression that they pose a revolutionary threat even if they do not.

[6] If it is difficult to obtain information from the general population, then the elite may have an incentive to facilitate these types of activities for the same reason as autocrats may want to introduce elections to obtain relevant information about voter preferences (e.g. Laurent-Lucchetti et al. 2024; Martinez-Bravo et al. 2022).

2.3 Top-down theories of democratisation and the political expedience hypothesis

While bottom-up theories of democratisation aim at resolving the democratisation puzzle, top-down theories of democratisation argue that it is not really a puzzle that a ruling elite (sometimes) agree to extend the voting franchise: it is beneficial for at least a subset of the incumbent elite to share power with other groups. The starting point is that the 'elite' consist of subgroups with different interests. A franchise extension can, therefore, resolve pre-existing within-elite tensions or give a subset of the pre-reform elite an advantage after the reform. The political economics literature offers four main theories viewing franchise reform as a top-down, voluntary, and peaceful process initiated by an incumbent elite who perceive an advantage of reforming. While different in the details, the four theories share the common assumption that franchise extension is the result of political expedience.

2.3.1 Pareto-improving extension of the franchise

The theory of suffrage reform developed by Lizzeri and Persico (2004) delivers the striking result that franchise extension can be a Pareto improvement in a democracy where a subset of citizens can already vote: it benefits, or at least does not harm, those who give up their monopoly on power. The theory is based on two main insights. First, it highlights a key distinction between public goods, which benefit everyone, and targeted redistribution, which is excludable and only benefits those receiving the transfers. Second, in a democracy, political parties compete to win elections under given suffrage rules, but they also want to maximise their vote share to make it easier to promote their agenda.

When universal suffrage is adopted, political parties no longer compete for the votes of a small subset of the population but must instead compete for the votes of the entire population. To understand why such a franchise extension can benefit everyone, start by observing that with a small electorate of elite voters, the political parties will find it optimal to use targeted redistribution to win elections. To maximise their vote share, political parties spread the funds available for redistribution over as large a number of voters as possible. But they need to give each elite voter a transfer that is equivalent to what he would have obtained if one of the two parties had offered public goods to avoid being out-competed. This means that some elite voters will not receive anything (as the funds run out). In short, the elite voters are not treated equally by the winning party: some are taxed (along with the non-voters) to buy the support of the rest.

By increasing the size of the electorate, a franchise extension changes the nature of political competition. It becomes too expensive for parties to compete on transfers, and they switch to offering public goods. All citizens benefit from the provision of public goods as they are non-excludable. Consequently, a franchise extension makes the excluded elite voters, who did not benefit from transfers beforehand, and the non-voters strictly better off. The section of the elite who previously benefited from transfers is no worse off because they obtained a transfer which just matched the value of the public good. A franchise extension can, thus, be a Pareto improvement.

This scenario arises when investment in public goods is sufficiently valuable. An implication of the theory, then, is that suffrage reform leads to more spending on public goods. In practice, urbanisation tends to increase the value of investing in the provision of public goods such as sanitation and clean water, and Lizzeri and Persico (2004) use the large investment in sanitation made by local urban authorities in the United Kingdom in the second half of the nineteenth century to illustrate this effect.[7] Other related instances of franchise extension could occur if property rights are better protected under democracy (Gradstein 2007) or if democracy enhances human capital accumulation (Bourguignon and Verdier 2000).

2.3.2 The franchise and post-reform electoral politics

Another rationale for top-down democratisation is that the newly enfranchised voters may support a different set of policies from those supported by the voters under the previous franchise or that they may vote for different political parties. Either way, this can give a subset of the incumbent elite an incentive to extend the franchise to gain a political advantage.

Motivated by nineteenth-century Western Europe, Llavador and Oxoby (2005) develop a top-down theory of democratisation in which factions within the incumbent elite may support franchise extensions in order to manipulate post-reform policy outcomes. They focus on the conflict between a landed elite whose economic interest is tied to agriculture and an industrial elite with an economic interest in manufacturing. They emphasise policies that enhance productivity in the manufacturing sector instead of transfers and pure public goods.

[7] It is clear that the local urban authorities responded to the public health crisis caused by urbanisation by investing huge sums in clean water and sewer systems (Aidt et al. 2010; Chapman 2024). However, many of the investments in clean water were made well before the second (1867) and third (1884–1885) reform acts (Harris and Hinde 2019). Moreover, the decisions were made by politicians elected on the local government franchise, which was different from the franchise governing national elections (Keith-Lucas 1952).

In their setting, the policy choice (the quantity of a productivity-enhancing, sector-specific public good) is determined by the median voter whose identity, in turn, depends on the voting franchise. Initially, only the landed and industrial elite can vote under a suffrage with a high income threshold that disenfranchises all workers. Each elite group is represented by a political party. It does not matter from a policy perspective who wins the election as the logic of the median voter theorem forces the two parties to propose the same policy. However, it matters from a reform perspective because the winning party can unilaterally decide to lower the income threshold that determines who can vote and enfranchise some or all of the workers. The motivation for a reform is that including workers in the electorate changes the identity of the median voter and, thus, the equilibrium policy emerging with the extended franchise.

This model suggests two paths to democracy. The first path is a full extension of the voting franchise to all workers sponsored by the landed elite. The landed elite has no interest in tax-funded policies that enhance productivity in the manufacturing sector. This economic interest is shared by the unskilled workers in agriculture. While unskilled workers everywhere benefit from a more productive manufacturing sector because the derived increase in labour demand pushes up unskilled wages, this is not, in general, sufficient to compensate for the taxes that the unskilled workers, along with everyone else, have to pay to fund the productivity-enhancing policy. By lowering the income threshold to zero and allowing all workers to vote, the landed elite can reduce public spending to a minimum if there are enough unskilled agricultural workers. The second path involves a partial franchise extension sponsored by the industrial elite that includes some high-skilled industrial workers in the electorate. These newly enfranchised voters benefit from spending on policies that improve productivity in manufacturing because the marginal product of labour (and their post-tax real wage) is increased. Accordingly, they agree with the industrial elite that spending should be higher.

Franchise extension in Llavador and Oxoby (2005)'s model is, therefore, linked to the structure of the economy: complete enfranchisement happens with a large agricultural sector, while partial reform happens where manufacturing is dominant. The extension of the franchise is supported by only a section of the elite and is not Pareto improving. Moreover, neither of the two political parties gains any electoral advantage by extending the franchise.[8]

In contrast, the prospect of party political *electoral* advantage plays a central role in Himmelfarb (1966)'s classic account of Britain's Second Reform Bill

[8] See also Pittaluga et al. (2015).

in 1867. The bill was carried by a Tory government after the Liberal Party's attempt at reform had failed. Himmelfarb (1966, 113) argues that the Tory Party's willingness to reform 'came from the belief that the lower classes were not only naturally conservative in temperament but also naturally Conservative in politics.... The Tories were democratic, one might say, because they assumed that the demos was Tory.' Along similar lines, Przeworski (2009) links women's suffrage to parties seeking to maximise their vote shares and conjectures that no party wants to enfranchise women unless it expects that the share of the vote it would receive from them would be larger than its current share in the male electorate.

2.3.3 Representation and taxation

An important mechanism behind voluntary institutional reform is exchange of political rights for tax payments. Cox et al. (2024), for example, stress such exchanges in their theory of the historical roots of representative forms of government in Europe. They argue that national elites gave cities the right to self-governance and extended representation in national parliaments to merchants in order to raise revenues, often to finance wars. Others, including Janowitz (1976) and Ticchi and Vindigni (2008), have argued that elites may use the promise of voting rights to motivate conscription armies.

Aidt et al. (2010) develop a mathematical theory of taxpayer democracy of the type common at the local level in Britain and elsewhere throughout the nineteenth century that illuminates the logic of the link between representation and taxation. In a taxpayer democracy, the right to vote is linked to (property) tax payments and, thus, encapsulates the maxim of 'no taxation without representation'. Under this type of suffrage, the local elite may want to manipulate the franchise because they seek to expand the tax base. Therefore, in a taxpayer democracy, suffrage reform involves a trade-off between sharing power and sharing the cost of funding public services.

The model of Aidt et al. (2010) considers an urban economy with three groups: the urban elite, the middle class, and the workers. The urban elite benefit more from the provision of productivity-enhancing public services than the other two groups. They initially control the city council and decide on the provision of public services. To fund these public services, the elite levy a property tax. The incidence of this tax falls mostly on the middle class. The urban elite can manipulate the boundaries of the local electorate by manipulating which properties are subject to the local property tax (endogenous franchise extension), or franchise extension can happen through national reforms that are exogenous to the politics of any particular city.[9]

In this context, partial reform, which extends the franchise to the middle class, can be a Pareto improvement if the tax base effect is sufficiently strong to increase the provision of public services. This gives the local urban elite a strong incentive to include the local middle class in the electorate. However, it is also possible that a forced partial extension of the franchise introduced by national legislation can be Pareto inferior. This happens when the tax base effect is weak and insufficient to overcome the local middle class's desire for low spending. In that case, the urban elite lose influence, the middle class pays more taxes (in exchange for the vote), and the unenfranchised working class is worse off because the extension of the franchise decreases public spending. Such a Pareto inferior extension of the franchise is associated with retrenchment, in contrast to the famous Meltzer-Richard hypothesis, which links franchise extension to fiscal expansion (Meltzer and Richard 1981). Nonetheless, further enfranchisement of the workers will lead to fiscal expansion because workers (for whom it is too costly to field their own candidates) will vote for a representative of the urban elite who will support higher levels of spending because of the expanded tax base. The model, therefore, predicts a U-shaped relationship between local government spending and the size of the electorate: franchise extension is associated with retrenchment at first before leading to fiscal expansion.

2.3.4 Constitutional bargaining and piecemeal suffrage reform

Congleton (2001, 2007, 2011) develops a top-down theory of democracy based on constitutional bargaining in which suffrage reform is the outcome of a bargaining process involving different subgroups within the elite.[10] His conceptual framework examines the relationship between 'King' and 'Parliament' (or 'Council'). Constitutional concessions represent a trade-off in a market for authority: granting the King access to more tax revenues versus giving Parliament more authority over various dimensions of policy-making. Typically, the King and Parliament have different preferences regarding the composition (and level) of public spending. Initially, the King possesses veto power over spending policy. Parliament can offer the King a transfer—interpreted as access to

[9] When the right to vote is linked to tax payments, property values, income, or education, the franchise evolves endogenously, as changing economic and social conditions enlarge or contract the set of citizens satisfying the given qualifications (Congleton 2004).

[10] See also Coll (2008); Munshi (2011); Horpedahl (2011); Nikolova and Nikolova (2017); and Tridimas (2021).

tax revenues—in exchange for a change in spending policy. The issue with this arrangement, however, is that in the absence of a mechanism to enforce the agreement, the King has an incentive to accept the payment and then revert to his preferred policy. Congleton's solution to this dilemma is constitutional reform: the two parties agree to a new power-sharing institution that cannot be unilaterally altered by either of them. The new institutional setting grants Parliament policy-making authority, either defined as veto or agenda-setting powers, over some spending decisions. This makes the exchange of tax revenue for a different policy mix an enforceable agreement because it grants Parliament the right to decide on some aspects of spending policy in the future. Consequently, the potential gains from trade in the market for authority can be realised. Exogenous shocks can lead to further constitutional reforms and a rearrangement of authority as new opportunities for additional beneficial trades open up.

As such, in Congleton (2011)'s framework, as in other top-down theories of democratisation, franchise extension and other constitutional reforms are the results of mutually beneficial bargaining inside the elite. Politicians implement major constitutional reforms because they expect to benefit, politically, and/or personally, from the new constitutional framework and the policies it enables. Fear of revolution or popular agitation does not trigger reform directly, as in some bottom-up theories, but can play an indirect role by shocking the system in a way that opens up new possibilities for mutually beneficial bargains between 'King' and 'Parliament'.

2.4 Three hypotheses about the causes of suffrage reform

We can summarise the theoretical discussion in the previous sections with these three hypotheses:

Hypothesis 1 *The threat of revolution hypothesis: Suffrage reforms happen because the incumbent elite with the power to change the existing institutions want to prevent a revolution from happening.*

Hypothesis 2 *The social movement hypothesis: Suffrage reforms happen because pivotal members of the incumbent elite with the power to change the existing institutions are persuaded by pro-reform social movements and public opinion to do so.*

Hypothesis 3 *The political expedience hypothesis: Suffrage reforms happen because it is expedient for pivotal members of the incumbent elite with the power to change the existing institutions and support reform.*

While the three hypotheses highlight very different theoretical mechanisms, they do not need to be mutually exclusive. In fact, they could, in principle, all operate at the same time. As we shall stress in the subsequent chapters, when suffrage reform is viewed as a process with many steps and many potential roadblocks that must be overcome for success, a natural conjecture is that different mechanisms come to the forefront at different points in the process and fade into the background at others.

2.5 Evidence on the three hypotheses

These three hypotheses have, of course, been subjected to empirical investigation, in many different historical contexts and with contemporaneous data. In particular, the historiographical literature on the threat of revolution (Maehl 1967; Royle 2000), on social movements (Tilly 1995), and on political expedience (Himmelfarb (1966); Congleton (2011, Chap. 13)) in relation to Britain's three reform acts in the nineteenth century is very rich. However, as Congleton (2011, 573) points out, there is a tendency that 'historical narratives were written with [particular] models in mind, and it is possible that factors focused on were given greater prominence than they deserve'. As a complement, there is a clear need for systematic econometric testing.

The political economics and political science literature have adopted two approaches to econometrically testing the competing theories of franchise extension. The first approach looks for evidence of the *consequences* of suffrage reform that are consistent with particular theories. The second approach directly focuses on the *causes* of suffrage reform identified by particular theories.

2.5.1 The consequences of suffrage reform

This approach starts from the premise that the causal mechanisms emphasised by the competing theories are too hard to quantify directly. As such, it contends that it is best to estimate the post-reform consequences and to assess whether they are consistent with specific theories.

Fiscal consequences: One branch of this literature takes a comparative approach and exploits the fact that many of the theories discussed above make precise predictions about post-reform outcomes related to public spending, redistribution, and taxation. Researchers have confronted these predictions with cross-country panel data from across the world (e.g. Boix 2001; Mulligan et al. 2004; Przeworski 2009), from Western Europe (e.g. Lindert 1994; Aidt and Jensen 2009), from Latin America (Aidt and Eterovic 2011), or from British municipalities (Aidt et al. 2010; Chapman 2018, 2024) with mixed results. For example, Aidt et al. (2006) find that franchise extensions in Western Europe before World War II were associated with investment in public services, which is broadly consistent with Lizzeri and Persico (2004)'s theory, but find little evidence of more spending on redistribution (as predicted by the theories of Acemoglu and Robinson (2000*b*) and Boix (2003)).[11] With this type of data, however, it is hard to establish that the observed consequences are causally linked to suffrage reform in general and even harder to link the conditional correlations that emerge back to particular theories.[12]

Stock market consequences: Another branch of this literature argues that the stock market reaction to particular suffrage reforms can be informative about the underlying causes that drive them. For this purpose, it borrows event study techniques from the financial economics literature to test the threat of revolution theory. It contends that if the stock market reacted positively to a successful reform or if it reacted negatively to violent unrest in the lead up to a reform, then the market participants and the politicians who undertook the reform might have been motivated by a threat of revolution. While Dasgupta and Ziblatt (2015) find evidence supporting the threat of revolution theory from the British sovereign bond market in 1832 and 1867, Turner and Zhan (2012) find that market participants were more concerned about the economic consequences of these reforms than about revolutionary threats.[13] Moverover, Cox and Saiegh (2022) attribute the British bond market reaction in 1832 and 1867 to the political risk of government turnover rather than to fears of revolution. These mixed results indicate how difficult it is to attribute stock market reactions to particular events in what is often a complex reform process.

Political consequences: Econometric testing of the political expedience hypothesis requires a more direct focus on the link between the political consequences of suffrage reform and the private interests of the politicians behind

[11] The accumulated evidence on the so-called Meltzer-Richard hypothesis (Meltzer and Richard 1981)—that franchise extension is associated with more redistribution—is surprisingly inconclusive (see the discussion in Seghezza and Morelli (2019) and Aidt, Winer and Zhang (2022)). Partly as a consequence, the empirical evidence on the link between democratisation and post-reform inequality is also mixed (Acemoglu et al. 2015), although recent work by Dorsch and Maarek (2015) shows that democratisation appears to drive extreme income distributions to a 'middle ground'.

[12] Aidt and Jensen (2013) argue that proxies for the threat of revolution can be used as instruments to isolate exogenous variation in the timing of suffrage reforms. They report evidence of a causal effect of franchise extension on total tax revenue in Western Europe during the long nineteenth century.

[13] Studies for other countries also find that stock market participants cared more about the economic consequences of a successful reform than about a potential revolution without reform. This includes Lehmann-Hasemeyer et al. (2014), who analyse Berlin stock market reactions to two suffrage reforms in the state of Saxony in 1896 and 1909, and Opitz (2018), who assesses the reactions to the 1905 Russian revolution of the Russian sovereign bonds listed on the Berlin and Saint Petersburg stock markets.

it. Berlinski and Dewan (2011) and Berlinski et al. (2014) pioneered such an approach in their study of the political consequences of Britain's Second Reform Act in 1867. The fact that the bill was sponsored by the Tory Party but it was the Liberal Party that increased its seat and vote shares in the first election after the reform in 1868 is commonly used as evidence that the threat of revolution (Acemoglu and Robinson 2000*b*), rather than expectations of party political advantage (Himmelfarb 1966), must have played an important role. However, by exploring the differential effect that the reform had on the increase in the number of voters in different constituencies, Berlinski and Dewan (2011) and Berlinski et al. (2014) are able to isolate the causal effect of the reform from constituency-level characteristics correlated with the voting population. They find that the reform was *not* causally linked, but was instead incidental to the victory of the Liberal Party in the 1868 election. It, therefore, appears that the Second Reform Bill did not give any political advantage to either the Tory Party or the Liberal Party.

In the long run, however, the Tories' reform gamble may have paid off, as the quantitative evidence of Ziblatt (2017) suggests. In light of the efforts made by the Tory Party in building a robust party organisation after 1832, Tory politicians attracted enough middle- and working-class voters to govern for twenty-three years between 1868 and 1905 under the voting franchises of the Second and Third Reform Acts. Larcinese (2024) uses an approach similar to that of Berlinski and Dewan (2011) to study the political consequences of universal male suffrage in Italy in 1912. He also fails to find a causal effect of the reform on the representation in parliament of parties considered 'social reformers'. These findings cast doubt on theories that view party political advantage as the driving force of suffrage reform.

2.5.2 The causes of suffrage reform

The second approach directly focuses on the causes of suffrage reform identified by particular theories and relates them to quantitative measures of democratic change. An important distinction is between causal triggers and structural causes. The structural causes determine if reform can happen—that is, if a society is ripe for reform. These are the state variables of the social system. The causal triggers determine the timing of reform, conditional on the structural causes. They can be thought of as shocks to the social system. The trigger and structural causes do not only operate at different time scales and with different speed; they also interact in complex ways. If, on the one hand, the configuration of structural causes is such that no causal trigger can induce reform, then nothing happens; if, on the other hand, the configuration of structural factors is such that reform is possible, its precise timing depends on the presence of a causal trigger.

An example can flesh this out in a more concrete way. In Acemoglu and Robinson's theory of franchise extension (e.g. Acemoglu and Robinson 2001), the level of inequality is a structural cause that affects the risk of revolution and the ability of the elite to prevent revolution via redistribution. A trigger cause is a negative income shock that opens the 'window of opportunity' and makes the threat of revolution real in the minds of the elite. What is needed, in this theory, for a democratisation to happen is that the level of inequality is sufficiently high to make a revolution worthwhile for the poor *and* that a recession creates sufficient discontent to motivate the elite to share power to prevent unrest turning into a revolution.

Many scholars in the comparative political economy literature on the structural causes of democracy have emphasised modernisation theory—that is, the hypothesis that democratisation is a logical consequence of economic growth, social progress, and advances in education (Lipset 1960; Rueschemeyer et al. 1992). This theory is, however, disputed empirically (see Acemoglu et al. (2008) for evidence against, and Gundlach and Paldam (2009), Boix (2011), and Paldam (2021) for evidence in favour). Przeworski and Limongi (1997) agree that the income level of a society does not matter for democratic reform per se but argue that it is important for the consolidation of democracy once a transition from autocracy has happened. Pre-reform inequality is another important structural factor that plays a role in many theories, including the threat of revolution theory. Dorsch and Maarek (2020) test this theory and find that inequality increases the chance of a democratisation but only, as predicted, when the 'window of opportunity' is open in a downturn—that is, the structural factor only operates in the presence of a trigger cause. Ansell and Samuels (2010, 2014) also stress inequality but distinguish between land and income inequality to show that they affect the likelihood of suffrage reform differently.

The empirical literature on trigger causes has largely focused on testing the two bottom-up theories—that is, the threat of revolution and social movement hypotheses—but there is also some promising micro-political econometric work on the political expedience hypothesis.

Testing the threat of revolution theory: The fundamental problem with any statistical test of the threat of revolution hypothesis is that the elite's perception of the threat is not directly observed. Researchers have engaged with this problem in two ways. The first approach is to use pre-reform information on social unrest which would have been available to the elites contemplating reform to proxy for the threat. Przeworski (2009), who pioneered this approach, finds a positive correlation between social unrest and franchise reforms in a world sample covering the nineteenth and twentieth centuries. Aidt and Jensen (2014) develop a more specific empirical test based on their theoretical model where leaders in one country can learn about the threat of revolution by observing revolutionary events in other countries. In a sample of suffrage reforms in Europe between 1820 and 1938, they find robust evidence that the threat of revolution, as measured by revolutionary events in neighbouring countries, was systematically related to the evolution of suffrage rights. This is consistent with Acemoglu and Robinson (2000*b*)'s theory of franchise extension and with international diffusion of information about revolutionary threats being an important transmission mechanism.

The second approach is to exploit the fact that the threat of revolution varies with economic conditions and shocks. Using this approach, Burke and Leigh (2010) and Brückner and Ciccone (2011) establish that democratic change happens when the 'window of opportunity' is open in a downturn. Aidt and Leon-Ablan (2016) extend this analysis by studying the link between economic shocks, riots, and democratisation. Similarly, Franck (2016) finds that economic shocks, in the form of floods, hampered the consolidation of democracy in late nineteenth-century France.

Testing the social movement hypothesis: Formal statistical testing of the social movement hypothesis is also hampered by measurement problems. Consequently, much of the existing evidence comes from detailed historical or contemporaneous case studies.[14] The seminal historical case study is Tilly (1995)'s investigation of public contention around the time of the Great Reform Act of 1832. He concludes that 'short of revolution, for successive popular mobilisations [the] parliamentary actions of 1828–34 deeply altered British politics.... The public meeting, the demonstration, the petition drive, the formation of specialized associations and related forms of social-movement politics became the standard means for pressing popular collective claims.... Mass popular politics had arrived on a national scale' Tilly (1995, 338–339). In his opinion, the reform movement and the extra-parliamentary agitation in the late 1820s and early 1830s played an important role for the Great Reform Act.

Going beyond such case studies is hard. Econometric tests of the hypothesis that social movements are a critical trigger of suffrage reform is hindered by the lack of comparable data that capture the strength of such movements over time and space as well as by the many potential confounding factors. Marino et al. (2020) attempt to overcome these problems in a panel study of 171 countries from 1971 to 2010 that explicitly models time-varying unobserved factors. They

[14] Contemporaneous cases include Bunce and Wolchik (2006) and Chenoweth and Stephan (2011) who argue that non-violent mobilisation was instrumental in bringing about democratisation in several countries in South Asia, Central and Eastern Europe, and Sub-Saharan Africa in the 1990s.

show that peaceful protest and agitation mattered both for triggering democratic reform and for democratic consolidation.[15]

An important historical case where social activism is thought to have played a pivotal role in obtaining voting rights is that of the women's suffrage movements, in particular in the United Kingdom and the United States. However, on this issue, quantitative evidence is also scarce, and most studies are descriptive and qualitative (e.g. Smith 1998; McConnaughy 2013; Adams 2014).[16] Teele (2018*a*)'s analysis of the suffrage movement in the United Kingdom, United States, and France represents a rare exception. She argues that some incumbent male politicians were considering women's suffrage with an eye to the party electoral advantage that it could bring. Teele (2018*a*) conjectures that they used the activities of women's suffrage movements to estimate the likely voting behaviour of women. The strongest supporting evidence come from the experience of the US states: Teele (2018*b*) shows that the size of the membership of the National American Women's Suffrage Association positively affected the likelihood of women's suffrage in the US states that gave women the right to vote before 1920. Furthermore, Morgan-Collins (2021) shows that the political preferences of female voters in the United States in 1920 varied with the strength of the women's suffrage movement in a county, suggesting that it is possible to learn about preferences by observing movement strength.

Testing the political expedience hypothesis: The hypothesis that has proved the hardest to test statistically is the political expedience hypothesis. The most promising approach to investigating political expedience as a causal driver of democratisation is to focus on particular reforms that were voted on by elected (pre-reform) parliaments. This makes it possible to study vote records and to relate the voting behaviour of certain politicians to their personal interest. Ziblatt (2008) pioneered this approach in his study of the failed attempt to reform the in-egalitarian 'three class' voting system in Prussia in 1912. He exploits the fact that the suffrage to the national parliament of the German Empire was universal (for men) at the time to assess how individual Prussian legislators would benefit or lose from the proposed Prussian reform had it passed. He finds that those who stood to gain electorally were more likely to support the reform, which is consistent with the political expedience hypothesis.

To sum up, the many comparative studies of structural and trigger causes of democratic change have clearly improved our knowledge. Still the literature suffers from many of the same weaknesses that haunt the comparative literature

[15] In contrast, violent protest has ambiguous consequences, as it favours initial democratic transitions but at the cost of threatening democratic consolidation.

[16] Adams (2014)'s careful study of women's suffrage across the world demonstrates that the general picture is complex. In many cases, such movements hardly existed or, if they did, only played a minor role.

on the consequences of democratic change. The comparative approach makes it hard to isolate causal effects. Where attempts are made to use instrumental variables to address this problem, as in the literature that uses weather shocks to induce exogenous variation in economic conditions that then trigger democratic change (e.g. Brückner and Ciccone 2011), the gap between what is being estimated and the underlying theoretical mechanism widens.

2.6 The micro-political process-focused approach

In this book, we argue that a new micro-political process-focused approach is required to improve our understanding of the relevance and importance of the three (types of) theories of franchise extension. We seek to study the theoretical mechanisms at the micro-political level. We neither take a bird's eye view of many democratisation episodes nor use the historical narrative to provide evidence of a particular theory. Instead we focus on one reform—the Great Reform Act of 1832—and we use micro-political data related to the causes which (might have) motivated the politicians who voted on reform and which were generated by that reform process itself to test the three competing theories. Schonhardt-Bailey (2006) and Ziblatt (2008) take approaches which are related to ours. While Ziblatt (2008), as noted above, deals with suffrage reform in Prussia, Schonhardt-Bailey (2006) deals with a different topic, namely, international trade and the repeal of the Corn Laws in the United Kingdom in the 1840s.

The advantages of this micro-political approach are manyfold. First and foremost, while it can be a useful abstraction to treat a democratic reform as one event, it is more accurate to describe such reforms as a process consisting of many important events. A successful reform has, typically, avoided numerous roadblocks that could have stopped it in its track. These roadblocks and the way they were overcome provide insights into the mechanisms of democratisation. Our approach is to leverage the process aspect and exploit the multiple events to explore the mechanisms of democratisation at the micro-political level.

Second, the reform process generates a wealth of micro data related to the identity of the main actors and their actions. Examples include data on socio-economic conditions of the politicians voting on the reform, information on votes and divisions in pre-existing parliaments, and data on the geography and intensity of violent protest and social unrest as well as on the activities of pro-reform social movements. These data are generated at different points in the process and enable quantitative, statistical tests of potential mechanisms. Most importantly, perhaps, these quantitative footprints are well-suited for formal testing of competing theories of suffrage reform within the common framework of a particular reform process.

Third, the approach highlights the multi-causal nature of democratisation and allows for the possibility that different causal mechanisms may operate with different intensities around different roadblocks within the same reform process. Conceptually, this is important because this diversity is lost in the comparative approach, where each process is treated as one successful democratisation event, and because the quantitative assessment of competing theories is not possible in the narrative approach.

Fourth, suffrage reforms are the results of choices made by individuals within the pre-reform elite with the power to change the existing institutions and rules. We want to understand what motivated them, why they decided to accept or even push for reform. Getting inside their heads is, of course, impossible. As a second best, our approach aims at linking the revealed choices of key decision makers to observable features of the environment in which they operated that capture elements of threats, social movement agitation, and self-interest. Studies of financial market reactions take a step in this direct by analysing particular reforms and by looking at different events in the reform process, but they focus on market participants, not the politicians involved. Comparative studies of the causes of democratisation focus on the outcome of successful democratisation processes (but ignore unsuccessful ones) and try to infer from this what might have motivated the politicians who made the process conclude with a successful reform.

The main weakness of our approach, which zooms in on a single reform process, is its limited external validity. The limitation arises from the fact that it is hard to generalise from particular cases. What are needed, then, are more studies applying the same methodology to other reform processes. Each study will provide one more piece of the overall puzzle, and in that way the generality of specific findings can be evaluated and judged. Such studies are beginning to emerge. Castaneda-Dower et al. (2018), for example, study the outcome of a reform in Tsarist Russia that instituted local governments in 1864. They use data on peasant disturbances between 1851 and 1863 to assess the impact of past unrest on the degree of local representation given to peasants after the reform. The results are in line with Acemoglu and Robinson (2000*b*): in places with a more permanent threat, the local elite could deal with the threat of revolution without sharing power.

PART II

HISTORICAL BACKGROUND

Chapter 3
Reform politics before 1830

3.1 Introduction

If the Great Reform Act of 1832 ends the era of the Unreformed Parliament, it is less clear when the 'Old Regime' began.[1] Was it in 1660, with the restoration of Charles II in the wake of the Second English Civil War? Or did it begin in 1688, with the Glorious Revolution that overthrew James II of England (James VII of Scotland) and the coming to power of William of Orange (William III of England) and Mary (Mary II of England)?

Whatever the precise starting point, it is generally agreed that the period between 1660 and 1832 was characterised by the continued rise of the political power of the British Parliament at the expense of the monarch (Jupp 2006; Congleton 2011). In 1762–1763, John Stuart, third Earl of Bute, commonly known as Lord Bute (1713–1792), was the last Prime Minister (or First Lord of the Treasury as the position was then called) to be directly appointed by the King without accounting for the makeup of Parliament. Afterwards, the Prime Minister needed to command a majority of support in the House of Commons (although not always needed on every bill), which made it harder for the King to control who would head his Cabinet.[2]

During the seventeenth and eighteenth centuries, most matters of internal dissent in Great Britain revolved around faith. A defining feature of the Old Regime was the delicate balance between the State and the Anglican Church that excluded from political life Catholics and, to a lesser extent, other branches of Protestantism that dissented from the Anglican Church. Nonetheless, ideas of liberty emerging from the American War of Independence and from the French Revolution did have an impact on political debates, and sustained calls for parliamentary reform had already begun in the 1760s.

[1] Many books engage with the period from the Second English Civil War to the time of the Reform Act and beyond, including Black (1993), Brewer (1989), Briggs (2000), Clark (1986), Clark (2000), Healey (2023), Hill (1967), Hilton (2006), Hoppit (2000), Langford (1976), Langford (1989), Namier (1957), O'Gorman (2016), Stone (1972), Thompson (1963), Turner (1999), and Wedgwood (1958). Dickson (1967) and Daunton (1995) focus on the economy of the period.

[2] However, even after the Great Reform Act, Queen Victoria (r. 1837–1901) still had enough clout in 1839 to enable William Lamb, second Viscount Melbourne (1779–1848) to remain Prime Minister and prevent Robert Peel (1788-1850) from replacing him. She was also supportive of the minority government led by Lord Derby (1799–1869) in 1858–1859, which briefly interrupted the premiership of Viscount Palmerston (1784–1865).

Peaceful and Violent Origins of Voting Rights. Toke S. Aidt and Raphaël Franck, Oxford University Press.
 DOI: 10.1093/9780197679746.003.0003

The era also marked the beginnings of the industrial revolution in England, which started in the second half of the eighteenth century and progressively lifted mankind out of the Malthusian trap.[3] The economic changes brought about by the industrial revolution created demands for democratisation and parliamentary reform. As Cannon (1973, 263) puts it, Edmund Cartwright (1743–1823), who invented the power loom, might have had done 'more to promote reform than his brother', Major John Cartwright (1740–1824), who campaigned for democratic principles throughout his life.

This chapter briefly reviews the politics of parliamentary reform between 1642 and 1830 (that is, before the reform process that culminated in the Great Reform Act began). In so doing, it stresses the longer-term trends in the political attitudes to democracy and in the wider debate about the proper role of the elected House of Commons within the unwritten English constitution.

3.2 From the English Civil War to the restoration of the monarchy in 1660

There were many political, religious, and economic causes of the English Civil War (1642–1651), and the warring factions had conflicting objectives. King Charles I (r. 1625–1649) and King Charles II (r. 1649–1651, 1660–1685) fought against the Parliament. Bishops and lay members of the Anglican Church of England fought against Catholics and members of other Protestant denominations. Some factions fought for political reform, ranging from the Diggers, who favoured early forms of agrarian socialism, to the Levellers, forerunners of advocates for manhood suffrage and who were wary of the ideas of common property proposed by the Diggers. The war ended when the army of King Charles II was defeated at Worcester in 1651. Oliver Cromwell (1599–1658), who dominated the 'Rump Parliament', then became Lord Protector of the Commonwealth of England, Scotland, and Ireland between 1653 and 1658.

Cromwell's rule was not democratic. However, within the parliamentary army that he had fought with during the civil war, some leaders of the Levellers, most famous among them John Lilburne (1614–1657), Richard Overton (d. 1664), William Walwyn (1600–1681), and John Wildman (c. 1621–1693), expressed democratic ideals in various manifestos, in particular the *Agreement of the People*.[4] This text is usually thought to have been the main influence

[3] Recent studies that aim at explaining the cause(s) of the industrial revolution, its timing, and location, include Acemoglu (2009), Allen (2009), de Vries (2008), Galor (2005), Galor (2011), Mokyr (2009), Jacob (2014), Ó Gráda (2016), and van Zanden (2009).

[4] The Levellers published several manifestos between 1647 and 1649. See Hart and Kenyon (2014) for an anthology of these texts.

during the Putney debates in 1647, which were held to decide on governance institutions for the Commonwealth (Woolrych 1987). During the debates, the most vivid expression of democratic ideas came from Thomas Rainsborough (1610–1648):

> For really I think that the poorest he that is in England hath a life to live, as the greatest he; and therefore truly, sir, I think it's clear, that every man that is to live under a government ought first by his own consent to put himself under that government; and I do think that the poorest man in England is not at all bound in a strict sense to that government that he hath not had a voice to put himself under... (Woodhouse 1951, 53)

Rainsborough's arguments were countered by Henry Ireton (1611–1651), Cromwell's son-in-law, who expressed the rationale for a limited franchise based on property:

> For my part, I think it is no right at all. I think that no person hath a right to an interest or share in the disposing of the affairs of the kingdom, and in determining or choosing those that shall determine what laws we shall be ruled by here—no person hath a right to this, that hath not a permanent fixed interest in this kingdom, and those persons together are properly the represented of this kingdom, and consequently are [also] to make up the representers of this kingdom, who taken together do comprehend whatsoever is of real or permanent interest in the kingdom. (Woodhouse 1951, 53–54)

John Lilburne started revising the *Agreement of the People* in November 1648 with Cromwell's support. Voting rights would be restricted to men paying taxes to fund poor relief, thus excluding beggars, servants, and many others who did not own property subject to taxation. There would be a reallocation of parliamentary seats from smallnomination (rotten) boroughs formerly controlled by peers to the rural counties. A reapportionment of seats was indeed included by John Lambert (1619–1684) when he drafted the first written constitution of Great Britain, known as the *Instrument of Government*, which was promulgated in December 1653 (Healey 2023, 285).

However, Cromwell's death in 1658 was to stop any attempt at democratic reform. His son Richard (1626–1712) proved unable to remain in power. Parliamentarians decided to call for new elections on 16 March 1660 under the pre–civil war voting rules and seat distribution. The elections resulted in a royalist majority that met in Westminster on 25 April 1660 and enabled the restoration of the monarchy under King Charles II.

3.3 From the restoration to the accession of George III in 1760

In the 100 years from the restoration of the monarchy under Charles II in 1660 to the accession to the throne of George III in 1760, Britain experienced important political changes. In 1688, the Glorious Revolution ushered in a new political era which ultimately led to the establishment of the House of Hanover, successively headed by the Protestant George I (r. 1714–1727) and George II (r. 1727–1760), and quashed all hopes of a Catholic king from the House of Stuart.[5] But the 1688 revolution, in spite of its important institutional and economic reforms, did not reform the voting suffrage or lead to any major redistribution of parliamentary seats.[6] Only two new towns were enfranchised between 1660 and 1760: Newark in 1673 and Durham in 1675. Likewise, the Acts of Union in 1707 (6 Ann. c. 11), which united England and Scotland into one kingdom and established the Parliament of Great Britain after its ratification by the Parliament of England and the Parliament of Scotland, also failed to modify election procedures and the distribution of seats in England and Wales.

Between 1660 and 1760, there was no major call, neither outside nor inside Parliament, for parliamentary reform. There was little appetite for challenging the political status quo. This was because any attempt at reform would be quickly associated either with the 'republicanism' and 'regicide' of Cromwell or with the 'popery' and 'tyranny' of James II. In that way, such attempts would be construed as a threat to both the monarchy and the Anglican Church of England. This is not to say that major thinkers like Locke (1689) or Hume (1752) did not write about parliamentary reform. But at the time, their writings had little impact on British politics, which was deeply concerned with the perpetuation of a Protestant monarchy.

The period, however, saw two new factions emerge in Parliament which would have a surprising longevity: the Tories and the Whigs. The factions first began to appear around the time of the Exclusion Crisis (1679–1681), when Parliament considered three successive bills which aimed at preventing the accession of the then presumptive heir to the throne, the future James II,

[5] In hindsight, it is tempting to paint the Jacobite movement (named after James II) as a romantic cause that was lost from the start and that was led by ineffective leaders mainly remembered nowadays for their derisive nicknames (James Francis Edward Stuart (1688–1766) was nicknamed 'The Old Pretender'; John Erskine, Earl of Mar (1675–1732) was known as 'Bobbing John'; Charles Edward Stuart (1720–1788) was nicknamed 'Bonnie Prince Charlie'). However, for the British ruling elite, the Jacobite cause represented a Catholic threat to the Protestant succession in which foreign powers were involved and which led to two uprisings (in 1715 and 1745). There was also some minor but genuine support within the British population for the Jacobites, which was only quashed by their defeat in April 1746 at the battle of Culloden (Langford 1976; Clark 2000).

[6] North and Weingast (1989) relate the Glorious Revolution to subsequent economic growth in England. Their argument has been subject to many more (and sometimes contradictory) analyses. See Pincus and Robinson (2014) for a general perspective.

because he was Catholic. Beforehand, the main parliamentary division was between 'Court' and 'Country'. The former group wished to serve Charles II, while the latter were wary of the King's intentions and sought to defend what they viewed as the general interest of the country. The names, Tory and Whig, first appeared in Parliament as insults hurled at opponents before being claimed as a sign of pride and self-identification. It is, indeed, usually understood that Tories were Irish bandits, while Whigs were militant Scottish Presbyterians (e.g. Hill 1996; Turner 1999; O'Gorman 2016), although Jupp (2006, 61) suggests that the term 'Whig' had its origin as Scottish slang for describing sour milk.

The membership of the two factions was fluid, and the shared ideological views were not fixed. Initially, the Whigs had opposed the accession to the throne of James II because of his Roman Catholic religion. They favoured a 'mixed constitution' which rested on the alliance between Parliament and the monarchy. They also thought that the interests of the State should prevail over those of the Church. As a result, they considered that the Anglican Church would be stronger if it were to allow for some measure of tolerance towards Protestant dissenters instead of seeking conformity at all costs. Conversely, the Tories thought that obedience to a one-state Church was of paramount importance. They undoubtedly would have preferred the king to be Protestant, but were willing to accept a Roman Catholic king who could enforce a one-state Church better than the Anglican Church itself. The Tories also subscribed to so-called divine right theory and accepted that the king's will should usually prevail over the wishes of Parliament. Nonetheless, between 1688, when James II was overthrown, and 1714, when the Elector of Hanover became King of Great Britain and Ireland under the name of George I, there were instances where Tories and Whigs as well as Country and Court politicians collaborated within government. After 1714, Tories were excluded for nearly fifty years from government because of their (actual and supposed) hostility towards the protestant Hanoverian monarch. Some historians (e.g. Namier and Brooke 1964, Vol I, 186) argue that neither a Whig nor a Tory party really existed until the last decades of the eighteenth century.

When party alignments began to form again after 1784, they no longer reflected the ideological differences of the late seventeenth century, if only because the Protestant monarchy had been firmly established by then. The Tory party of the late eighteenth century broadly represented the interests of the country gentry, the merchant classes, and various official administrative groups. It had become identified with Anglicanism and supported the Crown. Conversely, Charles James Fox (1749–1806) led a revived Whig party representing the interests of landed aristocrats, religious dissenters, and industrialists. These groups sought limited electoral and parliamentary reforms aimed at transferring power from the Crown to an elected House of Commons. Although it is common to refer to the Whigs and Tories as parties, they were not political parties in the modern sense but loose political factions with parliamentary leaders, core followers, and occasional supporters (Hill 1996).

3.4 From George III to the French Revolution

In the wake of George III's (r. 1760–1820) accession to the throne in 1760, a combination of long-term and proximate causes came together to make parliamentary reform a major political issue. Firstly, among the long-term factors, the onset of the industrial revolution and the tail-end of the 'industrious revolution' had increased the number of artisans, lawyers, industrialists, and merchants who wanted a say in public affairs. Secondly, under George I and George II, the number of peerages that became extinct had outpaced the number of new peers in the House of Lords. This led to more vocal demands from people outside Parliament who, given their land and wealth, felt entitled to a peerage. Thirdly, there had been a reduction in contested elections to the House of Commons in both the boroughs and the counties. This had closed off one path for men of means to win seats in the House of Commons. The underlying reason was not only that the government administration had strengthened its hold on many borough and county seats, but also that some aristocratic families had successfully stifled all electoral competition at the local level. Finally, in the second half of the eighteenth century, the American War of Independence (1775–1783) triggered calls for parliamentary reform in Britain. Many were dismayed that Lord North (1732–1792) remained Prime Minister through patronage and control of rotten boroughs when his government was losing the war. Others were inspired by the democratic ideas advocated by some of the colonists in America.

Two men were, in very different ways, proximate causes for sparking parliamentary agitation and demands for reform: King George III (r. 1760–1820) and John Wilkes (1725–1797).[7] In the 1760s, George III was still politically inexperienced.[8] He elevated his favourite, Lord Bute (1713–1792), to the position of Prime Minister, at the expense of the coalition led by the Duke of Newcastle (1693–1768) and William Pitt the Elder (1708–1778) that was successfully

[7] After a first mental breakdown between October 1788 and February 1789, King George III became permanently incapacitated in the latter years of his reign because of a mental illness which is usually attributed to porphyria. His son, the future George IV (r. 1820–1830) became Prince Regent in 1810.

[8] For various perspectives, see, for instance, Pares (1953), Namier (1957), Butterfield (1959), Foord (1964), Brewer (1976), and Thomas (2002).

waging the Seven Years' War (1756–1763).[9] Elite groups inside and outside Parliament, and the journalists who were their clients, did not directly criticise the King for choosing his ministers without asking Parliament for approval, as this was considered acceptable in the eighteenth century. However, they considered 'that the crown should be directed in the exercise of this public duty by public motives, and not by private liking and friendship' (Annual Register 1763, 41, as quoted by Butterfield (1959, 49)). Many aristocrats and other wealthy landowners were concerned that the King might disregard the views of both the House of Commons and the House of Lords, where they could voice their interests, and that he would support policies that they opposed. They began to wonder whether a new allocation of seats away from the patronage of the Treasury could prevent 'royal tyranny' from imposing its will on Parliament in the future.

The Wilkes affair of 1763–1774 became the starting shot for the early parliamentary reform movement outside Parliament and for the first attempt at reform inside the House of Commons (Rudé 1962; Wright 1970; Thomas 1996). John Wilkes was a journalist elected for the county of Middlesex in the 1768 General Election. His election was, however, annulled by the House of Commons, as were his subsequent victories in two by-elections in 1769. This led to the creation of the Society for the Supporters of the Bill of Rights. The members sought not only to pay Wilkes's debts but also to promote parliamentary reform. In the meantime, Wilkes's adventurous life led him to flee to France, but he was eventually re-elected for Middlesex in the 1774 General Election, and this time he was allowed to take up his seat. On 21 March 1776, he became the first member of Parliament (MP) to put forward a bill to reform the electoral system (Namier and Brooke 1985, 1286–1298).[10] The then Prime Minister Lord North appeared 'very jocular' when he replied that the 'honourable gentleman was not serious, nor ever meant his proposal should go to a committee' (Cobbett's Parliamentary History vol. 18, 1297). Without the support of other MPs, the House of Commons rejected Wilkes's proposal without a vote.[11]

[9] The Seven Years' War is usually seen as the first round in the fight for global dominance between Great Britain and France between 1750 and 1815. While France won the second round by enabling the independence of the United States of America (1775–1783), Great Britain won the first round (the Seven Years' War, 1756–1763) and the third round (the Revolutionary and Napoleonic Wars, 1792–1815).

[10] Prior to 1832, no reform bill proposal sought to extend voting rights to women. The first attempt was in 1867, when John Stuart Mill (1806–1873) took advantage of the debates preceding the Second Reform Act to introduce an amendment that would grant voting rights to all households, regardless of gender. His amendment was defeated by 194 votes to 73. It was not until after the Fourth Reform Act in 1918 that married women could vote, and not until the Fifth Reform Act in 1928 that all women were granted voting rights on the same terms as men in the United Kingdom (Aidt and Dallal 2008; Teele 2018*a*).

[11] Wilkes was seen as an adventurer, and this is the most likely reason why he did not find any support for reform among the Whigs led by Lord Rockingham (1730–1782) (e.g. Hoffman 1973; Langford 1973).

In 1776, another leading figure of the early reform movement, John Cartwright (1740–1824), who held the rank of major in the Nottinghamshire militia and was an officer in the English navy, began publishing pamphlets in favour of universal male suffrage, the secret ballot, and annual parliaments (following the logic that frequent elections would increase the cost of corruption and would thereby deter it).[12] Extra-parliamentary agitation was not restricted to the 'middling orders'. Christopher Wyvill (1740–1822), a major landowner and Anglican clergyman, formed the Yorkshire Association with other Yorkshire landowners in November 1779 and began campaigning for parliamentary reform.

With the defeat of the British army at Yorktown on 19 October 1781 in the American War of Independence and internal issues linked to the Civil List of the King, Wyvill sensed an opportunity for reform in 1782. He convinced William Pitt the Younger (1759–1806) to present motions in favour of parliamentary reform in the House of Commons. Pitt the Younger, the son of the former Prime Minister William Pitt the Elder, had just been elected to the Commons in 1781 in the nomination borough of Appleby.[13] Pitt's first proposal, which triggered the first major debate on parliamentary reform in the Commons, was defeated by 161 votes to 141 on 7 May 1782 (Cobbett's Parliamentary History vol. 22, 1416–1438). On 5 May 1783, Pitt's second motion, which aimed at increasing the number of county seats and at creating new seats in the larger boroughs, was also defeated by 243 votes to 149 (Cobbett's Parliamentary History vol. 23, 826–875). When Pitt the Younger presented his third reform motion on 18 April 1785, he had been Prime Minister since December 1784. However, even the clout which this position gave him was not enough. His proposal, which would redistribute seats from thirty-six rotten boroughs (that were controlled by patrons) to the counties and to London and would compensate the owners of the thirty-six disenfranchised boroughs for their loss of property, was defeated by 248 votes to 174 (Cobbett's Parliamentary History vol. 25, 432–478).

[12] The idea of annual parliaments had its origin in statuses (4 Ed. III c. 14; 36 Ed. III, c. 10) passed in the fourteenth century which stipulated that MPs should meet at least once a year (Randall 1916). The debate on the length of a Parliament intensified in the seventeenth century because of Charles I's intent to govern without consulting the MPs. In June 1640, the Scottish Parliament passed a 'Triennial Act' such that its members would meet at least once every three years (Healey 2023, 121). On 24 December 1640, in the House of Commons, MP William Strode (1694–1645) put forward a motion for annual parliaments. Strode's motion was modified at the parliamentary committee stage into a Triennial Act (16 Car. 1 c. 1), similar to that of the Scottish Parliament (Healey 2023, 132). Other Triennial Acts were passed in 1664 (16 Car. 2 c. 1) and 1694 (6 & 7 Wm. & Mar. c. 2). In 1716, Parliament passed a 'Septennial Act' (1 Geo. 1. St. 2. c. 38), which limited the duration of a Parliament to seven years. This rule was still in force in 1832, and was only repealed in 1911. In 1771, the Radical MP John Sawbridge (1732–1795) proposed a motion for shorter parliaments, which the House of Commons rejected without debate.

[13] Both men were actually named William Pitt. The monikers 'The Elder' and 'The Younger' are usually used to distinguish them.

While the attempts at reform in the 1770s and 1780s were ultimately unsuccessful, they did result in some minor steps towards more democratic institutions. For instance, the Parliamentary Elections Act 1770 (10 Geo III c. 16) sought to de-politicise the assessment of election petitions (complaining about electoral corruption), while the publication of parliamentary debates (which had been previously prohibited) was allowed from 1771 onwards. This increased transparency. Some minor attempts at weeding out corruption in two rotten boroughs were also successful. Following an election in 1770 in New Shoreham (Sussex), where some voters had received £34 for their vote, Parliament passed an Act in 1771 that disenfranchised sixty-eight electors by name and extended the franchise to freeholders in the nearby hundred of Bramber (Namier and Brooke 1985). In 1782, Parliament voted to extend the franchise to men living in the hundreds in the vicinity of the borough of Cricklade (Wiltshire), once again to limit electoral corruption.

3.5 The French Revolution and the Napoleonic Wars

Pitt the Younger remained Prime Minister without interruption between 1784 and 1801, and again between 1804 and 1806, until his death at age 46. Pitt considered himself an 'independent Whig' but this politics aligned him more with the Tories. Under his premiership, the main constitutional reform was the Acts of Union of 1800 (39 & 40 Geo. 3 c. 67). On 1 January 1801, the bill merged the Kingdoms of Great Britain and Ireland to establish the United Kingdom of Great Britain and Ireland. Pitt modified the franchise in Ireland and abolished some Irish boroughs that would not be represented in the new Parliament but without modifying the franchise or the distribution of seats in England, Wales, and Scotland.

In fact, very soon in his premiership, Pitt the Younger's early interest in parliamentary reform had waned. By 1792, there was again extra-parliamentary agitation for reform, but by that time, Pitt considered that reform 'was neither practical politics, nor to be desired' (Ehrman 1986, 86). This renewed agitation for parliamentary reform had its origin in the outbreak of the French Revolution in 1789 and the ideas of liberty that it projected. The calls were galvanised by opposition to Edmund Burke's (1729–1797) defence of the British Constitution in his *Reflections on the Revolution in France* published in November 1790. Burke (1790) saw social rights as an inheritance from the past based upon reverence for tradition and the existing constitution, and he rejected what he viewed as abstract and impractical ideas of universal rights. A new political order, he argued, could only emerge from old foundations, and it had to respect precedent. The (unreformed) British Constitution had shown its value as the bulwark against the inequities of the Old Regime in France and the violence of the 1789 revolution: it was, therefore, not in need of reform. Burke's defence of the British Constitution became the intellectual basis for the anti-reform Tory position in the five decades that followed. At the same time, however, the book's commercial and intellectual success sparked a counter-reaction which led many to write in support of the ideas emerging from the French Revolution.[14]

From the perspective of pro-reform agitation, the answer to Edmund Burke that would have the greatest impact was Thomas Paine's (1737–1809) book *Rights of Man*. It was published in two parts in 1791 and 1792 (Paine 1791–1792) and had sold more than 200,000 copies by 1793. In particular, the second part, published in 1792, in which Paine argued for democracy based on individual rights and universal male suffrage, was widely read. Calls for reform came from a range of societies, including the Society for Constitutional Information, the London Corresponding Society, and the Society for the Friends of the People. These organisations represented a range of opinions and had different objectives (Cone 1968; Goodwin 1979). For instance, many Whig opposition politicians from both houses of Parliament had joined the exclusive Society for the Friends of the People, which advocated for moderate reform. The more radical societies with a diverse membership of workers and artisans advocated, in line with the ideas of Major Cartwright, for annual parliaments, secret ballot, and universal male suffrage. Some even wanted to abolish the monarchy and aristocratic rule, while others sought to abolish private property and replace it with various forms of common ownership.[15]

Unlike Edmund Burke, who parted ways with a majority of his fellow Whigs over his opposition to the French Revolution, Pitt was not immediately hostile to the overthrow of the Old Regime in France (Ehrman 1986, 79–81). However, when the revolution became increasingly violent, he began the repression of radicals at home. Thomas Paine was notably indicted in May 1792 on a charge of seditious libel, and the repression legislation culminated with the suspension of habeas corpus in 1794 (Habeas Corpus Suspension Act 1794, 34 Geo. III, c. 54). That bill would be fiercely fought in vain by the Whigs, and in particular by Charles James Fox (1749–1806), their then leader in the House of Commons who had become a leading proponent of moderate parliamentary reform (Mitchell 1992).

[14] See the anthology of texts in Cobban (1960) or Ben-Israel (1968). See also Jones (2017, Chap. 2) on the influence of Burke's thought on political actors in the 1830s.

[15] The focus in the literature on radical societies advocating for parliamentary reform should not obscure the fact that there were also societies which opposed reform and offered strong loyalist support for the King and the Anglican Church before, during, and after the French Revolution and the Napoleonic Wars. Members of these societies were not only found among the propertied classes but also among sections of societies that were motivated by anti-Catholic sentiment (e.g. Black 1963; Dozier 1983).

If anything, the advocates for reform always tried to distance themselves from the excesses of the French revolutionaries. For example, in the House of Commons, Henry Flood (1732–1791) argued on 4 March 1790 that reformers supported a 'timely reform, and for this reason, that it renders revolutions unnecessary' (Cobbett's Parliamentary History vol. 28, 452–479). However, Flood's motion, which sought to extend the franchise to householders paying a minimum of 50 shillings in taxes per year, was rejected without a vote. The line of reasoning that reform would prevent a revolution was often invoked by pro-reform politicians as it allowed them to show their adherence to the British Constitution and criticise, at the same time, the French revolutionaries. In particular, Charles Grey (1764–1845), who would lead the reform government four decades later in 1830–1832, introduced a reform motion in the House of Commons in 1793 by arguing that 'it was impossible that any set of men, who had not actually lost their senses, should ever propose the French Revolution as a model for imitation' (Cobbett's Parliamentary History vol. 30, 787–925).[16] Unlike Flood's motion from 1790, Grey's reform proposal was voted on but defeated by 282 votes to 41 in the House of Commons. Charles Grey made another attempt at parliamentary reform in May 1797. He sought to introduce a single householder franchise in the boroughs, increase the size of the electorate in the counties, and institute single-member constituencies. Grey put his proposal forward at a time of great difficulty for Pitt's government, when the war against France was raging and a tax increase had provoked economic discontent. Nonetheless, Pitt was able to play on the fear of revolutionary France to defeat Grey's proposal by 256 votes to 91 on 26 May 1797 (Cobbett's Parliamentary History vol. 33, 644–735).

Pitt's repressive policies led to the dismantlement of many of the moderate reform societies. It became very difficult after 1795 to organise open political meetings, and censorship put an effective stop to extra-parliamentary radical agitation. Between 1797 and 1815, when the war against France ended, the reform question was, therefore, less central to British politics. Most Whigs, including Charles Grey, lost interest in the matter. It was not even a useful rallying cry for the Whigs, who remained in opposition, except for a brief period in 1806–1807 during the 'Ministry of All the Talents', a temporary coalition of Whigs and Tories.

Meanwhile, after the death of Pitt the Younger in 1806, leading members of his Cabinet, such as Henry Addington (first Viscount Sidmouth, 1757–1844), Robert Jenkinson (second Earl of Liverpool, 1770–1828), John Scott (Earl of

[16] This statement by Grey might have not convinced many, since his own sympathies with the French revolutionaries were well-known as he was one of the founders and leaders of the Society for the Friends of the People.

Eldon, 1751–1838), and Robert Stewart (Viscount Castlereagh, 1769–1822), joined forces. Unlike Pitt, who never wanted to build a party, they managed to reestablish the 'Tory party', which would control government until 1830.[17] The few attempts at reform from inside Parliament between 1797 and 1815 came from 'Radical' politicians who had been elected in the few open constituencies with many independent voters or from the more reform-minded Whigs. The first was made by Francis Burdett (1770–1844) on 15 June 1809.[18] He proposed to enfranchise householders, but his proposal was defeated by 74 to 15 votes (Hansard HC Deb, 15 June 1809, series 1, vol. 14, cc1041–1071). A year later, the Whig MP Thomas Brand (1774–1851) presented a motion for a household franchise and a reduction of the maximum duration of Parliament from seven to three years, but this was also defeated, by 234 to 115 on 21 May 1810 (Hansard HC Deb, 21 May 1810, series 1, vol. 14, 123–164). Brand's second attempt, on 8 May 1812, garnered even less support and was defeated by 215 to 88 votes (Hansard HC Deb, 8 May 1812, series 1, vol. 23, 99–161). Most Whigs were clearly not seriously committed to reform at the time.

3.6 Reform attempts after the Napoleonic Wars

In 1815, the international status of the United Kingdom was high. The policies of Lord Liverpool and Viscount Castlereagh had been instrumental in maintaining the international alliance against Napoleon and the allied coalition of armies that defeated the French army at Waterloo under the command of Arthur Wesllesley, first Duke of Wellington (1769–1852). However, with the end of the Napoleonic Wars, there was an increase in internal dissent and protest against the government of Lord Liverpool. This was spurred on by post-war economic distress and, notably, by the military discharge of former soldiers looking for civilian employment. In the volatile environment between 1815 and 1820, agitation in favour of parliamentary reform returned with an intensity not seen since the 1780s.

[17] The Tories supported the government of the Duke of Portland (1738–1809) between 1807 and 1809, of Spencer Perceval (1762–1812) between 1809 and 1812, of Lord Liverpool, who remained Prime Minister between 1812 and 1827, of George Canning (1770–1827) between April and August 1827, of Frederick John Robinson, first Earl of Ripon (1782–1859, also known as Viscount Goderich) between August 1827 and January 1828, and of the Duke of Wellington from 1828 until 16 November 1830 (Gash 1984; Derry 1990).

[18] Although a proponent of reform and radical politics, Burdett belonged to a political dynasty. Not only did his grandfather sit in the House of Commons, his own political career began in 1796 at the age of twenty-six, when he was returned for the rotten borough of Boroughbridge. He was then MP for the county of Middlesex between 1802 and 1807. From 1807 to 1837, he was MP for the borough of Westminster, renowned for its large and radical electorate. He became MP for Wiltshire North in 1837 and held that seat until his death on 23 January 1844.

Outside Parliament, the main advocates for parliamentary reform were Major John Cartwright (1740–1825), Henry Hunt (1773–1835), and William Cobbett (1763–1835). Through different means—Cartwright through the Hampden clubs, Hunt through his oratory, and Cobbett through his two-penny press (The *Political Register*)—they campaigned for reform but never developed a single united platform. They disagreed on the franchise—household suffrage or manhood suffrage—and had different goals. While Cobbett sought to redress the harm done to peasants by the industrial revolution, Hunt focused his efforts on the poor in urban industrial areas.

Inside Parliament, the main advocate for reform remained Francis Burdett. The extra-parliamentary reform agitation enticed him to renew his reform efforts in the House of Commons, but with little success. His reform motion in 1817 was defeated by 77 votes to 265 (Hansard HC Deb, 20 May 1817, series 1, vol. 36, c812) while his motion in 1818, in favour of annual parliaments, manhood suffrage, secret ballot, and constituencies of equal size, was defeated by 106 votes to 0 (Cannon 1973, 175).[19] Lord Liverpool's Tory government had no difficulties defeating reform motions inside Parliament. Outside Parliament, the emergence of an effective post-war reform movement was stopped by the government's willingness to repress dissidents (Brock 1973, Chap. 1).

The repression manifested itself in two ways. The first was violent repression of public meetings and riots. On Monday 16 August 1819, Henry Hunt was scheduled to speak at a large public pro-reform meeting at St Peter's Field in Manchester. In spite of the government's recommendations to let the meeting go ahead, the local yeomanry chose to disperse the participants, but ended up charging them, killing 11 and injuring more than 400 people. This tragic event, which quickly became known as 'Peterloo' (in an ironic twist on the name of the Waterloo battle), came after other episodes of disorders which had also been harshly repressed. This includes the Spa Fields riot in December 1816 and the Derbyshire rising of June 1817. The second aspect was the Six Acts of 1819, which were put forward by the government in the wake of Peterloo and adopted on 30 December 1819.[20] The Acts aimed at preventing large meetings and armed insurrection. They also increased the stamp duty on newspapers to hamper their

[19] Burdett found an intellectual justification for his motions in Jeremy Bentham's 1817 *Plan of Parliamentary Reform* (Bentham 1817). However, Bentham's utilitarian arguments were too abstract for his book to provide an effective political argument that would mobilise large sections of the population for reform (Dinwiddy 1984). For more discussion, see Bentham (1819), Cannon (1973, 175–176), Clark (2000, 151–164), and Barrell (2021).

[20] The Six Acts were as follows: Training Prevention Act (60 Geo. 3 & 1 Geo. 4 c. 1), Seizure of Arms Act (60 Geo. 3 & 1 Geo. 4 c. 2), Misdemeanours Act (60 Geo. 3 & 1 Geo. 4 c. 4), Seditious Meetings Act (60 Geo. 3 & 1 Geo. 4 c. 6), Blasphemous and Seditious Libels Act (60 Geo. 3 & 1 Geo. 4 c. 8), and Newspaper and Stamp Duties Act (60 Geo. 3 & 1 Geo. 4 c. 9).

circulation by making them too expensive for ordinary people to buy and toughened punishment against radical journalists guilty of 'blasphemy and seditious libel'.[21] After the Six Acts, Francis Burdett received a fine and was sentenced to three months in prison for his public remarks about Peterloo, while Henry Hunt was sentenced to two and a half years in prison.

Reform calls were nevertheless reignited by the 'Queen Caroline affair' in June 1820. The (future) George IV (r. 1820–1830) and his wife Caroline of Brunswick (1768–1821) had separated in 1796, shortly after the birth of their only daughter, Princess Charlotte of Wales. Before officially ascending to the Crown in 1820, George IV sought a divorce on the grounds of adultery. However, George IV was very unpopular, not least because of his own extramarital affairs. Queen Caroline's return from Italy to London attracted large crowds that came to support the woman who had been wronged. The affair undoubtedly excited the public because of the sexual promiscuity of the members of the ruling elite, but it also attracted reformers, such as Cobbett, who exploited Caroline's appeal as an 'ally of the people' in their reform agitation. Even though the affair somewhat died down when Caroline accepted a grant in early 1821, debates were reignited when she was refused entry at the coronation of George IV on 19 July 1821. She died shortly afterwards, on 7 August 1821.

After the Queen Caroline affair, as economic circumstances improved between 1820 and 1825, extra-parliamentary agitation for reform dwindled. Inside Parliament, the post-war reform calls and agitation had united the Tories in their opposition to reform. They considered that even a modest reform would set a dangerous precedent and feared that it would lead to the abolition of private property in Britain. However, their opposition was also motivated by self-interest since many of them were returned in rotten boroughs and many Tory peers owned nomination boroughs. At the same time, opposition Whig leaders, such as John Charles Spencer (third Earl Spencer, also known as Viscount Althorp, 1782–1845), Lord Grey, and Lord John Russell (1792–1878), remained amenable to moderate parliamentary reform. They considered themselves the political disciples of Charles James Fox, who had been a leading advocate of parliamentary reform from the 1790s onward. Nonetheless, many Whig backbenchers remained reluctant reformers because of the violence of the French Revolution, but also out of self-interest since some of them represented rotten boroughs (Mitchell 1967).

[21] Halévy (1923) saw the Six Acts of 1819 as an example of the repressive nature of Liverpool's government. More recent interpretations suggest that the laws were simply closing loopholes and were not strictly enforced (Derry 1990; Plowright 1996).

This power balance inside Parliament may explain why Lord John Russell focused his reform efforts on disenfranchising the most corrupt rotten boroughs.[22] His first attempt was a bill to disenfranchise Grampound (Cornwall) on 14 December 1819, which he expected to be defeated. He was, however, surprised, as were nearly all MPs, when Castlereagh, who represented Liverpool's government in the House of Commons, rose to second the motion. The borough of Grampound was disenfranchised in February 1821, and its two seats were added to the two existing seats in Yorkshire. In 1827 and 1828, however, arguments related to electoral corruption could not convince Parliament to disenfranchise the rotten boroughs of East Retford in Nottinghamshire and Penryn in Cornwall (Fisher 2009).

Indeed, the disenfranchisement of Grampound would prove to be an exception, and it was impossible to muster a majority for any reform measure for the next decade. John George Lambton (1792–1840, Lord Grey's son-in-law) failed on 17 April 1821 to obtain a majority in the House of Commons in support of householder franchise, equal-sized constituencies, and three-year parliaments.[23] Similarly, in 1822, Russell sought to disenfranchise 100 rotten boroughs and transfer their seats to the counties and to the new industrial centres. His proposal was defeated on 25 April 1822 by 269 to 164 votes (Hansard HC Deb, 5 April 1822, series 2, vol. 7, c139). Russell put again, on 24 April 1823, his 1822 proposal to a vote and was defeated 280 to 169. On 26 May 1826, Russell tried again, this time with a proposal against bribery in elections. The House of Commons was split equally, with sixty-two supporters and sixty-two opponents, but the Speaker of the House cast his vote against the bill. This final defeat led Russell to abandon all hopes of reform. The reform question was put on the back burner while the issues of rights to Catholics, the Corn Laws, and slavery in the West Indies rose to the top of the agenda.[24]

[22] John Russell was the third son of John Russell, sixth Duke of Bedford (1766–1839). He was only called, like other younger sons of aristocrats, 'Lord John Russell' as a matter of convention and courtesy. At the time of the Great Reform Act, he sat in the House of Commons, and he would not automatically be elevated to the House of Lords upon the death of his father. Nonetheless, Lord John Russell became a peer later in life, when Queen Victoria made him an earl in 1861.

[23] George Canning (1770–1827), who then led the Tory government in the Commons, called the vote in a poorly attended House of Commons just when Lambton had temporarily left the chamber for refreshments, and the motion was defeated with 55 votes against 43.

[24] The Corn Laws and Catholic emancipation cut across traditional party divisions. The Whigs usually sought to cut public spending, but many supported, chief among them Lord Grey, the protectionist Corn Laws because they were large landowners. As for Catholic emancipation, one of its notable proponents was the liberal Tory MP George Canning, but he could not always find support among the Whigs in the House of Commons or in the House of Lords.

3.7 The end of the Unreformed Parliament

In the late 1820s, three events contributed to putting reform back on the agenda. First, bad harvest and economic distress in 1829 renewed pressures for reform outside Parliament. Importantly, both Thomas Attwood's (1765–1838) Birmingham Political Union and Francis Place's (1771–1854) London Political Union were established at that time (LoPatin 1999). Through effective political agitation outside Parliament, these unions, along with hundreds of other reform societies, were to play an important role during the reform crisis in the following years.

Second, Lord Liverpool, who had held together the Tory party since 1812, had a stroke in 1827, and was replaced first by George Canning (1770–1827), then by Frederick John Robinson, first Earl of Ripon (1782–1859, also known as Viscount Goderich), and, finally, by the Duke of Wellington in 1828 (Jupp 1998). This succession of leaders substantially weakened the Tory party, which had split into two factions in the 1820s. While the Liberal Tories, who were usually found among the supporters of George Canning, favoured a cautious program of administrative reform and Catholic emancipation, the Ultra Tories led by Edward Knatchbull (1781–1849) and Sir Richard Vivyan (1800–1879) opposed administrative reform and were anti-Catholic. All factions, for which Wellington represented the middle ground, opposed parliamentary reform.

Third, after the 1828 by-election in the Irish county of Clare, which the Catholic lawyer Daniel O'Connell (1775–1847) won, Wellington's government was in a quandary.[25] It faced a rebellion in Ireland if O'Connell was not allowed to take up his seat in the House of Commons, or a split in the Tory party if he was, as this would make Catholic emancipation a reality. Wellington and the Tory leader in the House of Commons, Sir Robert Peel (1788–1850), decided to sponsor the Catholic Relief Act.[26] The Act admitted Roman Catholics to Parliament and to most public offices. It obtained a majority of votes in both houses of Parliament with Whig support and against the strongly held view of many conservative Ultra Tories (Machin 1964; Macaulay 2016).

The Catholic Relief Act dealt a blow to the Tory party and had the side-effect of making the group of Ultra Tories (temporarily) supporters of parliamentary reform. They feared that without parliamentary reform, a new Catholic party, solidly based on the Irish constituencies, might improve its position by buying up rotten boroughs. One of these Ultras, George Spencer-Churchill, sixth Duke of Marlborough and also known as the Marquess of Blandford (1793–1857),

[25] Under the idiosyncratic rules of the Unreformed Parliament, Catholics could run in the elections to the House of Commons but could not take their seat if elected.

[26] An Act for the Relief of His Majesty's Roman Catholic Subjects (10 Geo. 4 c. 7).

used this argument on 18 February 1830 when he presented a bill proposing that the rotten boroughs should be abolished and their seats transferred to the big cities and counties. The bill was defeated by 160 to 57, but it was significant in that it was supported by a core of Ultra Tories.[27] The Catholic question created tension amongst the Tories which would have important ramifications for the prospect of parliamentary reform, and Cannon (1973, 190) goes as far as to claim that 'the Catholic emancipation was the battering ram that broke down the old unreformed system'.

In sum, serious attempts at reform had been made between 1770 and 1792 and, again, in the post-war period (1815–1830). In both cases, calls for reform came from political movements outside Parliament as well as from Whig or Radical politicians inside Parliament. A central argument for reform was that it was needed to prevent violent political change. While all attempts failed (except for the disenfranchisement of the borough of Grampound), this combination of extra-parliamentary agitation, fears of revolution, and a willingness of part of the aristocratic elite to contemplate reform had created a powerful template for the reform process that started in 1830 and ended with the Great Reform Act of 1832.

[27] The Hansard HC Deb, 18 February 1830, series 2, vol. 23, c724 records the draft bill, but it mistakenly reports the votes of an amendment rather than the votes on the bill itself, which are reported in the Journal of the House of Commons vol. LXXXV, 70, 18 February 1830 (see Cannon 1973, 194, fn. 1).

Chapter 4
From the Unreformed Parliament to the Great Reform Act

4.1 Introduction

This chapter sets the stage for the constitutional drama that unfolded between November 1830 and June 1832 and resulted in the Great Reform Act of 1832.[1] It highlights salient features of the Unreformed Parliament and the events between November 1830 and June 1832 that subsequent chapters will focus on. The chapter concludes with an evaluation of the economic and political consequences of the Great Reform Act that provides some perspective on its actual importance.

4.2 The Unreformed Parliament

4.2.1 The legislative process

Before and after 1832, the British Parliament consisted of two houses: the House of Commons and the House of Lords. All the members of Parliament (MPs) in the House of Commons were elected, while the members of the House of Lords were appointed (directly or indirectly) by the King or had inherited their seats. The monarch in 1830, King William IV, formally appointed the government cabinet. Both MPs and lords could serve in the Cabinet; it was not unusual that the Prime Minister sat in the House of Lords rather than as an elected MP in the House of Commons.

The primary function of the House of Commons was to legislate. The House of Lords, however, had two functions. It was the final court of appeal for civil and criminal law, and it was the upper house of Parliament that could propose and veto legislation. The two houses of Parliament were, in theory, equal, but customary differences in their legal prerogatives had developed over the centuries, in particular in relation to financial bills.[2] This meant that legislation concerning

[1] This chapter draws, in some parts, on Aidt and Franck (2013).

[2] Following customary practices from the Middle Ages that the House of Lords would not discuss the details of the financial bills adopted in the House of Commons, the MPs explicitly asserted their

Peaceful and Violent Origins of Voting Rights. Toke S. Aidt and Raphaël Franck, Oxford University Press.
 DOI: 10.1093/9780197679746.003.0004

constitutional arrangements (as well as other bills) needed to obtain a majority in both houses before receiving royal assent and becoming law.

Most legislation originated from the House of Commons, either as public bills sponsored by the Cabinet or as private members' bills, and required a majority in the Commons before being considered by the House of Lords.[3] The voting procedure in the two houses was very similar, and each bill was given three 'readings'. The first reading of a bill in the House of Commons was a formal matter without debate. The second reading enabled the MPs to discuss the bill and its general principles. At the end of the second reading debate, a simple majority vote would take place—the MPs would divide into the two voting lobbies to indicate an aye or a nay—to decide if it would proceed to the committee stage. At the committee stage, the bill would be considered either by a select committee or, for major pieces of legislation, by the entire house. The articles of the bill would be investigated in detail, and amendments could be introduced (including by the opposition) before the bill was referred back to the full house. MPs were then asked to approve or reject each amendment by majority vote. The bill would proceed to the third and final reading (and vote), which was, typically, a formal matter.

After a bill had passed through these three stages in the House of Commons, it would be sent to the House of Lords, where the first reading also was a formal matter. After a second reading debate, the lords voted—with a roll call. If the bill obtained a simple majority, it would go through a committee stage similar to that in the House of Commons, and if it successfully cleared the committee stage, it would eventually be subject to a third reading. However, if the lords voted against a bill at the second reading, it would be thrown out. In that case, if the Cabinet wanted to persist, it would have to present a new bill in the Commons and start the process again. Bills amended by the House of Lords were sent back to the Commons for approval (or amendment) and would ultimately come back to them.[4] A bill that obtained a majority in the third reading in the House of Lords would be submitted to the Crown for royal assent.

ultimate authority in financial matters in resolutions passed in 1671 and 1678. In 1671, the House of Commons stated 'that in all aids given to the King by the Commons, the rate or tax ought not to be altered by the Lords' (Journal of the House of Commons, vol. IX, 235, 3 April 1671). Seven years later, it passed a broader resolution asserting its sole authority in all matters related to financial legislation (Journal of the House of Commons, vol. IX, 509, 3 July 1678). The Parliamentary Act of 1911 (1 & 2 Geo. 5. c. 13) formalised this custom.

[3] The House of Lords had the right to propose legislation directly, which was then considered by the Commons. By 1830, however, all major legislation came from the Commons, and the upper house operated mostly as a legislative backstop that occasionally blocked legislation coming from the Commons (Jones 2012, 160).

[4] If amendments made either by the House of Lords or by the Commons could not be accepted by the other house, then members of the two houses would meet to resolve the disagreement. If they could not reach an agreement, the bill would be dismissed; otherwise it would proceed to the next stage in the legislative process.

There was one major difference between the voting procedures in the two houses. The lords had the right to vote by proxy while the MPs in the Commons did not and had to be present in person.[5] Under this system, any lord could give a proxy to another lord for a whole session or only for specific instances.[6] Proxies were not used in a vote unless at least one peer asked for them to be counted, in which case they were counted separately from the votes of the lords who were present. This system made it hard to predict the strength of support or opposition to a bill in the Lords.

4.2.2 Peers and bishops in the House of Lords

All peers in the House of Lords were (directly or indirectly) appointed by the Crown or had inherited their seat, and they were not directly accountable to anyone. This made the House of Lords inherently conservative in its attitude to change and an unrelenting defender of aristocratic government (Turberville 1958; Smith 1992). The peers, either as members of the Lords or as patrons controlling the return of MPs to the House of Commons, dominated British politics.

The aristocratic peers in the House of Lords were less distinguished by their title (duke, marquess, earl, viscount, or baron) than by the (English, Scottish, or Irish) origin of their peerage, which determined whether they had an automatic hereditary right to sit in the House of Lords. There were two types of hereditary peers. Only a minority could show that their ancestors had attended a medieval parliament by writ of summons from the Crown. The majority had either received a peerage or had ancestors who had received a peerage through royal letters, sometimes quite recently. In most cases, the peerage was transmitted by male primogeniture, but in a few instances, royal letters might have enabled transmission through close relatives, including women.[7]

Holding an hereditary peerage of England, of Great Britain, or of the United Kingdom (from 1801 onwards) was a necessary but not sufficient condition for sitting in the House of Lords for life: one also had to be a twenty-one-year-old man who had not been declared insane and not been convicted of a felony. In addition, a peer had to be formally introduced to his seat, after swearing the oaths of political and religious allegiance that notably included the abjuration of Catholicism. Finally, three members of the royal family sat in the House of

[5] Proxy voting in the House of Lords was abolished in 1868 (Standing order 32 A of 31 March 1868).

[6] At any time, a lord could hold two proxies at most.

[7] In the Unreformed Parliament, the female holder of a peerage could not sit in the House of Lords and could not vote. In 1832, sixteen women held a peerage (Lodge 1832).

Lords and participated in the votes on the Reform Bill: the Duke of Cumberland (Ernest Augustus, 1771–1851), the Duke of Gloucester (William Frederick, 1776–1834), and the Duke of Sussex (Augustus Frederick, 1773–1843). Both the Duke of Cumberland and the Duke of Gloucester, respectively a brother and a cousin of William IV, opposed the reform, but the Duke of Sussex, who was also a brother of William IV, supported it.

There were three types of non-hereditary peers in the House of Lords: the Scottish peers, the Irish peers, and the archbishops and bishops of the Churches of England and Ireland. They were appointed for a fixed term, and their seats could not be inherited. In fact, many members of the Scottish and Irish peerage, as well as some of the bishops, did not automatically have a seat in the House of Lords.

First, under the Acts of Union of 1707 (6 Ann. c. 11) and with some minor changes afterwards, holders of the Scottish peerage were entitled to elect sixteen lords to the House of Lords. These sixteen lords were elected each time there was a general election to the House of Commons—that is, for a maximum of seven years.[8] Second, under the Act of the Union of Great Britain and Ireland (39 & 40 Geo. 3 c. 67) that became effective on 1 January 1801, twenty-eight Irish peers were elected for life by other holders of the Irish peerage. As such, the elections of Irish lords were de facto by-elections which took place after a peer had died.[9] Finally, the non-hereditary peers also comprised the higher echelons of the Church of England and of Ireland. The two archbishops (of Canterbury and York) and twenty-four other bishops of the Church of England sat in the House of Lords.[10] In addition, through a system of representatives, four members of the Church of Ireland had seats in the Lords.

4.2.3 The voting franchise and the social composition of the MPs

In 1830, the Unreformed House of Commons had 658 seats, which were divided between 188 county seats, 465 borough seats, and 5 university seats.[11] In England, there were 244 constituencies: 40 county, 202 borough, and 2 university

[8] After a Scottish peer had been given a British or United Kingdom peerage, and as a result, could sit automatically in Parliament, he could still take part in the election of the Scottish lords.

[9] An Irish peer who received a British or United Kingdom peerage did not lose his Irish seat in the House of Lords.

[10] The bishop of Soder and Man as well as the colonial bishops of Barbados, Calcutta, Jamaica, Nova Scotia, and Quebec did not have a right to sit in the House of Lords.

[11] The universities of Cambridge, Oxford, and Dublin were self-governing bodies that returned MPs on a franchise that granted the right to vote to all doctors and masters of arts at Cambridge and Oxford and to the provost, fellows, and foundation scholars at the University of Dublin. Cambridge and Oxford returned two MPs each to represent the two universities, while the University of Dublin only returned one.

constituencies. Each constituency returned, with a few exceptions, 2 MPs, for a total of 489 English MPs.[12] Wales had twenty-four constituencies, split between twelve counties and twelve boroughs, each returning one MP. Finally, Ireland had sixty-six constituencies, while Scotland had forty-eight.[13] The Great Reform Act itself only applied to England and Wales, but as we discuss below, subsequent legislation also reformed representation in Scotland and Ireland.

The rules which governed the elections to the House of Commons had not been modified in nearly two centuries prior to 1832. Despite the relocation of economic activity and internal migration, the new economic centres in the north of England and in the Midlands had no representation in 1830 but for Liverpool. Most borough constituencies were small market towns, and some constituencies established in the Middle Ages were largely depopulated. Consequently, a very small proportion of the population lived in boroughs with representation, and even fewer had the right to vote. We estimate that in England and Wales before the reform, there were approximately 461,788 (male) voters out of a total population in 1831 of 13,880,641 (see Table 4.6). While all counties had the right to return two (or, in the case of Yorkshire, four) MPs and the voters who could elect these MPs resided in the countryside, most urban areas were unrepresented. A useful metaphor for the political geography of the Unreformed House of Commons is to think of the borough constituencies as small islands of representation within the counties surrounded by scores of unrepresented cities, towns, and villages. Figure 4.1 illustrates this with the three borough constituencies of Colchester, Harwich, and Maldon in the county of Essex.

The MPs received no salary, those who wanted to run were subject to a high property qualification (Witmer 1943), and contested elections could be very expensive to win.[14] Unsurprisingly, the House of Commons was dominated by the landowning interest (Woolley 1938), and yet the MPs held a variety of occupations. Figure 4.2 illustrates the aristocratic nature of the Unreformed House of Commons very clearly. It shows data on the occupations and the social backgrounds of the MPs elected in 1830 and in 1831—the last two elections under the rules of the Unreformed Parliament. The MPs were army officers, lawyers or jurists, bankers, industry owners, merchants, and landowners, and some were 'dynasty heirs'—that is, they were immediately elected to the Commons in a 'safe' seat when they finished their education, reached majority, or both. Compared to the general population, the MPs were a highly selected group of educated men.

[12] Yorkshire and the City of London returned four MPs, while the boroughs of Abingdon, Banbury, Bewdley, Higham Ferrers, and Monmouth only returned one MP.

[13] An idiosyncrasy of Scotland is that three pairs of counties (Buteshire and Caithness, Clackmannshire and Kinross-shire, and Cromartyshire and Nairnshire) elected MPs in each alternate election.

[14] MPs only began to receive a salary in 1911.

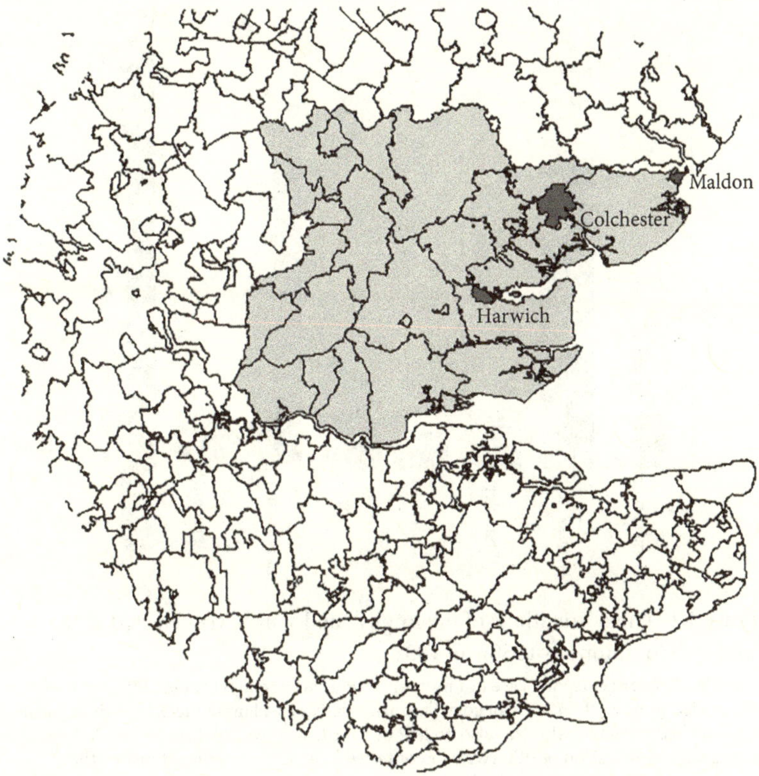

Figure 4.1 Parliamentary boroughs in Essex under the Unreformed Parliament

Note: This map shows the borders of the three parliamentary boroughs of Colchester, Harwich, and Maldon (marked in dark grey) within the county of Essex (marked in market in light grey). In Colchester and in Maldon, the right to vote was given to the freemen of the boroughs, while it was given to the members of the corporation in Harwich. Each of the boroughs returned two MPs. According to Philbin (1965), there were, in 1831, 1,084 voters in Colchester, 20 in Harwich, and 3,113 in Maldon. In addition, there were about 6,000 county voters in Essex who returned 2 MPs.

About 74 percent of them had attended secondary school, and 66 percent had also attended university. Almost 10 percent of the MPs had taken the Grand Tour. The Grand Tour was the educational rite of passage for the members of the British aristocracy to get them acquainted with classical and contemporary art and culture in Continental Europe, in particular in France and in Italy (Trease 1967; Hibbert 1987). The Grand Tour might be viewed as a proxy for open-mindedness and interest in continental philosophy and political ideas (see, in particular, Mitchell (2005, Chap. 5) on the Whigs' bond with France). Finally, many MPs served for many years, and the average length of tenure in the 1830–1831 parliament was eleven years.

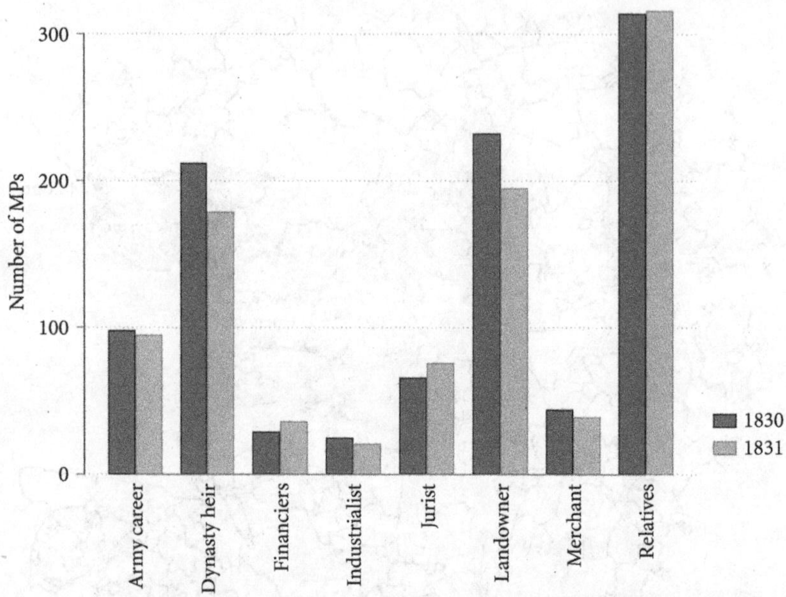

Figure 4.2 The occupations of the English and Welsh MPs elected to the House of Commons in 1830 and 1831

Note: The different categories are not mutually exclusive, and a particular MP can, therefore, be recorded in more than one category (e.g. army career and landowner). 'Relatives' mean MPs who had a relative who was also an MP or a lord, and 'dynasty heir' means MPs who were given a nomination or otherwise uncontested 'safe' seat when they finished their education, reached majority, or both.

Sources: Namier and Brooke (1964), Stooks Smith (1973), Thorne (1986), and various editions of Dod's Parliamentary Companion (Dod and Dod 1832).

The franchise rules of the Unreformed House of Commons were complex and had evolved idiosyncratically over the centuries. Unlike the counties, which all had the same franchise, whereby all men who owned freehold land or property worth at least 40 shillings a year could vote, there were six franchise types in the English and Welsh boroughs. In the freemen boroughs, all individuals with the freeman status were allowed to vote. The freeman status could be inherited, acquired by serving an apprenticeship in the borough, or received as an honour from the borough's corporation (that governed it). In some of the boroughs with a freeman franchise, freemen who did not live in the borough could come and vote. This created a group of so-called 'outvoters' whom candidates looking for support could pay to come and vote for them. In the scot and lot boroughs, inhabitants who paid the local property tax used to fund the Poor Law expenses (the poor rate) could vote. In the potwalloper boroughs, all the resident householders who 'had a family and boiled a pot' could vote. In the freeholder boroughs, the franchise requirement was the same as in the English counties. In the burgage boroughs, the owners of a property with an old form of tenure, called the burgage, could vote. These were often limited to plots of land that had formed the borough when it was first laid out and could be owned by a single person. In the corporation boroughs, only members of the local town council, called the corporation, could vote.

Table 4.1 shows the distribution of boroughs across the six franchise types and the approximate sizes of the electorates in 1830. The rules in the corporation, freeholder, and burgage boroughs typically resulted in very small electorates. In contrast, boroughs with scot and lot, potwalloper, or freeman franchise had relatively large electorates. There were, however, many exceptions, as sizes of the electorates varied within a given type. Moreover, elections to the Unreformed House of Commons were often uncontested (Cannon 1973, Appendix 3), and when a contest did take place, electoral corruption was ripe.[15]

4.2.4 Patrons and nomination seats

It is useful to think of the Unreformed Parliament along a line that measures the degree of aristocratic influence on the elections of MPs. At one end, there were the MPs for the most populous and independent counties, such as Yorkshire, and the two members for Westminster (in Middlesex), a borough with a large and independent electorate known for its radicalism. At the other end, there were the MPs for the so-called 'rotten' boroughs, such as Gatton and Old Sarum, which were almost entirely depopulated and were effectively owned by private individuals who nominated the MPs. Some constituencies (or rather the property with voting rights) were traded for huge sums of money. For example, the Irish (and at the time Tory-leaning) peer Du Pré Alexander, second Earl of Caledon (1777–1839), purchased the constituency of Old Sarum (Wiltshire) for £43,000 in 1802, while the Whig peer William Harry Vane, third Earl of Darlington (1766–1842), bought the constituency of Camelford (Cornwall) for £58,000 in 1815 (Thorne 1986).

As a rule of thumb, one can assume that the influence of patrons increases as one moves to the left across the columns and down across the rows of Table 4.1 towards the smaller boroughs. In many of the small borough constituencies, aristocratic patrons controlled the elections by buying votes, which was made possible by the absence of secret ballot. The voters either expected to be treated with food and drink in return for their vote, and that could be a very costly affair, or they expected a direct payment, as in Shaftesbury

[15] For an example of printed material during electoral campaigns before 1832, see Barker and Vincent (2001).

Table 4.1 The franchise types in the borough constituencies in England and Wales in 1830

	Franchise type						
Size of the electorate	Scot and Lot A	Potwalloper B	Freeman C	Freeholder D	Corporation E	Burgage F	Total
1. Over 5,000	1	1	5				7
2. 1,001–5,000	6	2	25	4			37
3. 601–1,000	8	5	11	1			25
4. 301–600	11	1	16				28
5. 101–300	8	5	12	1	1	10	37
6. 51–100	4		6		2	10	22
7. 50 or less	2		14		27	15	58
Total	40	14	88	6	30	35	214

Note: See Brock (1973, Table 2) for the coding of the English boroughs. For the Welsh boroughs, the coding is as follows: A3. Flint; A4. Haverfordwest; E7. Beaumaris; C2. Pembroke; C3. Cardiff; Carmartheren, and Montgomery; C4. Cardigan, Carnarvon, and Denbigh; C5. Radnor; C7. Brecon.

Sources: Brock (1973, Table 2) for the 202 English boroughs and own coding based on Philbin (1965) and Fisher (2009) for the Welsh boroughs.

(Dorset) and Stockbridge (Hampshire), where Richard Grosvenor, the second Earl Grosvenor (1795–1869), paid 20 guineas to each of 300 voters and £60 apiece to more than 100 voters (Sack 1980, 914). Outvoters, typically freemen with the right to vote in a borough but who lived elsewhere, and county voters would expect to get compensated for traveling to the polling place. In Colchester (Essex), for example, the Radical lawyer Daniel W. Harvey (1786–1863) told his outvoters in 1830 that they had become too expensive and had cost him £25,000 over the years, or more than £6,000 per election (Brock 1973, 101). Accordingly, it was in the interest of the candidates, whether supported by a patron or not, to avoid a contested election if possible, or for patrons to simply give up their influence when the cost did not match the benefit anymore. The very fact that the cost of controlling elections under the rules of the Unreformed Parliament had become so high gave some patrons reasons to think that *some* measure of reform of the election system would be beneficial as a means to reducing costs.

To quantify the influence of patrons on the election of MPs, we construct a patronage index. Based on the qualitative information provided by Philbin (1965), we divide the constituencies into five categories. We consider that there was a high degree of aristocratic influence in a constituency when (i) a single patron controlled the governing body of the borough or had ownership of the property to which voting rights were attached or when (ii) a single patron effectively nominated the MPs or a sharing arrangement between multiple patrons was in place, with each of the patrons nominating one MP without a contested election ('high influence'). We consider that patrons had an intermediate degree of influence when Philbin (1965) records that one, but not all the seats were controlled by a patron, or records evidence of rivalry between at least two patrons ('some influence'). We also single out the so-called Treasury boroughs, which were under the patronage of the government usually through employment ('Treasury borough'). Philbin (1965) explicitly characterises some constituencies as independent constituencies ('no influence'). Finally, we assume that there was a low degree of aristocratic influence when Philbin (1965) does not provide any specific information.

Table 4.2 shows that the majority of the English and Welsh constituencies were under some form of aristocratic or governmental influence in 1830 and that patrons directly controlled about 36 percent of the boroughs. The counties were, theoretically, more independent than the boroughs because of their relatively large electorates. Nevertheless, the landowning aristocracy also controlled the majority of county seats for two reasons. First, the farmers who could vote in the counties did not have the financial resources to stand up to the local landlords and openly vote against his interest or recommendation. Second, the aristocrats with an interest in the county expended large sums on getting voters to the polls and on treating them.

Table 4.2 Aristocratic influence and patronage in England and Wales under the Unreformed Parliament

Patronage index	English Boroughs	Welsh Boroughs	English Counties	Welsh Counties	English Universities	Total
High influence	73	2	8	4	0	87
Some influence	70	8	16	7	0	101
Low influence	25	1	10	0	2	38
No influence	20	1	5	1	0	27
Treasury borough	13	0	1[b]	0	0	14
Total	201[a]	12	40	12	2	267

Note: [a]We do not have information for New Sarum (or Salisbury).
[b]Hampshire would always return court nominees.

Source: Aidt and Franck (2013) based on Philbin (1965).

Table 4.3 Patrons in the House of Lords and the number of British seats in the House of Commons they controlled in the 1826, 1830, or 1831 General Election

Parliament elected in	Number of peers nominating MPs	Number of MPs nominated	Minimum nominated MPs per peer	Maximum nominated MPs per peer	Average nominated MPs per peer
1826	92	205	1	8	2.23
1830	98	214	1	9	2.18
1831	90	195	1	9	2.17

Note: The data refer to seats in England, Wales, and Scotland.

Source: Adopted from Sack (1980, Table 1 and Appendix).

Moreover, many of the aristocratic patrons who controlled seats in the House of Commons were peers who sat in the House of Lords. Table 4.3 shows that in 1826–1831 between 90 and 98 peers controlled between 195 and 205 seats in the House of Commons (Sack 1980). For instance, the Tory peer William Lowther, first Earl of Lonsdale (1757–1844) controlled as many as nine seats, mostly in the North of England in 1830–1831. This gave the peerage political influence, not only directly in the House of Lords, but also indirectly via their control of nomination seats in the House of Commons. Many of these seats were located in the small borough constituencies which were at risk of losing representation.

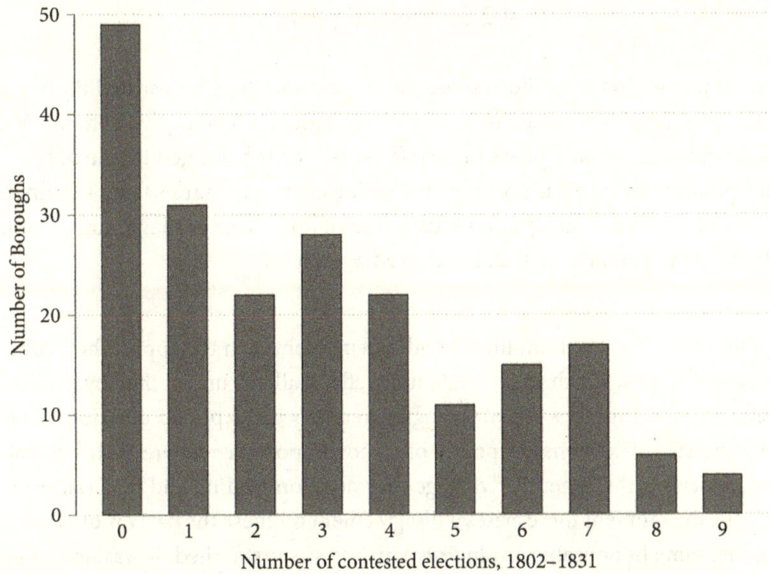

Figure 4.3 Number of contested general elections between 1802 and 1831 in the English borough constituencies

Note: There were nine elections within the period. The histogram includes Grampound which was disenfranchised and had its seats transferred to Yorkshire in 1826.

Source: Cannon (1973, Appendix 3).

Another way to quantity aristocratic influence on the election of MPs and the underlying electoral corruption is to count how many of the nine general elections held between 1802 and 1831 were contested in each constituency. Many elections were uncontested, partly because of patron control over the nomination of MPs and partly because competitive elections were, as we have seen, very expensive to run. Figure 4.3 shows that, in the vast majority of boroughs, less than half of the elections were contested. In a quarter of the boroughs, there was no contested election during the thirty years which preceded the Reform Bill. Only in four boroughs—Beverley (Yorkshire), Boston (Lincolnshire), Liverpool (Lancashire), and Maidstone (Kent)—were all nine elections contested. Although county elections could be particularly expensive, contested elections did take place in at least twenty-two of the forty English counties during the period, while no contest took place in eight of them. In Wales, contested elections were more common, with only three boroughs being entirely uncontested throughout the period (Philbin 1965).

4.2.5 Political parties

Political parties in the modern sense did not exist in the Unreformed Parliament (Hill 1996). Yet, as discussed in Section 3.3 in Chapter 3, many MPs in the House of Commons and many peers in the House of Lords belonged to one of the two main political factions: the Whigs or the Tories. Lord Charles Grey's definition is particularly illuminating as an illustration of how these parliamentary factions differed from modern parties. He viewed a party as

> [T]he connection of honourable and independent men to support their common principles, which they can do more effectually by united than by divided efforts. This supposes a general agreement on great public questions, and occasional concessions on points of minor importance where such become necessary for the general advantage; but none on leading and material principals; the moment there arises a disagreement on these the party is dissolved, on the same honourable ground on which it was first united. It was upon this principle, when very young that I originally connected myself with the Whig party, and I was glad to have the advantage of being assisted and directed in my course, whilst I sacrificed nothing of my independence, by those for whose experience, and integrity and talents I had the highest respect. (Grey to S. Whitbread, n.d. [May 1820], as quoted by Mitchell (1967, 7)).

The Tories had supported the governments appointed by the monarch from 1807 to 1830. They defended the constitutional role of the King and most were hostile to parliamentary reform. Conversely, the Whigs had a long history of supporting parliamentary reform, as we discussed in Chapter 3, but few were willing to go as far as universal male suffrage. Such ideas were reserved for the few Radicals elected to the House of Commons in Westminster and the larger provincial constituencies in 1830 and 1831 (Newbould 1990).

Since the Tory and Whig parties were loose organisations and it was common for MPs and peers to shift their allegiance over time, it is not straightforward to determine their political affiliation. We evaluated and compared the biographical information provided by Dod and Dod (1832), Namier and Brooke (1964), Stooks Smith (1973), Thorne (1986), and Fisher (2009) to construct a complete record of the political affiliations of all the English and Welsh MPs elected in 1826, 1830, and 1831. The House of Commons in 1826 and 1830 was dominated by the Tories, who held about 63 percent of the English and Welsh seats. After the 1831 election, which was fought almost exclusively on the reform question, as we discuss in detail in Chapter 6, the majority had shifted: 55 percent of the seats were held by the Whigs. Most peers in the House of Lords, including the bishops, also belonged to the Tory or the Whig parties, but some were independent. In 1830, the House of Lords was dominated by the Tories, and they held a solid majority amongst the lords. This dominance was the natural consequence of the successive Tory governments which had uninterruptedly ruled the United Kingdom between 1807 and 1830: the more recent peers had been created on the recommendation of Tory-led governments, which had also appointed all the bishops.

While the Whigs and the Tories were sufficiently organised to hold meetings, develop strategies, and organise their own patronage networks and party finance, they were unable to enforce party discipline, even on seemingly core issues such as Catholic emancipation or parliamentary reform (Macaulay (1848); Mitchell (1967, Chap. 1); Jupp (1998)). This meant that the MPs and lords had a large degree of agency and freedom to determine how they would vote on particular bills. Even MPs in nomination seats occasionally voted against the wishes of their patron. Sack (1980, Table 3) compares how MPs in nomination seats in the Commons and their sponsoring patrons in the House of Lords voted on the Reform Bill; he finds that 21.7 percent of these MPs voted aye when their patronal peer voted nay.

4.3 The legislative journey of the Great Reform Act

The reform process started with the 1830 General Election, which had been triggered by the death of George IV. The Tories, who had been in power since 1807 and who had opposed all previous attempts at parliamentary reform, won the election. The Duke of Wellington remained Prime Minister, with Sir Robert Peel as the leader in the House of Commons. They were supported by a weakened Tory party that was rife with internal conflict triggered by the split over Catholic emancipation.

The reform question had re-emerged during the 1830 General Election. This election had highlighted to the governing class many of the weaknesses of the old system, not least the cost of defending seats against self-made reform candidates who openly challenged nomination seats and triggered costly contests (Brock, 1973, 95–97). A number of candidates, notably the eminent Whig lawyer Henry Brougham (1778–1868), campaigned on the need for parliamentary reform. After the election, pressure was building inside and outside Parliament for some measure of reform. However, in a speech to the House of Lords on 2 November 1830, the Duke of Wellington categorically declared that he 'was not prepared to bring forward any measure of reform' and 'he should always feel it his duty to resist such measures when proposed by others' (Hansard, HL Deb, 2 November 1830, series 2, vol. 1, c53). This unsettled moderate Tories and hardened the stance against the government of the Ultra Tories who felt betrayed by Wellington and Peel over the question of Catholic emancipation. On 12 November 1830 in the Commons, the Whig MP Sir Henry Parnell (1776–1842) proposed a motion to refer the Civil List, which would settle the financial arrangements for the new King, to a select committee that was expected to reduce the grant. Wellington's government lost the vote on 15 November 1830 because the Whigs were joined by both moderate and Ultra Tories. Fearing another defeat the following day when Brougham was scheduled to present a motion for parliamentary reform in the Commons, Wellington resigned on the morning of 16 November 1830. On the same day, King William IV gave Charles Grey, who led the Whigs, an opportunity to form a government. This put the reform question firmly on the agenda. Grey made his intentions clear in the House of Lords on 22 November 1830, a few days after having been appointed Prime Minister:

> The principle of my reform is, to prevent the necessity for revolution.... The principle on which I mean to act is neither more nor less than that of reforming to preserve, and not to overthrow. (Hansard HL Deb, 22 November 1830, series 2, vol. 1, c613)

Grey and most of his colleagues were aristocrats who had little sympathy for radical democratic principles. He, therefore, carefully stressed to the committee appointed to draft the bill, which included amongst its four members Lord John Russell, that 'the reform was to be large enough to satisfy public opinion' and yet based on property and existing franchises, thereby ruling out manhood suffrage, and on existing territorial divisions, thereby ruling out electoral districts of equal size (Cannon 1973, 204). The constitutional status of the House of Lords was not up for debate. However, the expectation that many nomination borough constituencies controlled by the peerage would be disenfranchised posed a challenge to the control that the lords could exert over elections to the House of Commons.

The bill was meant to deal with anomalies that had accumulated over time and created the perception that the Unreformed Parliament was corrupt, unrepresentative, and allowed the House of Lords too much influence over who obtained seats in the Commons. The old political geography, which might have made sense in the Middle Ages, was out of synchronisation with the new economic geography of the 1830s. In short, the Whigs would give concessions to the new provincial merchant and manufacturing elite and disenfranchise the worst 'rotten' boroughs.

The committee members based their deliberations on the principle that the small boroughs needed to be disenfranchised. They used the rule that boroughs with less than 2,000 inhabitants would lose both seats and those with less than

4,000 would lose one, based on population data from the 1821 Population Census of Great Britain, and that their seats should be given to the large cities (with more than 10,000 inhabitants) and to the counties. They also favoured the secret ballot, five-year parliaments, and a uniform £20 franchise for the boroughs (giving the vote to householders who occupied a property, either as owner or tenant, worth £20 per year). They also wanted to cut down the cost of elections. This included disenfranchising outvoters immediately but otherwise allowing existing resident electors to retain their old rights to vote for life. However, when the proposal was presented to Lord Grey's Cabinet, the secret ballot was dropped. In addition, the £20 franchise, which had been suggested to counteract the effects of the secret ballot, was replaced with a £10 franchise, as many boroughs that were to keep their two seats hardly had any £20 voters.[16] It was also decided that the maximum duration of a parliament should remain at seven years. Finally, some adjustments to the redistribution of seats were introduced, but the principle upon which it was based remained.

On 1 March 1831, Lord Russell presented the first of three reform bills in the House of Commons. Table 4.4 gives an overview of how the MPs and the lords voted on the three versions of the bill over the following months. After nine days of debate, the initial bill passed the second reading in the House of Commons with a single vote, 302 against 301, on 22 March 1831. The turnout was unusually high (90 percent), and party affiliation was a very strong predictor of the MPs' vote: more than 96 percent of the Whigs and all the Radicals voted in favour, while more than 85 percent of the Tories voted against (see Table 4.4). Yet, the minority of about 15 percent Tories who supported the bill played a key role in getting it through the Commons. However, at the committee stage, Lord Grey's government was defeated on an amendment pertaining to the total number of MPs to be returned in England and Wales.[17] As a consequence and anticipating further defeats, Lord Grey asked the King to dissolve the Commons on 19 April 1831 and call a general election to settle the reform question. Between October 1830 and April 1831, the British Parliament received more than 3,000 petitions, mostly in favour of reform (e.g. Cannon (1973, 214) and Aidt and Leon-Ablan (2023)) and experienced a major rural uprising, the so-called Swing riots (Hobsbawm and Rudé 1973; Holland 2005). In this heated political atmosphere, the 1831 General Election was effectively a referendum on parliamentary reform. Many Tories were not returned, and the election gave the Whigs the majority

[16] In fact, even the £10 cut-off was so high that it would limit in some boroughs the electorate to very few voters. For example, Amersham (Buckinghamshire), with a population of 2,612, only had 25 £10 voters within its old parliamentary boundaries. As a consequence, a Boundary Commission was later in the process tasked with enlarging the boundaries of many of the smaller constituencies and in that way increase the number of houses within the constituencies worth £10 per year.

[17] The first version of the the bill implied a loss of thirty-one seats across England and Wales.

Table 4.4 How the MPs and lords voted on the three versions of the Reform Bill

	Bill	House	Votes for	Votes against
22 March 1831	Second reading of the first Reform Bill	Commons (elected in 1830)	Whig: 248; Radical: 6; Tory: 48; Total: 302 (235)	Whig: 8; Radical: 0; Tory: 293; Total: 301 (249)
6 July 1831	Second reading of the second Reform Bill	Commons (elected in 1831)	Whig: 316; Radical: 10; Tory: 41; Total: 367 (290)	Whig: 5; Radical: 0; Tory: 227; Total: 232 (208)
21 September 1831	Third reading of the second Reform Bill	Commons (elected in 1831)	Whig: 302; Radical: 10; Tory: 34; Total: 346 (282)	Whig: 5; Radical: 0; Tory: 232; Total: 235 (184)
7 October 1831	Second reading of the second Reform Bill	Lords	Whig: 119; Independent: 37; Tory: 2; Bishops: 2; Total: 160 (139)	Whig: 6; Independent: 22; Tory: 171; Bishops: 20; Total: 219 (165)
17 December 1831	Second reading of the third Reform Bill	Commons (elected in 1831)	Whig: 285; Radical: 4; Tory: 35; Total: 324 (275)	Whig: 4; Radical: 0; Tory: 158; Total: 162 (140)
13-14 April 1832	Second reading of the third Reform Bill	Lords	Whig: 122; Independent: 44; Tory: 18; Bishops: 13; Total: 197 (164)	Whig: 5; Independent: 23; Tory: 147; Bishops: 13; Total: 188 (142)
7 May 1832	Committee stage vote to postpone discussion of the disenfranchisement clause	Lords	Whig: 89; Independent: 31; Tory: 2; Bishops: 4; Total: 126 (120)	Whig: 6; Independent: 22; Tory: 126; Bishops: 16; Total: 170 (130)
4 June 1832	Third reading of the third reform bill	Lords	Total: 106	Whig: 1; Independent: 2; Tory: 19; Bishops: 0; Total: 22

Note: For the House of Commons, the votes refer to all MPs, including those elected in Scotland and Ireland. The votes in parentheses refer to the MPs from England and Wales only. For the House of Lords, the votes include all peers, including those with Scottish or Irish peerage. The votes in brackets refer to the lords with English, British, or United Kingdom peerages, and to the bishops.

Sources: Hansard HC Deb, 22 March 1831, series 2, vol. 2, Division List; Hansard HC Deb, 6 July 1831, series 2, vol. 4, Division List; Hansard HC Deb, 21 September 1831, series 2, vol. 7, Division List; Hansard HC Deb, 17 December 1831, series 2, vol. 9, c547; Hansard HL Deb, 7 October 1831, series 2; Hansard HL Deb, 7 October 1831, series 2, vol. 8, c339-344; Hansard HL Deb, 13 April 1832, series 2, vol. 12, c453-455; Hansard HL Deb, 7 May 1832, series 2, vol. 12, c725-728; and Hansard HL Deb, 4 June 1832, series 2, vol. 13, c373.

that they needed to get the Reform Bill through the House of Commons without devastating amendments.

Lord John Russell introduced the second version of the Reform Bill shortly after the election on 24 June 1831. Except for minor adjustments related to the boroughs that were to lose seats, it was identical to the first version of the Reform Bill. At the second reading on 6 July 1831, it passed with a solid majority of 367 against 232, reflecting the outcome of the 1831 General Election. At the committee stage, it was nevertheless amended by the Tories, but still it passed with a comfortable majority at the third reading on 21 September 1831.[18]

The next day, on 22 September 1831, the government presented the bill to the House of Lords. The Lords rejected the bill after five days of heated debate on 7 October, leading to a parliamentary deadlock. At the same time, unrest broke out in many parts of the country, and an alarming rise in political militancy was observed. It was in this volatile political environment that Lord John Russell presented the third version of the Reform Bill in the House of Commons on 12 December 1831 with modifications aimed at winning over the Tory lords—the so-called waverers—interested in a compromise. The bill passed the second reading with a majority of 324 against 162 on 17 December 1831 and proceeded through the committee stage without any significant amendments.

In the months leading up to the presentation of the new version of the bill to the House of Lords, Lord Grey had suggested to a reluctant King William IV that the creation of additional Whig peers might be needed to pass the reform. With that threat hanging in the air, the third version of the bill was presented to the House of Lords on 26 March 1832. The waverers did not want to risk any creation of Whig lords and strategically calculated that the bill could be amended in the committee stage after the second reading. Only the hardliner Tories, including Wellington and the Ultra Tories who opposed reform on principle, voted against, but with the votes of the waverers and support from the bishop of London, the bill passed the second reading in April with a narrow majority of nine votes, seven of which were proxy votes that could not be used at the committee stage. And, unsurprisingly, things went wrong at the committee stage, where the Tory leaders were ready to introduce a series of significant amendments. As soon as the committee stage opened on 7 May 1832, Lord Grey found himself in minority on a critical amendment that would undermine a key element of the Reform Bill: the discussion of the disenfranchisement of the small borough constituencies was to be postponed. The waverers, who had helped the bill in

[18] The Tory amendment was an important clause suggested by the Marquis of Chandos (1776–1839). The Chandos clause gave the right to vote in the counties to tenants-at-will who rented property worth at least £50. It was a clear attempt to shift the balance of the bill towards the landowning aristocracy. Acknowledging that another general election would be counter-productive, Lord Grey allowed a third reading of the bill with the Chandos clause.

the second reading, had joined forces with the hardliners. For Lord Grey, this was an indication that major amendments would follow.

The next day, Lord Grey informed King William IV that he would resign failing the creation of enough Whig peers (around fifty) to carry the bill in the House of Lords. Upon the King's refusal to create such an unprecedentedly large number of new peers, Lord Grey stepped down. The King's message to any new Tory government was, however, very clear: any government had to undertake an extensive reform measure to 'secure tranquility in the land'. This put the Tories in a dilemma for which they had no solution. Robert Peel, the only Tory with any chance of commanding respect (and a majority of MPs) in the Commons, declined to lead a pro-reform Tory government. In the end, the Duke of Wellington had to resort to the speaker of the House of Commons—Charles Manners Sutton (1780–1845)—as his proposed Commons leader, but it soon became clear that a Sutton-Wellington government did not command support in the House of Commons.

All these parliamentary dealings took place in an atmosphere of heightened social unrest and heated reform-related agitation, subsequently known as the Days of May. Pro-reform agitation, stirred in part by reform activists such as Thomas Attwood and Francis Place and their political unions, led to a spike in pro-reform meetings, demonstrations, and riots and to a surge in the number of petitions against Wellington and the Tories. Francis Place sought to add economic stress to the political confusion. While property owners should withhold taxes, investors should withdraw their assets from banks, he argued. The slogan ran: 'To stop the Duke [of Wellington], go for gold'. Talks of an armed uprising were reported throughout the country. While the reform societies and political unions probably did not aim to start a revolution or civil war, their activities could have triggered one nonetheless, and many leading politicians, including Lord John Russell himself, feared a potential violent uprising during the Days of May.

In the end, the attempt to form a Tory government failed, and Lord Grey was recalled by William IV on 18 May 1832. Even though the newspapers did not report anything at the time, their private correspondence shows that the King gave Grey an unconditional promise that he would create fifty new Whig peers if need be (see Grey 1867, Vol 2, 426–437). After the return of Grey to power, the bill went very quickly through the various legal stages in the House of Lords. It only spent seven days in committee. The vote on the third reading took place on 4 June 1832. Not wishing to lose their majority in the Lords, many anti-reform Tories abstained, and only 22 hardliners opposed the bill openly, while 106 peers vote for it. The bill had then garnered majority support in both houses, and the King gave it royal assent on 7 June 1832, with some reluctance. He refused to give his royal assent in person, most likely at the request of his wife Queen Adelaide (1792–1849), who feared that Radical politicians would be elected to the reformed House of Commons (Brougham 1871, Vol 3, 203–204). He even forbade any celebrations that would involve the illumination of government buildings and fireworks in the royal parks (Ziegler 1971, Chap. 17, 220).[19]

4.4 The consequences of the Reform Bill

For nineteenth century 'Whig historians' like Macaulay (1848) and Stubbs (1873), the Great Reform Act consecrated the triumph of the Whig ideas of liberty and progress over revolution and violence. For *them*, as for later historians writing in the Whig tradition (e.g. Butler 1914; Trevelyan 1920), the Act was *great* because it was an important stepping stone on the journey from an oppressive past to modern forms of liberal democracy and constitutional monarchy. For contemporaries, it brought undeniable changes to the political system but without universal suffrage, the secret ballot, and annual parliaments, it disappointed many radicals. O'Gorman (2016, 374) concludes that 'the working classes were cheated out of representation in 1832'. As documented by Gash (1953) and Salmon (2002) amongst others, it is clear, moreover, that many features of the Unreformed Parliament persisted after 1832, most importantly the political dominance of aristocrats and landowners. In that sense, at least, Lord Grey did achieve his objective of 'reforming to preserve, and not to overthrow'. Yet, the Great Reform Act set in motion or at least accelerated important political and legislative processes that contributed to reforming the British political and administrative system over the following decades.

4.4.1 The Reform Bill's main features

While different from the first bill (Parliamentary Papers, 1830–1831, Bills and Acts, vol. 22, II.197 (247)) presented to the Commons two years earlier, the final bill (2 & 3 Will. 4. c. 45), which was given royal assent on 7 June 1832, was nevertheless based on the same main principles (see Brock 1973, Table 3): the electoral system should be based on property and not on individual rights

[19] Since William IV did not attend Parliament to give the bill his assent, it was the Clerk of the Crown who pronounced the traditional formula in French 'Le Roi le veult' (The King wants it). According to Whig politician Sir Denis Le Marchant (1795–1874), just after the Clerk of the Crown had said those words, he received an anonymous note reading: 'It surely would have been more appropriate if you had said "Le canaille le veult".' (Aspinall 1952, 273) (*canaille* is French for scoundrel).

while seats should be redistributed to eliminate the most blatant corruption and to better match the new economic geography. Still, many features of the Unreformed Parliament persisted: both boroughs and counties elected MPs, voting remained open (i.e. not secret), and the maximum duration of a parliament was kept to seven years.

The borough and county franchises. The bill created a uniform franchise in the boroughs based on occupation of property. Initially, the draft bill sought to give the right to vote to local occupiers (as owners or tenants) of properties with an annual value of at least £10. However, this was augmented with the requirement that the occupier needed to pay the local local property tax (the rate) on the property in full and had been in residence for at least twelve months.[20] This innocent-looking change, in practice, disenfranchised many tenant occupiers who rented their properties and where the landlords (i.e. the owners) paid the rate on behalf of the tenants under a system known as compounding (Salmon 2002). The new franchise allowed voters with ancient voting rights to keep them for life if they lived in the borough. Outvoters, mostly freemen who did not live in the borough that had granted them freedom, were, however, disenfranchised so that only freemen living in the borough could qualify.

In the counties, the franchise continued to be based on the 40-shilling freeholders, who previously qualified for the vote, with £10 copyholders and long leaseholders (sixty-one years) included. The Chandos amendment added £50 tenants-at-will if occupiers and short leaseholders (for twenty years).[21] The inclusion in the county franchise of the £10 copyholders, many of whom owned urban property, implied a certain degree of urban penetration into the counties. In effect, it meant that owners of £10 properties in urban areas could vote in the county, if they did not qualify to vote in a borough constituency (because they did not live there).

Seat redistribution: The Great Reform Act redistributed seats away from small and in some cases 'rotten' boroughs to larger towns and cities and to the counties. The guideline adopted to determine which boroughs should wholly or partially lose representation was initially based on population numbers as recorded in the 1821 Population Census of Great Britain. However, in the final bill, the fifty-six boroughs in Schedule A of the Act that lost representation entirely as well as the thirty boroughs in Schedule B that lost one seat were determined with reference to a formula devised by Thomas Drummond (1797–1840), the civil servant who chaired the Boundary Commission. The

[20] Lodgers could also obtain the vote, as long as the value of the occupied property divided by the total number of lodgers exceeded £10 per year and the other requirements were satisfied.

[21] The voting franchise was also extended to certain mortgagees, annuitants, and shareholders in landed property of sufficient value, and to certain office-holders, beneficed clergy, irremovable schoolmasters, parish clerks, and sextons (typically bell ringers and gravediggers).

formula was designed to measure the relative importance of each constituency in an objective way that avoided the issues related to inaccuracies in the population numbers from the 1821 census and to the risk that population numbers in the 1831 census had been strategically inflated. It was based on the number of inhabited houses and total property tax payments (Robson 2014, 74). In the original Schedules A and B, 107 boroughs had been singled out to lose representation; in the final bill, only 56 boroughs were disenfranchised entirely, while the number of single-member constituencies was reduced from 46 to 30. Schedules C and D listed the towns in England and Wales to obtain representation for the first time. The 22 English towns (14 of which were industrial towns) in Schedule C would get two seats, while the 19 English towns and Merthyr Tydfil (Glamorganshire) in Wales in Schedule D with a population of more than 10,000 would obtain one seat. The original bill had only 13 of the largest towns in Schedule C and 18 in Schedule D. During the parliamentary process, 10 more English towns with more than 10,000 inhabitants were added to Schedule D, taking the total to 28. Concerns about creating too many single-member constituencies, however, capped Schedule D at nineteen English constituencies (but added Merthyr Tydfil (Glamorganshire) as number twenty). Rather than denying representation to nine of the towns allocated to Schedule D, the nine biggest of them were given a second seat and moved to Schedule C: the final Schedules C and D would have twenty-two and nineteen English constituencies, respectively. In addition, Swansea (Glamorganshire) in Wales, which had previously been part of Cardiff (Glamorganshire), became an independent borough constituency. Weymouth and Melcombe Regis (Dorset), which had previously returned two MPs each, were taken to be one borough and together elected only two MPs after the reform.

Twenty-six English counties were divided into two constituencies with the right to elect two MPs each (i.e. adding two new seats per county), while each of the three Ridings of Yorkshire also obtained two seats (increasing the county total from four to six). Compared to the initial draft of the bill, additional seats were given to seven English and three Welsh counties in the final bill as part of the attempt to make the bill more acceptable to the large landowners.

Table 4.5 provides an overview of the changes in the geography of representation. It shows the change in the number of constituencies and seats in the boroughs and counties of England and Wales. The most significant effects were in England, where the number of borough constituencies were reduced by fifteen and eighty seats were lost. The English counties, in contrast, gained a total of sixty-two new seats, so that the net result was a loss of eighteen English seats.

Voting procedures: The bill standardised the voting practices, and local authorities would have to compile a register of voters before each election. Voting

Table 4.5 The effect of the Reform Bill on the geography of representation

	Constituencies			Seats			
	Pre	Post	Δ	Pre	Post	Δ	Comments
				Boroughs and universities			
England							
Surviving 2-seats	110	110	0	220	220	0	No change
Surviving 1-seat	4	4	0	4	4	0	No change
City of London	1	1	0	4	4	0	No change
Schedule A[a]	56	0	−56	111	0	−111	All seats lost
Schedule B	30	30	0	60	30	−30	1 seat lost
Schedule C	0	22	22	0	44	44	2 seats gained
Schedule D	0	19	19	0	19	19	1 seat gained
Weymonth	1	1	0	4	2	−2	2 seats lost
University	2	2	0	4	4	0	No change
Subtotal (E)	204	189	−15	407	327	−80	
Wales							
Surviving 1-seat	12	12	0	12	12	0	No change
Schedule D	0	1	1	0	1	1	1 seat gained
Swansea	0	1	1	0	1	1	1 seat gained
Subtotal (W)	12	14	2	12	14	2	
				County constituencies			
England							
2-seats	39	6	−33	78	12	−66	Undivided
4-seats	0	52	52	0	104	104	26 split in two
3-seats	0	7	7	0	21	21	Undivided
Isle of Wight	0	1	1	0	1	1	1 seat gained
Yorkshire	1	3	2	4	6	2	2 seats per riding
Subtotal (E)	40	69	29	82	144	62	
Wales							
1-seat	12	9	−3	12	9	−3	
2-seats	0	3	3	0	6	6	
Subtotal (W)	12	12	0	12	15	3	
County total	52	81	29	94	159	65	
Borough total	216	203	−13	419	341	−78	
England total	244	258	14	489	471	−18	
Wales total	24	26	2	24	29	5	
Total (E and W)	268	284	16	513	500	−13	

Note: Schedules A to D refer to the appendix tables in the final version of the bill that specified which boroughs would lose and gain seats. In the headings, 'pre' refers to before the reform, 'post' refers to after, and 'Δ' is the difference between the two.

[a]Higham Ferrers in Schedule A had only one seat pre-reform; the rest had two.

Sources: Representation of the People Act 1832 (2 & 3 Will. 4. c. 45), Brock (1973, Table 5), and Vincent and Stenton (1971).

would take place over two days throughout the country, and not as was the case before 1832 over several days or weeks. The number of polling stations was to be increased to make it easier for voters to vote. These measures were devised to reduce the cost of elections. However, the bill preserved open voting, thereby doing little to reduce vote buying.[22]

Boundaries of the borough constituencies: The Reform Act implied a significant territorial expansion of many of the surviving borough constituencies into surrounding districts and it subdivided twenty-six counties that previously had been one large constituency into two smaller ones. However, to avoid endless discussions, the bill itself left open the details of how this was to be done. The Boundary Bill (2 & 3 Gul. IV, c. 64), which built on the work of the Boundary Commission, filled in the gaps and received Royal assent on 11 July 1832, five weeks after the adoption of the Great Reform Act. As many as 112 of the 146 English borough constituencies that survived the reform saw a territorial expansion, and in many cases a very significant one (Salmon 2009, 395). The underlying hope was to ensure a minimum of 300 £10 voters in each constituency, but an unintended consequence was, in many cases, to add rural areas to the urban boroughs.

4.4.2 Short-term consequences

The size of the electorate in England and Wales: The new suffrage rules entailed an overall increase in the size of the electorate in England and Wales. It is, however, difficult to accurately quantify this increase as the number of voters before the reform is uncertain and the post-reform registration system only gives a partial picture. The fundamental problem is that there was no registration system before 1832: eligibility to vote could therefore only be established in constituencies were elections were contested and only for those voters who wanted to claim their right. The reform introduced a system of registration, so that systematic information on the number of registered voters exists after 1832. However, since it could be cumbersome to register and even for some county voters required payment of a fee, the number of registered voters likely underestimates the eligible number of voters.[23]

[22] Part of the radical agenda to reduce vote buying was to reduce the duration of a parliament to one year (O'Leary 1962). The logic of holding yearly parliaments was that the resulting increase in electoral contests would make vote buying and excessive treating of voters unaffordable.

[23] Overestimation is also possible insofar as some voters who qualified under both the old pre-reform and the new post-reform rules were sometimes (mistakenly) registered twice and, therefore, double counted.

Table 4.6 The number of voters before and after the Reform Bill

Category	Pre-reform voters (c. 1831)			Post-reform voters (1832)			
	Voters (Local officials)	Max. polled voters	Voters (His. of Par.)	Reg. voters 1832	New voters 1832	Old voters 1832	Δ voters (4) - (3)
	1	2	3	4	5	6	7
England (E)							
Boroughs							
Sch. A	5,882	3,754	5,579	0	0	0	–5,579
Sch. B	4,432	2,649	4,243	9,219	7,711	2,285	4,976
Surviving[a]	132,128	119,200	158,476	178,841	111,361	66,221	20,365
Sch. C & D[b]	0	0	0	82,529	82,579	0	82,579
Borough total	142,442	125,603	168,298	270,639	201,451	68,506	102,341
Counties		188,380	266,232	336,401			70,169
Total (E)[c]		313,983	434,530	607,040			172,510
Wales (W)							
Boroughs	7,324	5,703	7,298	10,807	5,515	4,405	3,509
Counties		13,600	19,960	24,893			4,933
Total (W)		19,303	27,258	35,700			8,442
Total (E&W)		333,286	461,788	642,740			180,952

Note and sources: 'Voters (Local officials)' is the local officials' estimate of the number of borough voters in 1831 reported to the Boundary Commission in 1831 (PP, 1831–1832, vol. 36, XXXVI.489 (607 112 209)) supplemented in a few cases with information from PP, 1830–1831, vol. 10, X.53 (338) for England. For Wales, the data are constructed from the full Boundary Commission Report (PP, 1831–1832, vol. 38-41, XXXVIII.1, XXXIX.1, XL.1, XLI.1 (141)). 'Max. polled voters' is the maximum number of voters who polled between 1802 and 1831 in the boroughs as reported by local officials to the Boundary Commission (PP, 1830–1831, vol. 10, X.23 (204) and PP, 1830–1831, vol. 10, X.53 (338)). For the counties, we report the number of voters who polled in the last contested county election as recorded in Cannon (1973, Appendix 4). 'Voters (His. of Par.)' is the voters in the boroughs and counties recorded in Fisher (2009). 'Reg. voters 1832' is the number of voters who were registered for the 1832 General Election. For the boroughs, this is recorded in Salmon (2002, Appendix 3); for the counties, the data are sourced directly from McCalmont's Parliamentary Poll Book (Vincent and Stenton 1971). 'New voters 1832' and 'Old voters 1832' record, respectively, the voters who registered under the new £10 suffrage and the ones who registered under old pre-reform suffrage rules (Wade 1834).

[a] 'Surviving' is the boroughs that did not lose seats.

[b] Merthyr Tydfill in Wales was listed in Schedule D in the bill. To avoid double-counting, we include its voters within the Welsh boroughs.

[c] The two university constituencies in England are excluded. They had 2,496 (Oxford) and 2,269 (Cambridge) registered voters in 1832 (Fisher 2009).

Table 4.6 records estimates of the number of voters on the eve of the reform (c. 1831) and in the first post-reform election held in December 1832. The local officials overseeing elections in the boroughs were in 1831 asked to report to the Boundary Commission how many voters were eligible to vote in their borough (column 1) along with the maximum number of voters who had voted in any election between 1802 and 1831 (column 2). On their estimate, there were 142,442 English borough voters in total (and 7,324 in Wales), with the maximum number polling in England being 125,603 (and 5,703 in Wales). Fisher (2009) estimates the English borough electorate to be larger, around 168,298 (column 3),[24] while Cannon (1973, Appendix 4) puts the number at 156,000.[25] The 5,579 voters in the disenfranchised boroughs in Schedule A lost their right to vote. The total pre-reform county electorate was 1.6 times larger than the pre-reform borough electorate, while the total number of pre-reform voters in Wales was 27,258. Column 4 reports the number of registered voters in 1832. The borough electorate in England increased by 102,341 to 270,639, while the county electorate increased by about 70,000. For England and Wales combined, the Reform Bill added 180,952 voters, which is an increase of 39 percent. Additional insights can be obtained from columns 5 and 6, where the English borough voters in 1832 in the constituencies that survived the reform ('Sch. B' and 'Surviving') are split between those who registered under the new £10 rule and those who registered under one of the old franchises. In these constituencies, 36 percent of the total number of voters registered in them (68,505 out of 187,578) were registered under the old rules. If all the old franchises had been discontinued immediately, then the expansion of the English borough electorate would have been 33,153 rather than 102,341. Finally, 80 percent of the new borough voters came from the forty-two newly created constituencies in Schedules C and D.

Another way to put the aggregate effect on the size of the electorate into perspective is to compare it with the 'natural' growth in the electorate before and after 1832. Since the franchise rules before and after in different ways were linked to economic and social conditions, the electorate evolved organically as changing circumstances enabled more (or fewer) individuals to quality. Salmon (2009, 394) reports that the electorate grew by 37 percent between 1821 and 1831 in the English boroughs that survived but only by 16 percent between 1831 and 1832

[24] Part of the difference can be attributed to the fact that some officials did not give an estimate. Fisher (2009) and the research team involved with the History of Parliament project were able to fill many of these gaps and to validate or adjust, as appropriate, other estimates by consulting local sources.

[25] O'Gorman (1986, 37) assumes that 20 to 30 percent of voters abstained: he, therefore, estimates the English and Welsh (borough and county) electorate under the Unreformed Parliament (c. 1831) to be between 410,000 and 450,000 men. This is similar to the estimate given by Wade (1834), who estimates the number of borough and country electors before 1832 to 435,000 in England and Wales, and to the total arrived at by Fisher (2009) of 461,788 (Table 4.6, column 3).

Table 4.7 The change in the size of the electorate and in electoral turnout before and after the Reform Bill in the surviving borough constituencies in England and Wales

	1	2	3	4	5	6	7
	N	mean	median	st. dev.	min.	max.	< 0
Δ number of registered voters	144	145	143	991	−4,424	6,504	43
Δ registered voters in % of pop.	144	−1.41	0.15	9.18	−89.8	10.1	69
Δ turnout rate	69	10.4	8.79	21.5	−44.5	68.5	20

Note: The maximum sample size of borough constituencies that existed before and after (surviving constituencies) is 158, but data are missing for some boroughs, and the actual sample size (N) is between 69 and 144. Row 1 shows statistics for the absolute difference between the registered voters in each borough in 1832 and the number of voters reported by local officials for the electorate in 1831. Row 2 shows the difference in percentage points between the registered voters in 1832 relative to the population inside the new boundaries and the local officials' estimate of the electorate in 1831 relative to the population inside the old boundaries. Row 3 reports the percentage points change in the turnout rate. The pre-reform turnout rate is calculated as the number of voters who polled in the last contested election between 1820 and 1831 (if any) and the number of voters reported by local officials to the Boundary Commission in 1831. The post-reform turnout rate is for the 1832 General Election and calculated as the number of voters who polled in percentage of registered voters. Column 7 records the number of boroughs with a contraction in the electorate or in turnout.

Sources: See the note to Table 4.6. The data on the pre- and post-reform populations come from the reports of the Boundary Commission and take into account that the boundaries of many constituencies were changed (larger areas included) (PP, 1831–1832, vol. 36, XXXVI.321 (232) for England and PP, 1831–1832, vol. 38–41, XXXVIII.1, XXXIX.1, XL.1, XLI.1 (141) for Wales).

because of the reform. In the decade after the reform, the growth in registered voters was even smaller, only 10 percent, partly reflecting the natural decline in the population of voters enfranchised under the pre-1832 rules.[26] Viewed in this perspective, the franchise extension of 1832 looks modest.

While the aggregate data in Table 4.6 tell a story of franchise extension, albeit a modest one, they hide very diverse experiences that tell a story of franchise contraction in many cases, as emphasised by Salmon (2009). Table 4.7 and the two histograms in Figure 4.4 provide information on the distribution of the change in the size of the electorate in the constituencies that survived the reform and where it is possible to make a direct 'before and after' comparison. It is striking that about 30 percent of these boroughs experienced a *reduction* in the absolute number of voters (Table 4.7, row 1 and Figure 4.4, panel A), while only 145 voters were added to the average constituency, and half the 158 surviving boroughs welcomed less than 143 new voters. Some boroughs experienced a substantial reduction. In Westminster (Middlesex), the number of voters fell by 4,424, while in the Essex borough of Maldon, it fell by 3,284 voters. The franchise contraction

[26] The number of registered voters in 1839 was 207,425 compared to 188,060 in 1832 (Salmon 2002, Appendix 3).

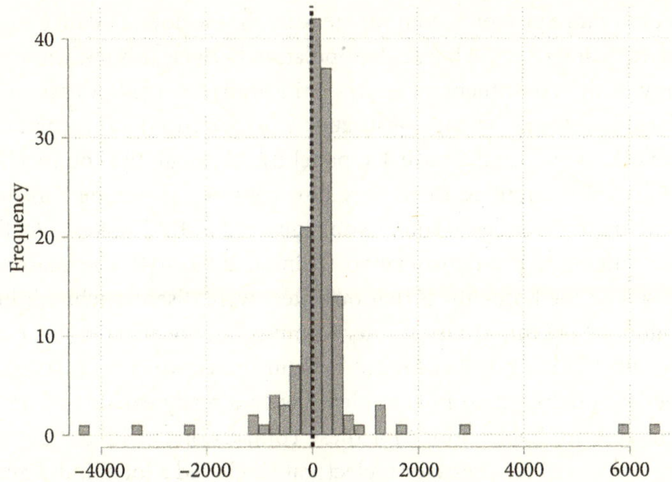

Panel A. Δ electorate (absolute).

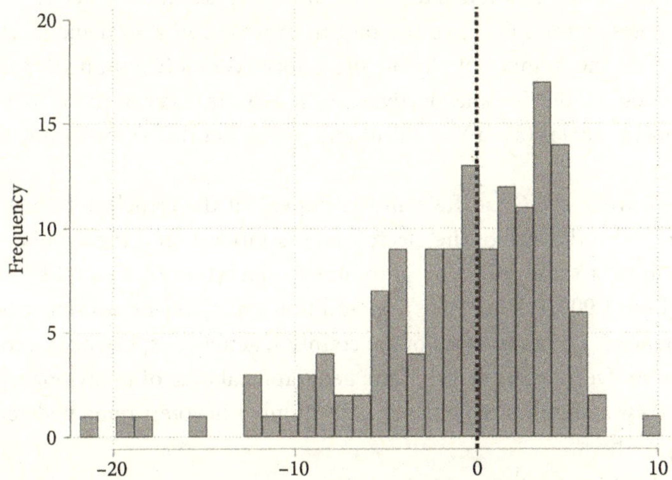

Panel B. Δ electorate per capita (percentage points).

Figure 4.4 The change in the size of the electorate between 1831 and 1832 in the surviving borough constituencies in England and Wales

Note: Panel A shows the difference between the pre-reform number of voters reported by local officials and the post-reform number of registered voters; panel B shows the difference between the pre-reform number of voters reported by local officials and the post-reform number of registered voters in percent of the respective populations. The sample is the borough constituencies in England and Wales that kept at least one of their seats. Maldon (fall of 90 percentage points) excluded in panel B. Negative numbers indicate a franchise contraction.

Source: See the notes to Tables 4.6 and 4.7.

effect is even more pronounced if we measure the electorate relative to the pre- and post-reform size of the borough population because this takes into account that many of the constituencies were significantly enlarged. Measured in this way, almost half the surviving constituencies experienced a franchise contraction (Table 4.7, row 2 and Figure 4.4, panel B). Although the county electorate increased in most counties, there were four counties, including Yorkshire and Suffolk, where the number of voters who registered in 1832 was smaller than the estimated number of pre-reform voters (Salmon 2009, 404). One reason for the contractions in the boroughs is that outvoters were disenfranchised: in places like Maldon, where this group of voters dominated, the effect on the electorate could be substantial. But this cannot explain the contraction in Westminster and other boroughs where non-residents were already excluded from voting before the reform. Explanations for these contractions include the possibility that the estimates of the pre-reform electorate included a lot of individuals who could not actually vote, in particular in constituencies that were rarely contested (Salmon 2009, 389–390). An alternative possibility is that the officials who made the estimates in the middle of the reform process had a strategic incentive to overestimate the number of eligible pre-reform voters (Cannon 1973, 290). In the counties, the decline may partly be related to a transfer of voters to new borough constituencies (as in Yorkshire) and to the fact that some simply failed to register.

In sum, while the Great Reform Act *did* extent the franchise to new voters, the increase in the size of the electorate was modest, and the number of voters remained a small minority of the total population of about 13 million in England (and 904,312 in Wales). In addition, many of the surviving borough constituencies, and even some of the counties, actually experienced a franchise contraction. Despite the fact that the geographical area of many borough constituencies was significantly enlarged, the number of voters remained below 200 in many of them.

Change in the geography of representation: The other major component of the bill was, as shown in Table 4.5 and discussed above, the change of the geography of representation in the House of Commons: seats had been distributed from the small constituencies, many located in the Southwest of England, to fourteen of the large and fast-expanding industrial towns in the Midlands and the North of England and to other urban areas. Nevertheless, the south continued to be over-represented compared to the industrial north (O'Gorman 2016, 370). The newly enfranchised urban constituencies such as Birmingham and Manchester added many new urban voters to the electorate. However, in many of the smaller boroughs, boundary changes meant that rural electors were added to the urban voters, and vice versa. Over time, many of these new electors became less dependent on a single major landowner or employer. As a result, more parliamentary elections in the 1830s and 1840s were contested than before the reform (Wright 1970, 54) and, as political parties became better organised, were fought along party lines (e.g. Dewan et al. 2020). Figure 4.5, panel A, compares the three last elections (1826, 1830, 1831) before the reform to the three first elections (1832, 1835, 1837) after in the 158 surviving borough constituencies and records the fraction that had none, 1, 2, or 3 contests. Before the reform, 40 percent of the boroughs had no contests; afterwards, this had dropped to less than 10 percent. Moreover, only 10 percent of the boroughs witnessed contested elections in the last three campaigns before 1832; in contrast, all three post-reform election were contested in just about half the boroughs. Figure 4.5, panel B, exhibits the change (in percentage points) in the turnout rate in the surviving boroughs where at least one contest took place before and after. For about 80 percent of these boroughs, electoral participation increased, but there is a non-negligible tail of boroughs where it declined. In sum, although less than half the seats were contested in any single post-reform election in the 1830s, the reform *did* result in more elections being competitive and spurred more electoral participation in the places with a contest.

Scotland and Ireland: The Great Reform Act legislated for England and Wales, but soon after it had gained royal assent, reform bills for Scotland and Ireland were passed without much controversy (e.g. Jupp 1967; Brash 1974; Hoppen 1984; Walker 1992).[27] In terms of seat redistribution, there was no significant change in the geography of representation in either Scotland or Ireland. Scotland obtained eight additional seats and Ireland obtained five more, but no existing constituency was disenfranchised in either nation.

The new voting franchise for the two nations was similar to that adopted in the English and Welsh borough and county constituencies. This enlarged the electorate considerably. In Scotland, Jupp (2006, 232–245) estimates that the electorate grew from 1,303 in 1831 to 32,251 in 1832 and 46,000 in 1839 in the boroughs and from 2,500 in 1831 to 33,562 in 1832 and 48,000 in 1839 in the counties. Fry (1992) argues that the Scottish Reform Bill broke the system of patronage that Henry Dundas (1742–1811) and his son Robert (1771–1851) had built. As a result, while not a single Scottish seat had been contested in 1826, many were in the 1830s. Moreover, Scottish MPs elected to the House of Commons after 1832 were no longer the silent and steadfast supporters of the Tory cabinets that they had been since the late 1770s.

An important effect of the Irish Reform Act was to counteract the 'Parliament Elections Act' (10 Geo. 4. c. 8) from 1829. By restricting the voting franchise to

[27] 'An Act to amend the Representation of the People in Scotland' (2 & 3 Will. 4. c. 65) and 'An Act to amend the Representation of the People in Ireland' (2 and 3 Will. 4. c. 88) became law on 17 July and 7 August 1832, respectively.

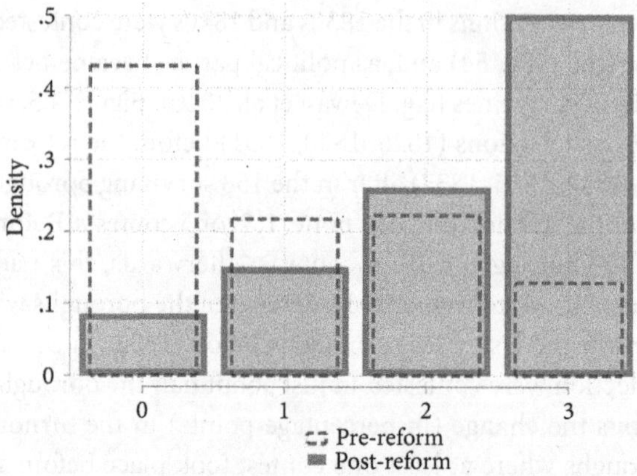

Panel A. Number of contested elections.

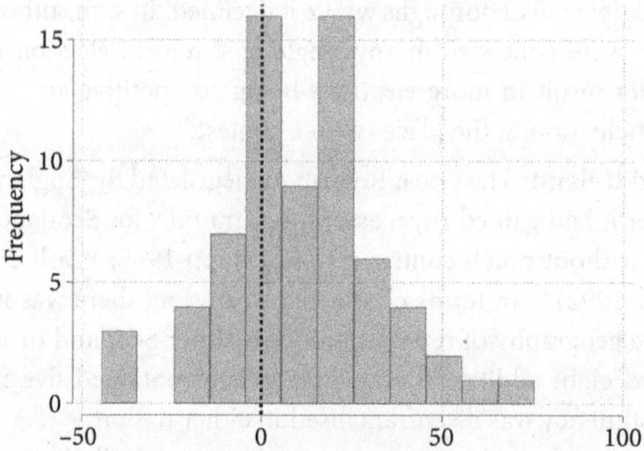

Panel B. Δ turnout rate (percentage points).

Figure 4.5 Contested elections and the turnout rate before and after 1832

Note: Panel A shows the distribution of how many of the three last elections before (1826, 1830, 1831) and the three first elections (1832, 1835, 1837) after the Great Reform Act, respectively, that were contested in the 158 English and Welsh borough constituencies that were represented both before and after. Panel B shows the difference in the turnout rate before and after 1832 for the surviving English and Welsh borough constituencies with contested elections. The pre-reform turnout rate is calculated as the number of voters who polled in the last contested election between 1820 and 1831 (if any) relative to the number of voters reported by local officials to the Boundary Commission in 1831. The post-reform turnout rate is for the election in 1832. It is calculated as the percentage of voters who polled out of the registered voters.

Sources: Pre-election polled voters: PP, 1831–1832, vol. 36, XXXVI.489, 607 (112 209) supplemented in a few cases from PP, 1830–1831, vol. 10, X.53 (338). Pre-reform voters: see note to Table 4.6. Post-reform data: Salmon (2002, Appendix 3).

freeholders with a title to property worth £10 per year, instead of 40 shillings (£2) per year as was previously the case, this act had reduced the electorate in the Irish counties from somewhere between 160,000 and 212,270 in 1820 to about 37,000 in 1831. As a consequence of the new county suffrage, the Irish county electorate grew to 60,597 in 1832 and to 78,259 in 1839. The growth of the electorate in the Irish boroughs was more modest, from 21,394 in 1831 to 29,471 in 1832 and 43,814 in 1839.

Patron influence and electoral corruption: Many features of the Unreformed Parliament, such as patron influence or government control in the small boroughs and electoral corruption more generally, did not, however, disappear swiftly. Large landowners continued to dominate and influence many elections. Gash (1953, Chap. 9) suggests that after 1832, as many as fifty boroughs with seventy members in England and Wales were controlled by peers and/or landlords, and usually returned members of the proprietor's family. Similarly, there remained several boroughs where the government retained or gained the power to control the return of MPs (Gash 1953, Chap. 12). One of those boroughs was the constituency of Chatham (Kent), where the newly enfranchised voters were dependent on the Admiralty and, hence, on the government of the day (Seymour 1915, Chap. 4).

Figure 4.6 illustrates how the Reform Bill affected patron influence in the borough constituencies. We divide the boroughs into three groups with a low, medium, or high degree of patron influence. Panel A compares the degree of patron influence for all the English and Welsh borough constituencies before and after the reform. Panel B restricts the sample to the constituencies that survived the reform. Before the reform, only 20 percent of all boroughs and 30 percent of the surviving ones were classed as low influence; after, this had risen to about 60 percent. For the surviving boroughs, this does not reflect a reduction in the number of boroughs fully controlled by a patron, but a marked reduction in boroughs with some degree of patron influence (Figure 4.6, panel B).

As such, the Great Reform Act did not eliminate electoral corruption overnight, as is evident from the long sequence of Bribery Acts adopted throughout the nineteenth century (e.g. Seymour 1915; O'Leary 1962; Salmon 2002).[28] One of the reasons it failed in this regard is that voting remained open. The secret ballot had been considered in 1831 but ultimately rejected by Lord Grey. It was not until the Ballot Act of 1872 that voting became secret ('An Act to amend the Law relating to Procedure at Parliamentary and Municipal Elections', 35 & 36

[28] While the Bribery Acts passed in 1839 ('Election Petitions Act' (2 and 3 Vict. c. 38)) and 1841 ('Parliamentary Elections Act' and 'Controverted Elections Act ' (4 and 5 Vict. c. 57, 58.)) sought to strengthen parliamentary investigations of petitions related to election irregularities, it was the Bribery at Elections Act in 1842 (5 and 6 Vict. c. 102, 463, clauses 20-22) that first defined illegal payments to a voter as 'head money' or 'corrupt treating at elections'. The Bribery Act 1854 ('Act to consolidate and amend the Laws relating to Bribery, Treating, and undue Influence at Elections of Members of Parliament' (17 and 18 Vict. c. 102, 217–220, clauses 2–23)) provided the first exact definition of electoral bribery. Additional acts followed, in particular 'An Act for the better prevention of Corrupt and Illegal Practices at Parliamentary Elections' (46 and 47 Vict. c. 51) passed in 1883, which limited campaign spending.

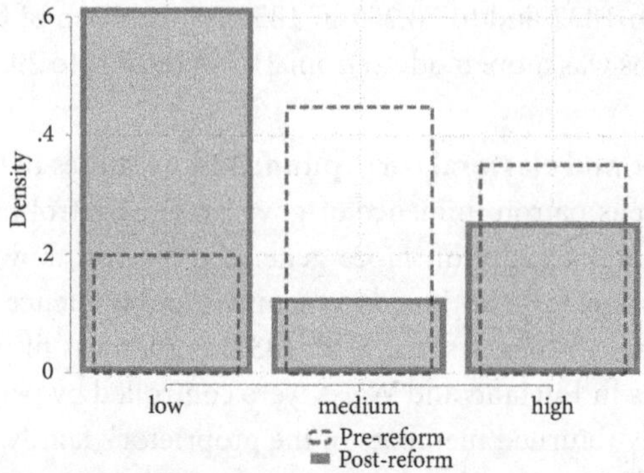

Panel A. All borough constituencies.

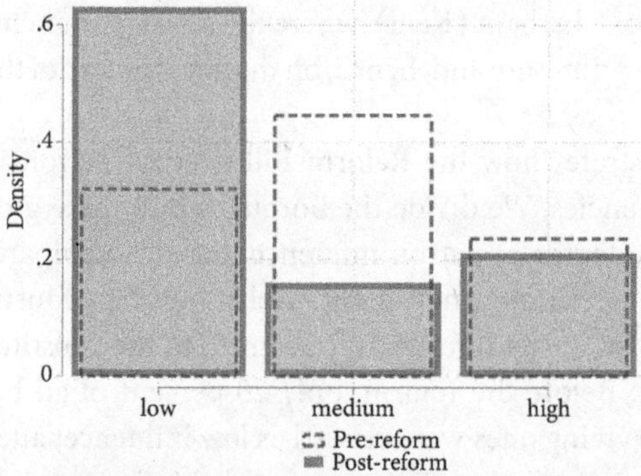

Panel B. Surviving borough constituencies.

Figure 4.6 The effect of the Reform Bill on the patronage index in the English and Welsh borough constituencies

Note: The patronage index is coded as follows. Pre-reform: 'low influence', if Philbin (1965) records no patronage and at least one contested election took place between 1820 and 1831; 'medium influence' if Philbin (1965) records partial control of the borough by a patron or if no contested election took place between between 1820 and 1831; 'high influence' if Philbin (1965) records that all seats were controlled by patrons. Post-reform: 'low influence' if Gash (1953) records no proprietor, family, or government control and at least one contested election took place between 1832 and 1839; 'medium influence' if Gash (1953) records that half of the seats were proprietor or family controlled, or if the seats were government controlled or if there were no contested elections between 1832 and 1839; 'high influence' if Gash (1953) records that all seats were proprietor, family, or government controlled. The patronage index for the pre-reform period used in the statistical analysis and summarised in Table 4.4 is defined slightly differently. The alternative coding is used here to make the pre-reform index comparable to the post-reform index. Panel A shows the distribution of the patronage index for all the English and Welsh borough constituencies before and after the Reform Bill, including those in Schedule A that got disenfranchised and the newly created boroughs in Schedules C and D; panel B shows the distribution of the patronage index for the surviving English and Welsh borough constituencies.

Sources: Philbin (1965) and Gash (1953, Appendix D and G, 193–205 and 337).

Vict. c. 33). One major reason that opposition to the secret ballot had softened by 1872 was that it had become sufficiently uneconomical to buy votes. Not only had voters become more economically independent, but political parties had also become better at mobilising voters on party platforms, and it had become uncommon that elections were not contested (Stokes et al. 2013; Aidt and Jensen 2017; Kasara and Mares 2017; Kam 2017).

The Members of Parliament: We can gauge the effect of the Great Reform Act on the elections immediately after the reform in 1832, 1835 and 1837, which returned Whig majorities, by considering two questions: (i) were the MPs elected in the disenfranchised boroughs able to get elected elsewhere, and (ii) did the the socioeconomic make-up of the House of Commons change?

Woolley (1938) studies these questions carefully and concludes in relation to the first that 'it cannot be maintained that the overwhelming majority of [the members for the disenfranchised boroughs] was permanently excluded from parliament.' (Woolley 1938, 256). Many of them found seats in other boroughs, and many of the MPs who had been elected to surviving borough seats were reelected to these seats after the reform. This was, in part, due to the fact that the aristocratic influence remained high, not only in the counties, but also in the small boroughs. In fact, only 37 percent of the MPs elected in 1833 were new members (which should be compared with the corresponding figure for the 1826 election, which was 26 percent); the rest had previously been elected under the old rules (Woolley 1938, 242).

As for the second question, given the relative modest increase in new MPs, it is not surprising that the socioeconomic composition of the 1833 House of Commons looked very similar to what it had been before the reform. It remained dominated by landowners (who were often relatives of peers).[29] Yet, there was a small increase in the number of MPs with a background in trade, finance, or industry. Before the reform, merchants, bankers, and manufacturers had, at a cost, been able to win seats in the small (corrupt) borough constituencies. The Great Reform Act made it easier for the rising middle class and the industrial elite to win seats in the new constituencies where the aristocratic influence was weaker. The new franchise, thus, gave these groups a stronger foothold in the Commons (Ansell and Samuels 2014), but there was no sudden increase in the shares of middle-class radicals or of merchants and manufacturers (O'Gorman 2016, 370). Many were actually discouraged from running for election by the high cost of contesting elections and by the social violence that often surrounded election campaigns (Wright 1970, 52). Others were prevented from running because of the property qualifications which had been adopted in 1710 and were only abolished in 1858 (Witmer 1943). In essence, the landed elite continued to dominate British politics after the Reform Bill.

[29] Berlinski et al. (2014) show that the aristocratic nature of the House of Commons remained unaltered even after the Second Reform Act of 1867.

4.4.3 Medium- and long-term consequences

It is very difficult to attribute medium- and long-term changes in the British political system to one event such as the Great Reform Act, and a direct causal effect is virtually impossible to establish. Yet, the short-run effects of the reform—a different electorate, voter registration, and a new distribution of seats—most likely interacted with other social and economic factors to bring about many subsequent changes. These include further administrative and institutional reforms, the rise of modern political parties, and civic society mobilisation.

Administrative and institutional reforms: The decade following the Great Reform Act saw the British Parliament adopts a sequence of important administrative and institutional reforms. A sequence of Whig cabinets dominated until 1841 (when the Tories returned to power). This allowed the Whigs to pursue a broader agenda of administrative reform aimed at asserting parliamentary control (Cox et al. 2023) and to respond to the demands from the new middle-class electorate. The first reform abolished slavery in 1833.[30] This was followed by the Poor Law reform in 1834.[31] There had already been calls in the 1820s to reform the Poor Law system, if only because of its continuously rising and ultimately unsustainable cost. The reform of the Poor Laws combined parishes into Poor Law Unions and entailed a return to 'indoor relief' where recipients of relief had to live in workhouses (Boyer 1990).[32] This was, in turn, followed by other reforms through the 1830s and the 1840s.[33] This included the Municipal Corporations Act of 1835[34] that created a standardised organisation of the municipal boroughs, where local property taxpayers would elect a council to manage their town. This gave the new corporations freedom to respond to local concerns and

[30] 'An Act for the Abolition of Slavery throughout the British Colonies; for promoting the Industry of the manumitted Slaves; and for compensating the Persons hitherto entitled to the Services of such Slaves' (3 and 4 Will. 4. c. 73).

[31] 'An Act for the Amendment and better Administration of the Laws relating to the Poor in England' (4 and 5 Will. 4 c. 76).

[32] The reformed system, whose most memorable criticism came in the form of Charles Dickens's novel *Oliver Twist* (Dickens 1838), was far from being 'pro-poor', even though some of the younger Whigs, such as Lord John Russell, had genuine social concerns. The reform was aimed at satisfying demands for economy coming from the middle-class ratepayers who funded the system.

[33] Significant policies of religious tolerance had been implemented under the Unreformed Parliament: the repeal of the Test and Corporations Acts in 1828 enabled Protestant dissenters to hold military and civil office as well as to become members of town corporations. The Catholic Relief Act removed similar discriminatory policies against Catholics in 1829. However, it was only in 1858 that similar legislation was adopted to enable Jews to sit in Parliament ('An Act to provide for the Relief of Her Majesty's Subjects professing the Jewish Religion' (21 and 22 Vict. c. 49); it would only be with 'An Act to amend the Law as to Oaths' (51 and 52 Vict. c. 46) in 1888 that atheists could solemnly swear instead of swearing to God.

[34] 'An Act to provide for the Regulation of Municipal Corporations in England and Wales' (5 and 6 Will. 4 c. 76).

empowered commercial interests locally. It also included successive factory acts in the 1830s and 1840s, which notably regulated the working hours of children (Nardinelli 1990) and the establishment of the income tax in 1842 (Aidt and Jensen 2009). Moreover, as argued by Schonhardt-Bailey (1991, 1994, 2006), a more representative Parliament whose constituents from the industrial sections of society would benefit from free trade was necessary for the repeal of the Corn Laws implemented by a Tory government led by Robert Peel in 1846.

The emergence of modern political parties: The Great Reform Act most likely accelerated the emergence of modern political parties. For Ostrogorski (1902), the registration clause meant that voters needed local party representatives to help them in the revision courts and that this led to the establishment of permanent local party associations. Kam and Newson (2021) argue that the new registration requirement put a premium on literacy because the complex registration system meant that candidates could challenge the register in registration courts, where illiterate voters found it difficult to defend themselves. As the spread of literacy over time reduced this disadvantage, candidates had an incentive to contest elections. This, in turn, increased the cost of campaigning which subsequently led to the organisation of parties with programmatic policy platforms as a cost-cutting devise. Another perspective is that of Cox (1987), who emphasises that economic development and modernisation had increased the demand for legislation in the years after the bill. He argues that the congestion of the agenda created the need for party discipline in Parliament and that, in turn, was the trigger for the development of modern parties at the constituency level.

The political mobilisation of civic society. The struggle for the reform had been a politicising experience, not only for the middle class that had mobilised extra-parliamentary groups and boosted political unions across the country, but also for working-class radicals who had joined the middle class-led political unions or formed their own organisations. This had manifested itself in demonstrations, public meetings, and reform-related petitions submitted to the houses of Parliament on an unprecedented scale (Tilly 1995). O'Gorman (2016, 364) concludes that 'the role of public opinion during the Reform Crisis can hardly be overestimated'. Equally important, the politicising effect of the agitation around the reform question had long-term effects: the newly enfranchised borough constituencies experienced an increase in activism relative to the old constituencies in the decades that followed the reform (Aidt and Leon-Ablan 2023). In this way, representation in the House of Commons boosted grass-root activism, and this, in turn, fed into Chartist reform agitation in the 1840s (Thompson 1984).[35] The

[35] Francis Place drafted with William Lovett (1800–1877) the *People's Charter* in 1838. On Francis Place and the Chartist movement, see Briggs (1959), Ward (1973), Walton (1999), and Chase (2007).

reform agitation had demonstrated the power of extra-parliamentary agitation and that demonstration had long-term effects.

Seen in this perspective, the Great Reform Act was arguably 'great' despite its limited short-run effects. It enabled reform in other areas, it accelerated the emergence of modern political parties, it served to mobilise civic society, and it was the first in a sequence of reforms of the British political system. In the words of O'Gorman (2016, 371), 'The reform door had been opened and, it would never again be in the power of the politicians to close it'.

PART III

A MICRO-POLITICAL ANALYSIS OF THE GREAT REFORM ACT

The historical narrative makes it clear that the Reform Bill had to overcome five key roadblocks before it finally received royal assent on 7 June 1832. These roadblocks were as follows:

Roadblock	Source of opposition	When	What happened
1	Cabinet	16 November 1830	The King appoints Lord Grey as Prime Minister, who then forms a reform-friendly Whig government.
2	Commons	22 March 1831	The Reform Bill wins a majority of one in the House of Commons.
3	Electorate	April–June 1831	The Whigs win a majority of seats in the 1831 General Election, which is, effectively, a referendum on reform.
4	Lords	October 1831 to May 1832	Stalemate in the House of Lords: the Reform Bill is rejected, then approved, and then amended, resulting in Lord Grey resigning as Prime Minister.
5	Lords	May–June 1832	The King promises the reinstated Lord Grey to create new pro-reform lords if need be. The House of Lords approves the Reform Bill on 4 June 1832.

We want to understand how Lord Grey ultimately found ways around these roadblocks. But we want to move beyond the historical narrative and inquire into the causal forces that were critical in pushing the Reform Bill through each roadblock. The theoretical work on suffrage reform, discussed in Chapter 2, points to competing causal mechanisms that could have played a role. To investigate this, we build a large micro-political dataset that enables us to investigate four of the roadblocks in detail with modern statistical tools: the vote in the House of Commons on 22 March 1831 (roadblock 2), the 1831 General Election (roadblock 3), and the votes related to the stalemate in the House of Lords between October 1831 and May 1832 (roadblocks 4 and 5). The next three chapters are devoted to this task.

Chapter 5
The cliffhanger: the vote in the Commons on 22 March 1831

5.1 Introduction

On the night between 22 and 23 March 1831 at 3 a.m. in a packed House of Commons, the MPs divided on the second reading of the first version of the Reform Bill after a prolonged and heated debate between the pro-reform Whigs and the anti-reform Tories.[1,2] It was a cliffhanger. It was not until the tellers reported back that it became clear that the bill had passed with a majority of one vote and narrowly avoided hitting the second roadblock.

In this chapter, we investigate how the Whig leadership managed to garner that critical majority. Arguably, a few additional votes against the bill could have stopped, or at least delayed, the reform. It is clearly important to understand why this did not happen. From a theoretical perspective, the critical 22 March 1831 vote, precisely because it was so close, offers a unique opportunity to evaluate the relative importance of the three prominent theories of democratisation discussed in Chapter 2: the threat of revolution hypothesis, the social movement hypothesis, and the political expedience hypothesis.

To test the threat of revolution hypothesis, we need to measure and quantify the threat of revolution as perceived by the MPs at the time, which, of course, cannot be directly observed (by us). We get around this difficulty by quantifying the degree of actual violent unrest preceding the second reading of the Reform Bill and use that as a proxy for the perceived threat of revolution. Between Lord Grey's announcement of parliamentary reform in November 1830 and the vote on 22 March 1831, England experienced high levels of social unrest. This included a major violent rural uprising—the Swing riots, which we shall explore in greater detail in Chapter 6—and violent confrontations between workers and law enforcement in many of the fast-expanding industrial cities in the north of England and in London (Tilly 1995). Geographical dispersion in the intensity of violent unrest enables us to directly evaluate the effect of fears

[1] This chapter is based on Aidt and Franck (2019).
[2] We follow the convention to date the vote to 22 March 1831, when the last day of debate started.

Peaceful and Violent Origins of Voting Rights. Toke S. Aidt and Raphaël Franck, Oxford University Press.
 DOI: 10.1093/9780197679746.003.0005

of revolution by comparing the votes of MPs elected in areas with high levels of violent unrest to those elected in areas with low levels.

During the same period, England also experienced a surge in public demand for democratic reform from civic society and social movements such as the Birmingham Political Union, the National Union of the Working Classes, and hundreds of other smaller reform unions (Horn and Tilly 1988; LoPatin 1999). This allows us to test the social movement hypothesis and to establish if members of the elite unsure about the costs and benefits of parliamentary reform were swayed by extra-parliamentary pro-reform agitation. For this purpose, we relate the scale of peaceful mass mobilisation through public meetings and demonstrations related to parliamentary reform in the areas where the MPs were elected to their vote on the bill. We also explore the fact that thousands of petitions related to the reform question were presented to the House of Commons (Leys 1955). We use the volume of petitions originating from particular constituencies to measure lobbying for and against the reform, and in that way, we quantify the role of targeted lobbying on the vote of the MPs elected in those constituencies.

We can directly evaluate the extent of self-interested voting because the bill's two main features—redistribution of seats and reform of the suffrage rules—allow us, when combined with detailed bibliographic information, to predict whether an MP would personally benefit or lose from the bill. In particular, the draft bill listed the constituencies to be disenfranchised and the places, including the expanding industrial cities in the Midlands and in the north of England, that were to gain representation. Moreover, the bill changed the voting franchise in the counties in favour of the landowners. These features allow us to measure the geography of expected gains and losses, and in that way, we test the political expedience hypothesis.

The results of our empirical analysis show that conditional on party affiliation, the MPs' votes were influenced by violent social unrest in urban (but not rural) areas, by peaceful agitation and expressions of mass support for reform, and by political expedience. A 'horse race' between the competing theories demonstrates that petitions and public agitation related to the reform question had more influence on the MPs' votes than fears of revolution created by exposure to violent urban unrest. The bill passed with a one-vote majority; two additional nays were all that was needed to block it. We evaluate counterfactual scenarios to understand if violent urban unrest, reform agitation, or political expedience were substantive enough to switch at least two votes. We find that they were.

5.2 Voting on The Great Reform Act: the data

5.2.1 Reform support in the House of Commons

Out of the 658 MPs elected from across the United Kingdom to the House of Commons, only 27 (including 18 from England) were not present for the second reading on 22 March 1831, with a further seven seats unfilled on the day. This was an unusually large turnout. The net result, after 20 MPs including the four tellers were paired off and the Speaker of the House followed tradition and abstained, was a one-vote majority (302 vs. 301). Table 5.1 shows the breakdown of the vote. For the English seats, we report the votes separately for the Tories, Whigs, and the four Radical MPs. For Wales, Scotland, and Ireland, we report the totals. The majority of the 489 English MPs and of the 45 Scottish MPs voted against the bill, while the majority of the 100 Irish and of the 24 Welsh MPs supported it. The opposition in England came almost exclusively from the Tories, while the Radical MPs and the vast majority of the Whigs voted in favour. However, party discipline was imperfect: the thirty-seven Tory MPs who deviated from the party line were critical for the bill's success.

Our statistical analysis focuses on the 489 MPs elected in the 244 English constituencies. The unit of analysis is, therefore, an English seat in the House of Commons. These MPs were elected in the 1830 General Election and served in the parliamentary session between 26 October 1830 and 22 April 1831. We exclude the Scottish and Irish MPs because we do not have data on social unrest and social movement agitation in Scotland and Ireland, but we include Wales in some robustness checks (it makes no difference). For each of the 466 English MPs who were present and voted on 22 March 1831, we create the dummy variable *yes vote*, which is equal to 1 if the MP supported the bill and equal to 0 if he voted no (excluding the Speaker). This is our measure of reform support. For the total sample of the 489 English seats, we also create the dummy variable *present*, which is equal to 1 if the MP elected to a seat was present in the House of Commons for the vote and 0 if not (excluding the four vacant English seats and the Speaker). This allow us to analyse what explains the absence of the eighteen non-voting MPs.

5.2.2 Violent unrest and social movement agitation

Violent unrest and peaceful social movement agitation reached very high levels in the early 1830s (Stevenson 1992; Bohstedt 2010). Tilly (1995, Table 2.2)

Table 5.1 The breakdown of the second reading vote in the House of Commons on 22 March 1831

	England				Wales	Scotland & Ireland	United Kingdom		
	Whig	Tory	Radical	Total	All MPs	All MPs	Gross total	Paired off and tellers	Net total
Yes	188	37	4	229	14	69	312	10	302
No	8	229	0	237	10	64	311	10	301
Absent	9	9	0	18	0	9	27		
Vacancies	1	3	0	4	0	3	7		
Speaker		1		1			1		
Total	206	279	4	489	24	145	658		

Note: The category 'absent' includes the MPs who could have been present but were not. The category 'vacancies' refers to seats where a by-election was due. The seats were Evenham (both seats vacant due to bribery), Colchester (one ineligible elected), and Durham City (one ineligible elected) in England; Nairnshire in Scotland (vacated); and Clare (one ineligible elected) and Londonderry (one ineligible elected) in Ireland. The Speaker (a Tory, elected in Scarborough) abstained. Eight MPs were paired off, and two MPs were appointed tellers on each side of the issue.

Sources: Hansard HC Deb, 22 March 1831, series 2, vol. 2, 719–826 contains the division list reporting all votes cast. It also lists those who were absent, those who were paired off, and those who were tellers. The party affiliations of the English MPs elected in 1830 are constructed from information in Dod and Dod (1832), Namier and Brooke (1964), Stooks Smith (1973), Thorne (1986), and Fisher (2009).

Table 5.2 The number of participants involved in violent unrest and peaceful agitation by major regions between 1 January 1828 and 22 March 1831

Region	All protest	Violent unrest			Peaceful agitation			Reform agitation
		All	Rural %	Urban %	All	Meetings %	Gatherings %	%
Southeast	154,023	20,507	73.4	26.6	133,516	48.3	51.7	10.5
East Anglia	45,181	7,293	37.5	62.5	37,888	71.8	28.2	15.8
Midlands	252,853	16,306	3.3	96.7	236,547	46	54	70.8
Southwest	133,721	6,623	94.3	5.7	127,098	32.6	67.4	7.6
North	374,192	14,519	0	100	359,673	38.7	61.3	26.4
London	239,294	29,756	0	100	209,538	77.9	22.1	20.3
Wales	3,142	40	0	100	3,102	25.1	74.9	2.9
All participants	1,202,406	95,044	25.9	74.1	1,107,362	49.2	50.8	30.2
All events	2,726	546	39.0	61.0	2180	87.5	12.5	18.3
Av. participation	441	174	630	1155	508	286	2068	836

Note: Southeast includes Berkshire, Buckinghamshire, Hampshire, Kent, Oxfordshire, Surrey, and Sussex; Southwest includes Cornwall, Devon, Dorset, Gloucestershire, Somerset, Wiltshire, and Monmouthshire; East Anglia includes Bedfordshire, Cambridgeshire, Essex, Hertfordshire, Huntingdonshire, Norfolk, and Suffolk; Midlands includes Derbyshire, Herefordshire, Leicestershire, Lincolnshire, Northamptonshire, Nottinghamshire, Rutland, Salop, Staffordshire, Warwickshire, and Worcestershire; North includes Cheshire, Cumberland, Durham, Lancashire, Northumberland, Westmorland, and Yorkshire; London includes the City of London, Westminster, and Middlesex; Wales includes all the counties of Wales. All protest is equal to violent unrest plus peaceful agitation; meetings and gatherings sum to peaceful agitation, and rural and urban violent sum to violent unrest. Reform agitation is reform-related peaceful events (and expressed in percentage of all peaceful agitation). The row titled 'all events' records the number of events and ave. participation is the number of participants per event. The number of participants is calculated from Horn and Tilly (1988)'s best estimate and for those events where they do not have an estimate, we assume that ten people were involved (this is the cut-off for being included in their database).

Source: Own construction using data from Horn and Tilly (1988).

estimates that several million individuals participated in these activities. Violent unrest had to be put down by force, and at least 91 were killed and more than 2,000 were arrested (Tilly 1995, 97). The largest wave of rural violent unrest was the Swing riots. They took place between August 1830 and March 1831, when rioting landless agricultural labourers threatened local officials and farmers with violence, burned hayricks, smashed threshing machines, and destroyed other types of private property (Hobsbawm and Rudé 1973). Urban violent unrest included instances of violent street confrontations (for example, in Derby in 1830 and in Bristol in 1831) and turbulent strikes (for example, in Barnsley, Bethnal Green, Coventry, Manchester, and Spitalfields in 1829). The major events were widely reported in the local and national newspapers. For instance, both *the Morning Chronicle* and *the Times* reported in their 10 November 1830 editions that after a meeting near Radical activist Richard Carlile's (1790–1843) ramshackle building (called the Blackfriars Rotunda) on 9 November 1830 about 1,000 to 1,500 persons confronted a detachment of the police with cries of 'Down with the police!', 'No Wellington', and 'No Peel'. Home Secretary Robert Peel described it in the House of Commons as 'some unpleasant collisions between the police and the mob at Temple Bar, and other parts of the Strand' (Mirror of Parliament, 10 November 1830, as quoted by Tilly (1995, 314)). There were two hallmarks of violent unrest during the period: on the one hand, it was unrelated to parliamentary reform and instead caused by a variety of special economic and social demands; on the other hand, it helped stir up fears of a revolution.

However, most of these extra-parliamentary activities and events were peaceful expressions of public opinion often orchestrated by social movements and reform unions. Partly due to less-blatant government repression of organisations in the late 1820s, urban political associations, such as the Birmingham Political Union or the National Association for the Protection of the Workers, had become sufficiently organised to mobilise peaceful mass meetings (Thompson 1963, Chap. 14). In the lead-up to the division on the Reform Bill in March 1831, they organised public meetings in support of the reform, which, on occasion, attracted thousands of participants. In other instances, freeholders, parishioners, or religious congregations met publicly to express their views on the reform question (Tilly 1995, Table 7.3). These events were announced in the local newspapers and often reported in the London-based national newspapers after the fact. For instance, a large peaceful demonstration in favour of reform was held in London on 12 October 1831. The following day, *the Morning Chronicle* described it as 'about 300,000 inhabitants of the metropolis—chiefly tradespeople and industrial artisans, with the Parochial Officers at their head—walked in procession from their respective parishes to St. James's Palace' (Tilly 1995, 329). Unlike violent unrest, many of the peaceful meetings and gatherings that took place during the period were directly linked to agitation for or against parliamentary reform and organised by reform movements.

Individuals, groups, or organisations could also petition Parliament directly (Leys 1955; Jupp 1998). According to the record in the *Journal of the House of Commons* (JHC), more than 3,000 petitions related to parliamentary reform were received between November 1830 and June 1832 (see Aidt and Leon-Ablan 2023). These petitions were presented in the House of Commons and often used by MPs to start debates. Some of them were signed by thousands of people, such as one received by the MP John Savile Lumley (1788–1856) in March 1831 from '2,500 most respectable persons' (Hansard HC Deb, 22 March 1831, series 2, vol. 3, c705) amongst the freeholders of the county of Nottingham petitioning in favour of the reform. Others represented the views of smaller and more select groups such as the petition from the University of Cambridge against the reform (Hansard HC Deb, 22 March 1831, series 2, vol. 3, c706). The petition system allowed organised groups and movements outside the ruling elite and outside the areas with parliamentary representation to lobby and make their views on the reform question known.

To test the social movement hypothesis, we need to quantify the MPs' exposure to public opinion, agitation, and mass mobilisation. We draw on two sources to do this. First, as we noted above, it was common for political unions and other social movements to send petitions to the House of Commons either in support of, or in opposition to, specific bills or issues. These petitions are recorded in the *Journal of the House of Commons* (1828–1831, vol. 83–86). Based on word searches of the names of the 244 English constituencies, we count the number of petitions related to the reform campaign which originated from each constituency between 1 January 1828 and 22 March 1831.[3] We code the variable *petitions* as the difference between the number of petitions for and those against parliamentary reform. This measures constituency-level agitation in favour of reform and enables us to test if the MPs were influenced by the views of the people living in the constituencies in which they were elected and by the organisations that represented them. Second, to quantify the broader patterns of agitation and social movement mobilisation, we draw on Horn and Tilly (1988) and Tilly (1995). They collected information on various forms of 'popular protest' in England between 1828 and 1834 from textual analysis of eight London-based periodicals (*Annual Register*, *Gentleman's Magazine*, *Hansard's Parliamentary Debates*, *London Chronicle*, *Mirror of Parliament*, *the Morning Chronicle*, *the Times*, and *Votes and Proceedings of Parliament*). Tilly (1995, 63) defines 'popular protest' as an event where '10 or more people gather in a publicly accessible place and make claims on other people, including holders of power, claims which if realised would affect the interests of their object'. Each event is characterised by several elements describing date and location,

[3] During the parliamentary session of 1828, 1829, and 1830 (up to the election held in July to September), only 20 petitions related to parliamentary reform were received, while 400 were received between 14 September 1830 and 22 March 1831. This does not include petitions from unrepresented areas.

an estimate of the number of people involved, who was making the claim, and against whom the claim was directed. We use participation in three types of peaceful events that happened between 1 January 1828 and 22 March 1831 as proxies for agitation and mass mobilisation at the constituency level. Meetings involved organised events where a group of individuals congregated with prior notice. Gatherings were more spontaneous and included street protests of various sorts, including demonstrations, which remained peaceful and non-violent.[4] While meetings and gatherings enable us to study different types of peaceful agitation, some of these meetings and gatherings were not related to the reform question. Our third and main proxy for reform agitation uses the classification of Horn and Tilly (1988) to single out the subset of peaceful meetings and gatherings which were related to the reform question.[5] This provides us with a direct measure of reform agitation.

To test the threat of revolution hypothesis, we also draw on Horn and Tilly (1988). We single out the events between 1 January 1828 and 22 March 1831 that involved violent unrest. We contend they can be used as a proxy for the MPs' perceptions of the threat of revolution. We further subdivide violent unrest into unrest that took place in rural areas and unrest in urban areas.[6] Violent unrest in urban areas might have been perceived as being more threatening than unrest in the countryside (Do and Campante 2009).

During the period from 1 January 1828 to 22 March 1831, Horn and Tilly (1988) record 2,726 events. For many of the events, they give an estimate of the number of individuals involved and for each type of event, we calculate the number of individuals involved in them.[7] It is important to take this into account, as, for instance, a small meeting with 10 individuals involved would have been

[4] Horn and Tilly (1988) also record the number of delegations. Since there were very few of those (less than 1 percent of all events), we combine them with the meetings.

[5] The quality of these data is remarkable. They were hand-collected over a twelve-year period in the 1970s and 1980s by a research team led by Charles Tilly and coded independently by several researchers (Horn and Tilly 1988). The very labour-intensive collection method minimises, if not eliminates altogether, false positives. By definition, the dataset does not include minor events with less than ten people involved, and it does not include events that happened but were not reported in the national newspapers, which were the primary sources. This will tend to underestimate protest. Tilly (1995, 398) compares his data from the national newspapers with information extracted from *the Lancaster Gazette* (a regional newspaper) and concludes that 'local and specialised periodicals sometimes reported more events within their own purview than our national periodicals, but not always and rarely with significantly more detail'. For our purpose, it is appropriate to focus on the main events that made it to the national newspapers as these are the ones that were most likely to catch the attention of the MPs.

[6] Horn and Tilly (1988) do not make a rural-urban distinction. We proxy violent rural protest by the violent events related to the Swing riots and violent urban protest by the residual number of violent events. While all the Swing riots were rural in nature, there might be some element of rural protest in the proxy for violent urban protest, but most would have been urban.

[7] Horn and Tilly (1988) code the information on the number of people involved as a lowest, best, and highest estimate to reflect the fact that the sources do not always give a precise number. We use the best estimate under the assumption that this is also the number than the MPs at the time would have associated with the event. For events where no information is provided, we assume that ten individuals were at least involved, as otherwise the event would not have been coded in the database. This means that the estimates of the number of people involved is a lower bound.

perceived very differently from a large public demonstration with thousands of participants, such as the reform-support meeting in Manchester on 8 March 1831, which according to *the Times* was attended by 3,000 people.[8] We consider that each MP was influenced by the number of participants in the events which occurred in the county where his constituency was located. This is reasonable because counties were natural information hubs for the constituencies, and each county had a newspaper which reported local news and those from London (see below, for a discussion of newspaper circulation). For each event type and each MP, we code the variables *violent unrest* and *peaceful agitation* as the number of people participating (in 10,000s) in events involving violence and peaceful agitation, respectively, in the home county of the MP's constituency, and *all protest* as the sum of the two. We further disaggregate *violent unrest* into *violent rural* and *violent urban* to capture the distinction between violent events in the countryside and in towns and cities, respectively. We also disaggregate *peaceful agitation* into *meetings* and *gatherings*, and code the variable *reform agitation* as participation in reform-related peaceful meetings and gatherings.[9]

Table 5.2 shows the distribution of violent unrest and peaceful agitation recorded between 1 January 1828 and 22 March 1831, classified by the type of event and disaggregated within the six main regions of England and Wales. Most of the events were peaceful, but 20 percent of them did involve violence. The average number of participants was 441 people. Violent events in rural areas involved fewer individuals than violent events in urban areas. While there were many more meetings than gatherings, gatherings had substantially larger average participation (2,068 compared to 286 people). Reform-related meetings and gatherings constituted 18.3 percent of all peaceful agitation events, with participation of 30.2 percent of all individuals involved in peaceful agitation. Figure 5.1, panels A and B, maps the geographical distribution of the participants in peaceful agitation and violent unrest across the English and Welsh counties, respectively.[10] Peaceful agitation took place mainly in the industrial towns in the North and the Midlands, as well as in and around London. Violent unrest was concentrated in the hinterland of London (mostly rural unrest) and in the north of England (mostly urban unrest).

Figure 5.2 plots participation in peaceful agitation (measured on the right-hand y-axis) and violent unrest (measured on the left-hand y-axis) in England

[8] *The Times* (London, England), Tuesday, 8 March 1831; p. 4; Issue 14481.

[9] While we report results with the total number of participants, we find similar results if we normalise this number by the total population or by the number of adult males (Table C5.1 in the supplementary material appendix). We can also replicate the results with the variables coded by summing up the number of events by county, irrespective of the number of people involved (Table C5.2 in the supplementary material appendix). The supplementary material appendix is available at www.oup.com/us/peacefulandviolentorigins

[10] Figure C5.1 in the supplementary material appendix reports the geographical distribution of the participants in gatherings and meetings. The supplementary material appendix is available at www.oup.com/us/peacefulandviolentorigins

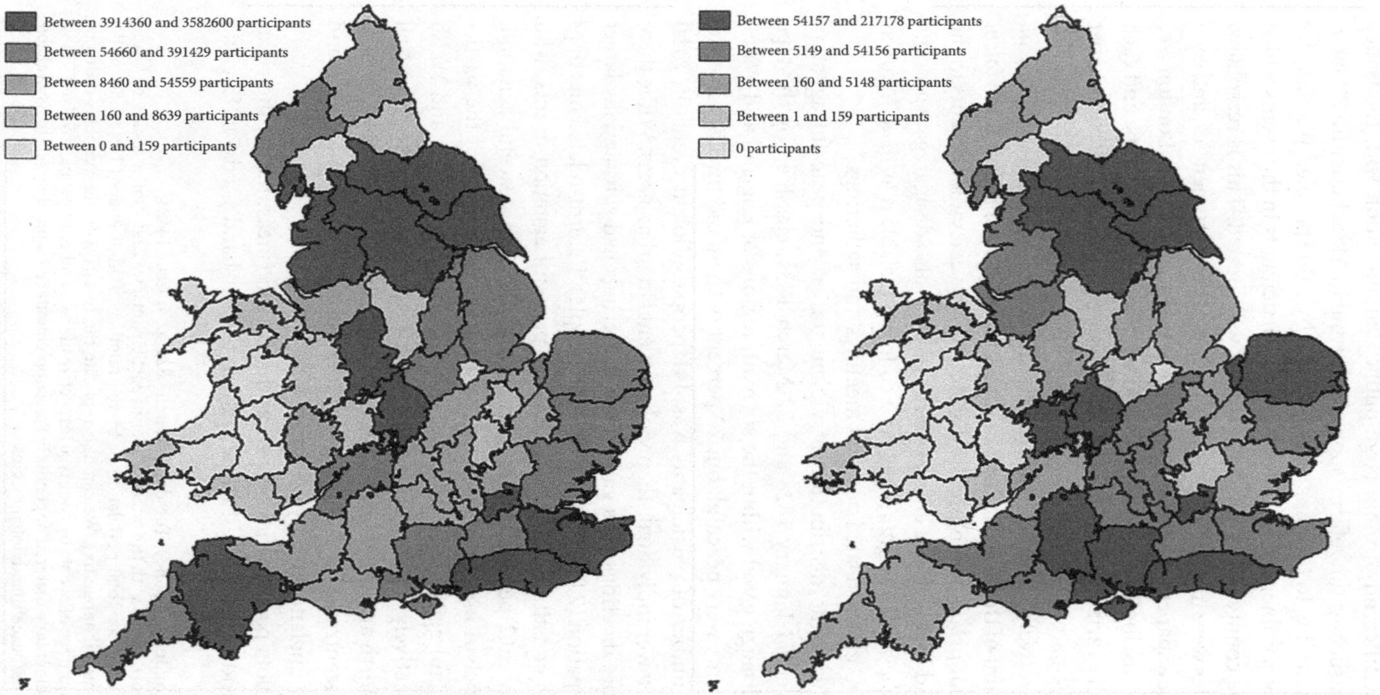

Panel A. Participants peaceful agitation.

Panel B. Participants violent unrest.

Figure 5.1 The spatial distribution of the number of participants in violent unrest or in peaceful agitation in the English and Welsh counties between 1 January 1828 and 22 March 1831

Source: Own construction using data from Horn and Tilly (1988).

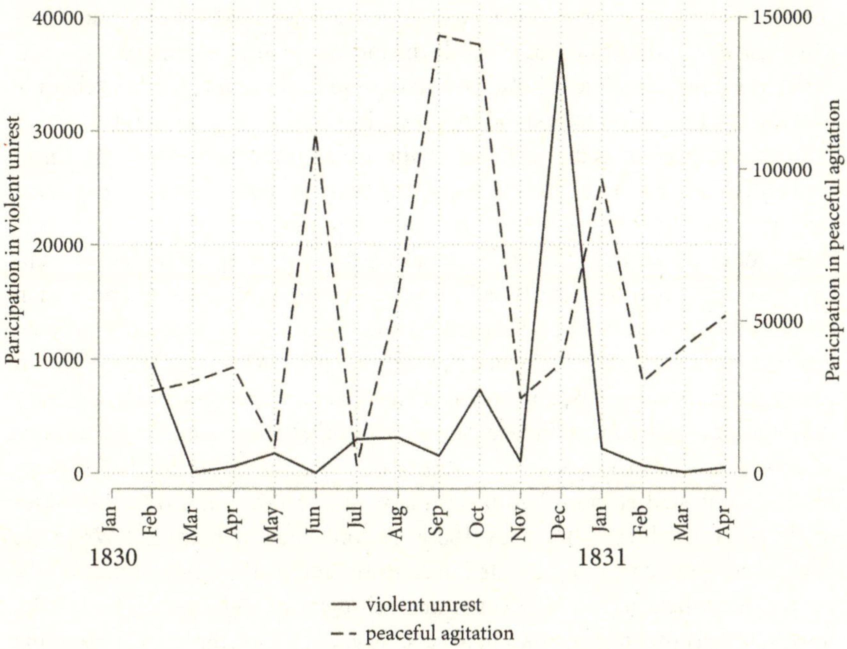

Figure 5.2 Violent unrest and peaceful agitation over time, 1830–1831

Note: The figure displays the number of participants in violent unrest and peaceful agitation in England and Wales between January 1830 and April 1831 by month. The dotted line, measured on the right-hand y-axis, graphs the number of participants in peaceful agitation (meetings and gatherings) while the solid line, measured on the left-hand y-axis, graphs the number of participants in violent urban or rural unrest.

Source: Horn and Tilly (1988).

and Wales by month for the period between January 1830 and April 1831. We note that participation in peaceful agitation activities grew in the period leading up to the vote on the Reform Bill. The peak in May 1830 was a large meeting with more than 100,000 participants in Warwickshire, and the high level of peaceful agitation during the summer of 1830 corresponds to the polling period of the 1830 General Election. Violent unrest was more concentrated in time. The spike in violence, which occurred in November and December 1830, corresponds to the peak of the violent Swing riots instigated by landless agricultural labourers.

5.2.3 Political expedience

To test the political expedience hypothesis, the details of the draft bill enable us to identify prospective winners and losers. Obviously, the MPs elected in the constituencies which were scheduled to be disenfranchised by the bill had a personal reason to vote against it. We code the indicator variable *disenfranchised* as equal to 1 if the constituency that an MP represented was included in Schedule A of the draft bill[11] and thus stood to lose all its seats, and 0 otherwise.

Patronage played, as discussed in Chapter 4, an important role in the Unreformed Parliament. The MPs elected in the borough constituencies controlled by patrons might have been under pressure to oppose reform because the new rules would undermine the old system of patronage even in the constituencies that continued to exist. Based on the contextual information about each constituency provided by Philbin (1965) and the complete record of contested and uncontested elections provided by Cannon (1973, Appendix 3) used to construct the *patronage index* introduced in Chapter 4, we construct a binary indicator of aristocratic influence, *patron controlled*. It is coded as 1 if the constituency was under full or partial control of a local patron or by the Treasury or if no contested election had taken place since 1802, and 0 otherwise. Out of the 244 English constituencies, 188 were controlled by patrons.[12] While the patrons controlled who represented the constituencies, they did not necessarily control how the selected MPs voted on each piece of legislation. They could, however, exert pressure in relation to specific votes, for example, by threatening not to select the MP at the next election, and had a strong incentive to do so with regard to the Reform Bill.

The Reform Bill was a threat to the political influence of the landed elite because it aimed at redistributing seats from the small 'rotten' borough constituencies in the countryside to the expanding industrial cities in the north of England and in the Midlands and to other large towns. At the same time, the draft bill sought to extend the existing voting franchise in the counties to include £10 copyholders and various types of leaseholders, and to increase the number of county seats from 80 to 144. These new voters often owed their livelihood to the local landlords, and their vote could be influenced by the landed elite. As such, this franchise extension was seen by many contemporaneous observers as an attempt to compensate the landed interest for the loss of their influence in the disenfranchised rural boroughs (Brock 1973, 222). To capture the role of the landed interest, we code the indicator variable *landed interest* as 1 if an MP was elected to a county seat, and 0 if he was elected to either a borough seat or to one of the university seats.

[11] PP, 1830–1831, Bill and Acts, vol. 22, II.197 (247).

[12] The number is consistent with the information on the lords who controlled nomination boroughs (Sack 1980) and with the estimate for 1793 given by Hammond and Hammond (1911, 19).

As a more general measure of the expected benefit of seat redistribution, we construct the variable *net seat gain*. It codes the difference between the number of seats that would be allocated to each county and to the borough constituencies located within its borders by the Reform Bill and the number of seats in the Unreformed Parliament.[13] MPs elected in a particular county would have a ready-made network of supporters in that area enabling them to take advantage of the new seats to be established post reform. In fact, as we discussed in Chapter 4, we know that many MPs who had been elected to seats that were abolished were elected to other seats after the reform. This variable, therefore, measures the extent to which the MPs supported (opposed) the reform because of seat gains (losses) in 'their' county.

5.2.4 Political and economic control variables

Party affiliation: As noted above, 'party affiliation' is a strong predictor of how an MP voted. The Reform Bill was sponsored by the Whig leadership and supported by most Whig MPs (only eight English Whig MPs voted against). It was strongly opposed by the Tory leadership and most backbench Tories, yet thirty-seven English Tory MPs voted for the bill (see Table 5.1). We control for 'party affiliation' with the variable *Whig/Radical*, which is coded as 1 if the seat was held either by a Whig or one of the few Radical MPs and 0 otherwise. Our tests, accordingly, isolate the influence of social movement agitation, political expedience, and threat of revolution on the forty-five MPs who voted against the 'party line' and whose votes were pivotal.

Newspaper circulation: Newspaper circulation can be used to proxy for the general flow of information. In the 1830s, London was the information hub of Britain (e.g. Aspinall 1973). The MPs had access to the major London newspapers and to local newspapers from the area in which they were elected, and they could mail copies free of charge to, for instance, family and patrons (Barker 2000). Many of the newspapers were supportive of reform (Jupp 1998) and reported extensively on the proceedings in Parliament. The newspapers were also a major source of information on public support for reform and on violent unrest, and the national newspapers often reported on meetings and other

[13] In the results reported below, we use the final seat distribution to calculate the expected gain/loss in seats. The final seat distribution is different from the one originally proposed in the schedules of the bill that was second read on 22 March 1831. It makes no difference to the results which version we use.

reform-related events outside London.[14] Newspapers were subject to stamp duty, which was levied on each sheet of paper. This made most newspapers too expensive for ordinary people. The accounts of the Stamp Office report the stamp duty paid by each newspaper. This makes it possible to estimate newspaper circulation within each county. We code the variable, *local newspapers*, as the estimated number of newspapers sold per year in each county in 100,000s.[15]

Economic fundamentals: Based on information from the 1831 Census of Great Britain, we consider two aspects of the economic environment: employment concentration and population density. First, we measure employment concentration in each constituency with a Herfindahl index, *emp. Herfindahl index*. It is computed as the sum of the square of the share of individuals in each census registration district working in agriculture, in trade, as professionals, or in other occupational categories.[16] *Emp. Herfindahl index* varies between 0 and 1: a value closer to 1 implies that employment is concentrated in fewer sectors. Second, we code the variable *population density* as the number of individuals per inhabited house in the constituency, as recorded in the 1831 Census of Great Britain. We conjecture that areas with more concentrated employment structures and higher population density could articulate reform support (or opposition) more effectively.

Personal characteristics of the MPs: We account for the possibility that the personal and professional characteristics of the MPs might have influenced their votes. As discussed in Chapter 4, from the bibliographical notices compiled by Fisher (2009) and other bibliographical sources, we obtain information on the MPs' age, education, and occupation. We also record years of service in the Commons as a proxy for experience and information on whether they had traveled on the Grand Tour. Table 5.3 reports descriptive statistics for the variables used in the main analysis.[17]

[14] See, for example, *the Times* (London, England), Friday, 4 March 1831; p. 4; Issue 14478; *the Times* (London, England), Tuesday, 8 March 1831; p. 4; Issue 14481, or *the Times* (London, England), Friday, 11 March 1831; p. 4; Issue 14484.

[15] The sources used for this calculation are Wadsworth (1955), PP, 1833, vol. 32, XXXII.613 (569) and PP, 1833, vol. 32, XXXII.605,607 (502 657). Section C5.1 in the supplementary material appendix explains the details behind the calculation. The supplementary material appendix is available at www.oup.com/us/peacefulandviolentorigins

[16] The occupation categories are those tabulated in the 1831 Census of Great Britain, and each constituency is matched to the Census registration district that is the closest geographical unit.

[17] Supplementary material appendix C5.2 provides an overview of definitions and sources. The supplementary material appendix is available at www.oup.com/us/peacefulandviolentorigins

Table 5.3 Descriptive statistics related to the second reading on 22 March 1831

	Obs.	Mean	Std. Dev.	Min.	Max.
	Seat-level variation				
Support for parliamentary reform					
Yes vote (second reading)	466	0.49	0.50	0	1
Members of Parliament					
Whig/Radical	484	0.43	0.50	0	1
Age (of MP)	484	44.9	13.1	21	79
Army career	484	0.19	0.39	0	1
	County-level variation				
Public protest participants (10,000s)					
All protest	489	3.60	5.88	0.001	25.9
Violent unrest	489	0.26	0.43	0	2.98
Peaceful agitation	489	3.34	5.68	0.001	25.6
Rural violent	489	0.11	0.21	0	0.83
Urban violent	489	0.15	0.41	0	2.98
Meetings	489	1.61	2.93	0.001	16.3
Gatherings	489	1.72	4.20	0	21.1
Reform agitation	489	0.71	2.12	0	15.1
Expected consequences of reform					
Net seat gain	489	−4.01	9.51	−28	12
Institutional controls					
Local newspapers	489	16.6	62.3	0	303
	Constituency-level variation				
Public protest					
Petitions	489	1.46	2.83	−2	27
Expected consequences of reform					
Disenfranchised	489	0.23	0.42	0	1
Patron controlled	489	0.76	0.43	0	1
Landed interest	489	0.17	0.37	0	1
Demographic and economic controls					
Emp. Herfindahl index	489	0.76	0.073	0.24	0.86
Population density	489	5.58	0.84	3.92	9.79
Distance to London (inverse)	489	0.02	0.11	0.002	0.88

Note: The sample is restricted to the 489 English seats. The statistics for the MPs exclude the four unrepresented English seats and the Speaker of the House. Definitions and sources of the variables are provided in the text.

5.3 Empirical strategy

Our statistical tests of the threat of revolution, the social movement, and the political expedience hypotheses relate violent unrest, peaceful agitation and petitions, and political expedience to each MP's vote for or against reform on 22 March 1831. We estimate the following probit model:

$$Prob\,(yes\ vote_{k,d,c} = 1) =$$

$$\Phi\left(\alpha_0 + \mathbf{threat}_c\alpha_1 + \mathbf{movement}_{d,c}\alpha_2 + \mathbf{expedience}_{d,c}\alpha_3 + \mathbf{X}_{k,d,c}\alpha_4\right), \quad (5.1)$$

where Φ is the distribution function of the standard normal distribution, *yes vote* is equal to 1 if MP k elected in constituency d in county c voted in favour of the bill, and 0 if he opposed it. The vector **threat** represents combinations of the various measures of violent unrest (*violent unrest*, *rural violent*, and *urban violent*); the vector **movement** collects combinations of the variables that proxy for social movement agitation and public opinion (*peaceful agitation*, *meetings*, *gatherings*, *reform agitation*, and *petitions*); the vector **expedience** collects the four measures of political expedience (*net seat gain*, *disenfranchised*, *patron controlled*, and *landed interest*); and the vector **X** represents the control variables (which are, in the main specification, *local newspapers*, *emp. Herfindahl index*, *army career*, and *population density*). We control for *Whig/Radical* in all specifications.

The statistical model is hierarchical: seats belong to constituencies which are located within counties. Since our main explanatory variables are measured at the county or the constituency level, they are perfectly correlated within those clusters. It is also likely that the errors are correlated for seats and constituencies within a given county. To avoid basing inference on standard errors, which are likely to be downwards biased, we report standard errors that are clustered at the county level (Cameron and Miller 2015).

Nine Whigs and nine Tories from England were not present in the House of Commons for the vote on 22 March 1831. The date for the second reading of the bill was known in advance, and the second reading itself followed several days of debates. It is unlikely that any of the absent MPs were unaware of the intensity of the discussions, or that they were uninformed about when the final vote would approximately take place. Since any one of the absent MPs could have been pivotal had they been present, it is important to consider their participation decisions. For most of them, we know why they were not present. Table 5.7, which provides detailed information on this question for each of the absent MPs, shows that by far the most common reason was poor health or planned absence to attend to private business. Yet, it is possible that the decisions of some of these MPs not to attend on that day was influenced by how they would have voted had they attended. For example, the absent MPs might have decided not to attend because they, as in the case of William Henry Litton Earle Bulwer (1801–1872), did not want to confront their patron or because they were discouraged from taking the trip to London by fear of social unrest. If this were the case, our estimates of equation 5.1 would suffer from a selection bias. We can correct for such a bias using a Heckman-probit model (Van de Ven and Praag 1981). This entails estimating a selection equation that models the probability of being present for the vote and then adjusting the outcome equation (equation 5.1) for the selection effect. We consider that two variables can be excluded from the outcome equation because they explain the MPs' presence in the House of Commons for the vote, but are (plausibly) unrelated to the MPs' vote decisions. First, the distance from an MP's constituency to London directly affected how troublesome it was to get to London, if the MP was not residing at the time in his London residence, but arguably did not have any direct impact on the vote decision. Second, the MP's age would be a factor, and it is reasonable to suppose that old age could explain why an MP was not present at 3 a.m. in the morning when the vote was taken. We, thus, write the selection equation of the Heckman-probit model as

$$\begin{aligned} &Prob\left(present_{k,d,c} = 1\right) = \\ &\Phi(\beta_0 + \mathbf{threat}_c\beta_1 + \mathbf{movement}_{d,c}\beta_2 + \mathbf{expedience}_{d,c}\beta_3 + \mathbf{X}_{k,d,c}\beta_4 \\ &+\beta_5 distance_d + \beta_6 age_k + \beta_7 age_k^2), \end{aligned} \tag{5.2}$$

where Φ is the distribution function of the standard normal distribution, *present* is equal to 1 if MP k elected in constituency d in county c was present in the House of Commons on 22 March 1831, and equal to 0 if he was not. The variable *distance* is the inverse crow-fly distance (in kilometres) from each constituency to London, and the variable *age* and its square control for the age of the MP in a flexible manner. The other variables are defined as above.

5.4 Results

5.4.1 Public protest versus political expedience

In Table 5.4, we start by presenting our estimates of the effect of all protest (whether related to threat of revolution or to social movement agitation) and of the four variables capturing political expedience (*net seat gain*, *disenfranchised*, *patron controlled*, and *landed interest*) on the probability that the 466 English MPs present voted in favour of the Reform Bill on 22 March 1831.

Table 5.4 The probability that an MP voted in favour of the Reform Bill on 22 March 1831: probit and Heckman-probit estimates

	1	2	3	4	5	6
	Yes vote					Present
		England only		Including Wales	Heckman-probit	Selection equation
All protest	0.014 (0.0067)**	0.015 (0.0074)**	0.015 (0.0071)**	0.015 (0.0072)**	0.016 (0.0071)**	−0.34 (0.14)**
Net seat gain	0.0074 (0.0035)**	0.0066 (0.0038)*	0.0071 (0.0038)*	0.0073 (0.0039)*	0.0053 (0.0037)	0.0029 (0.011)
Disenfranchised	−0.066 (0.080)	−0.090 (0.090)	−0.099 (0.091)	−0.099 (0.091)	−0.068 (0.075)	−0.44 (0.35)
Patron controlled	−0.084 (0.10)	−0.11 (0.10)	−0.10 (0.10)	−0.072 (0.098)	−0.080 (0.090)	−0.57 (0.33)*
Landed interest	0.21 (0.070)***	0.27 (0.065)***	0.27 (0.065)***	0.31 (0.062)***	0.24 (0.060)***	−0.07 (0.27)
Whig/Radical	0.83 (0.029)***	0.84 (0.029)***	0.84 (0.029)***	0.84 (0.028)***	0.81 (0.029)***	−0.30 (0.17)*
Local newspapers		−0.00013 (0.00032)	−0.00020 (0.00029)	−0.00015 (0.00032)	−0.00028 (0.00027)	0.0027 (0.0011)**
Emp. Herfindahl index		−1.03 (0.51)**	−1.18 (0.53)**	−1.07 (0.52)**	−1.05 (0.46)**	0.69 (0.95)
Population density		−0.026 (0.041)	−0.026 (0.039)	−0.029 (0.040)	−0.030 (0.035)	0.070 (0.14)

Army career			−0.16	−0.11	−0.10	−0.57
			(0.087)**	(0.087)	(0.074)	(0.21)***
Distance (inverse)						18.0
						(11.9)
Age of MP						0.062
						(0.034)*
Age of MP (squared)						−0.00076
						(0.00038)**
Observations	466	466	466	490	484	484

Note: Columns 1–4 report probit estimates of the probability that an MP voted yes (marginal effects evaluated at the mean of the explanatory variables). Constant not shown. Standard errors in parentheses are clustered at the county level. In columns 1–3, the sample is the English MPs who were present in the House of Commons on 22 March 1831, and in column 4, the Welsh MPs are included. Column 5 reports Heckman-probit estimates for the 484 English MPs who could have voted (marginal effects reported). Column 6 reports the selection equation; the outcome variable *present* is coded 1 if the MP was present and 0 otherwise. The Wald test of independence between the selection and outcome equation is associated with a p-value of 0.0001. We, therefore, reject that the two equations are independent and selection may be an issue. * = Significant at the 10 percent level; ** = Significant at the 5 percent level; *** = Significant at the 1 percent level.

This allows us to assess the importance of self-interest versus fears of revolution and social movement agitation combined. In this and subsequent tables, we report marginal effects evaluated at the mean of the explanatory variables. Column 1 reports a parsimonious specification, while we progressively add controls in columns 2 and 3. Column 4 reports the results from a sample which is extended with the seats in Wales. Columns 5 and 6 report results from the Heckman-probit model.

The results show that unrest and agitation generally conceived, and self-interest, all mattered. The point estimate on *all protest* is significant at the 5 percent level, the coefficient is stable, and it does not matter if Wales is included in the sample or not. Intuitively, if the home county of an MP had been exposed to an increase of one standard deviation in the number of protest participants (58,000), this would have increased the probability that he voted in favour of the Reform Bill by 8.7 percentage points (column 3). The estimation results also show that some dimensions of political expedience, as proxied by the *net seat gain*, *disenfranchised*, *patron controlled*, and *landed interest* variables, mattered for the MPs' vote decisions. In the preferred specification in column 3, MPs representing the landed interest were 27 percentage points more likely to support the bill than other MPs. MPs from constituencies in counties that stood to gain additional representation were also more likely to vote for reform: an increase in *net seat gain* of one (creating one extra seat within the county) increased an MP's likelihood of voting for the bill by 0.7 percentage points. In contrast, neither the MPs elected in the Schedule A boroughs which stood to lose representation (*disenfranchised*), nor those elected in constituencies dominated by a local patron (*patron controlled*) were more likely than the other MPs to oppose the bill.

Further inspection of Table 5.4 confirms that Whig and Radical MPs were much more likely to support the bill than Tory MPs. *Whig/Radical* controls for the ideological predisposition of the MPs. Consequently, we estimate how public protest and political expedience caused the MPs to deviate from this predisposition or from the wishes of the respective party leaderships. We also observe that MPs from constituencies with a higher employment Herfindahl index, and, therefore, with a more concentrated employment structure, were more likely to oppose the bill. The circulation of local newspapers and population density are negatively correlated with support for the bill, but not statistically significant. Column 3 includes the only personal characteristic that was significantly related to the MP's vote decision: MPs with an army career were 16 percentage points less likely to support the bill than other MPs.[18]

[18] Table C5.3 in the supplementary material appendix reports probit estimations that include all the various personal characteristics (age, years in parliament, occupation, and social circumstances). The supplementary material appendix is available at www.oup.com/us/peacefulandviolentorigins. After applying a general-to-specific algorithm only the indicator variable *army career* is significant at the 10 percent level.

Table 5.4, columns 5 and 6, report the result of the Heckman-probit model that accounts for self-selection regarding the presence of MPs in the House of Commons on 22 March 1831. The three variables used to identify the selection equation in column 6 have the expected signs, but the (inverse) distance to London is insignificant. The polynomial in age is, however, significant and suggests a sharp decline in the attendance probability around the age of forty-one years. The selection correction has little influence on the outcome equation in column 5, and the results related to *all protest* and to political expedience are not modified, except for the fact that *net seat gain* becomes insignificant.[19]

5.4.2 Violent unrest and peaceful agitation

The results reported in Table 5.4 support the political expedience hypothesis and demonstrate that overall exposure to public protest—a combination of violent unrest and peaceful agitation—increased support for the Reform Bill. In Table 5.5, we present results on the threat of revolution and the social movement hypothesis, respectively, by making a distinction between violent unrest and peaceful agitation; we further disaggregate violent unrest into rural and urban violence, and peaceful agitation into meetings, gatherings, and reform agitation. Since some of these variables are highly correlated,[20] we enter them one by one before presenting a 'horse race' regression.

In Table 5.5, columns 1 and 2, we disaggregate *all protest* into violent unrest and peaceful agitation. We see that the positive effect of *violent unrest* is imprecisely estimated while *peaceful agitation* influences the MPs' vote decisions significantly. An extra 10,000 peaceful agitators in the home county of an MP increase his support for reform by 1.6 percentage points. The further decomposition of *violent unrest* in Table 5.5, columns 3 and 4, into *rural violent* and *urban violent* unrest, however, shows that the variable that isolates violent unrest in urban areas, *urban violent*, had a significant and large positive effect of the probability of voting yes, while violence in the countryside (*rural violent*) did not have an effect. An extra 10,000 participants in violent unrest in urban areas within an MP's home county increase his support for reform by 24 percentage points. This result is consistent with the threat of revolution hypothesis and

[19] Table C5.1 in the supplementary material appendix reproduces the results reported in Table 5.4, column 3 with different codings of the main variables. The results are similar when, instead of the number of participants, we use the number of events, the number of participants per capita, or the number of participants per adult male. Furthermore, *net seat gain* has a positive and significant effect in the Heckman-probit model if we code the variable as percentage rather than as absolute gain.

[20] Table C5.4 in the supplementary material appendix reports partial correlations between these variables. The supplementary material appendix is available at www.oup.com/us/peacefuland violentorigins

suggests that what the MPs feared most was an urban uprising. It is also consistent with the observation that many MPs did not reside in the countryside for most of the winter months, even if they owed property there. Consequently, many of them had not been directly exposed to the Swing riots (in the winter of 1830–1831), which were the largest violent rural revolt in our sample period.

Table 5.5, columns 5 and 6, disaggregate *peaceful agitation* into *meetings* and *gatherings*. Both types of agitation had a positive effect on the MPs' likelihood of voting yes. For each additional 10,000 participants in meetings or gatherings, the probability of a yes vote from the MPs elected in the county experiencing the additional agitation goes up by 2.1 and 1.7 percentage points, respectively. In Table 5.5, column 7, we single out those meetings and gatherings which Horn and Tilly (1988) identified as being explicitly related to the reform question (*reform agitation*), and we observe a highly significant positive effect of this type of agitation. The point estimate on *reform agitation* indicates that an extra 10,000 participants in reform-related agitation and mass protest would have increased support for reform by 2.5 percentage points. Furthermore, Table 5.5, column 8, shows that petitions in favour of reform originating from a constituency increased the probability of a yes vote from the MPs elected in that constituency by 0.027 percentage points per additional petition. Taken together, these results support the social movement hypothesis, and suggest that peaceful agitation from extra-parliamentary groups, organisations, and movements helped convince some MPs that reform was needed and desirable.

In all these specifications, we consider one (unrest or agitation) variable at the time. In Table 5.5, column 9, we report the results of a 'horse race' specification which pitches the two variables *rural violent* and *urban violent* that capture the threat of revolution against the two variables *reform agitation* and *petitions* that capture peaceful reform-specific agitation and lobbying (related to the social movement hypothesis). We find that *reform agitation* and *petitions* are statistically significant while *rural violent* and *urban violent* are not. This suggests that peaceful agitation aimed specifically at the reform question had a stronger influence on the MPs than urban violence and the fears of revolution that such unrest may have stoked.[21]

[21] Table C5.5 in the supplementary material appendix reports additional regression results where we exclude the MPs elected in the City of London, in Westminster, and in the county of Middlesex. The motivation for this robustness check is that London, as the capital, was the centre of political agitation. The results are less precisely estimated, but otherwise similar to those reported in Table 5.4. The supplementary material appendix is available at www.oup.com/us/peacefulandviolentorigins

Table 5.5 The effect of violent unrest and different types of peaceful agitation on an MP's probability of voting in favour of the Reform Bill: probit estimates

	1	2	3	4	5	6	7	8	9
					Yes vote				
Violent unrest	0.11								
	(0.11)								
Peaceful agitation		0.016							
		(0.0075)**							
Rural violent			−0.19						−0.20
			(0.15)						(0.16)
Urban violent				0.24					0.055
				(0.081)***					(0.13)
Meetings					0.021				
					(0.0099)**				
Gatherings						0.017			
						(0.0098)*			
Reform agitation							0.025		0.019
							(0.0094)***		(0.011)*
Petitions								0.027	0.023
								(0.0069)***	(0.013)*
Net seat gain	0.011	0.0070	0.0100	0.0098	0.0087	0.0088	0.0094	0.012	0.0087
	(0.0028)***	(0.0039)*	(0.0033)***	(0.0031)***	(0.0036)**	(0.0032)***	(0.0033)***	(0.0029)***	(0.0042)**

continued

Table 5.5 *continued*

	1	2	3	4	5	6	7	8	9
					Yes vote				
Disenfranchised	−0.080	−0.100	−0.081	−0.078	−0.095	−0.092	−0.085	−0.039	−0.045
	(0.088)	(0.090)	(0.087)	(0.089)	(0.091)	(0.087)	(0.088)	(0.090)	(0.097)
Patron controlled	−0.096	−0.10	−0.10	−0.080	−0.091	−0.11	−0.097	−0.076	−0.064
	(0.11)	(0.10)	(0.10)	(0.11)	(0.11)	(0.10)	(0.10)	(0.11)	(0.11)
Landed interest	0.25	0.27	0.25	0.25	0.26	0.26	0.25	0.26	0.25
	(0.066)***	(0.065)***	(0.066)***	(0.065)***	(0.065)***	(0.066)***	(0.067)***	(0.064)***	(0.066)***
Controls	Yes	Yes	Yes	Yes	Yes	Yes	Yes	Yes	Yes
Observations	466	466	466	466	466	466	466	466	466

Note: Probit estimates. Marginal effects evaluated at the mean of the explanatory variables. Constant not shown. Standard errors in parentheses are clustered at the county level. Sample restricted to the English MPs who were present in the House of Commons on 22 March 1831. *Peaceful agitation* is the sum of *meetings* and *gatherings*. *Violent unrest* is the sum of *rural violent* and *urban violent*. Controls included are *Whig/Radical, local newspapers, emp. Herfindahl index, population density*, and *army career*. When tested down by a general-to-specific algorithm, *petitions* is significant at the 1 percent level, and *reform agitation* is significant at the 5 percent level in column (9). * = Significant at the 10 percent level; ** = Significant at the 5 percent level; *** = Significant at the 1 percent level.

5.4.3 Two counterfactual scenarios

We design two counterfactual scenarios to assess the magnitude of the estimated effects as well as to evaluate if the threat of revolution, social movement agitation, and political expedience exerted a sufficiently powerful effect on the MPs to be considered pivotal in the outcome of the vote. In the first counterfactual scenario, we analyse what would have happened if the MPs who attended the second reading on 22 March 1831 had been exposed to other levels of violent unrest (*urban violent*) and reform-related agitation (*reform agitation* and *petitions*) than the actual levels they were exposed to. We also analyse what would have happened if the significant variables related to political expedience (*net seat gain* and *landed interest*) had taken different values. For each variable, we determine its value at the 1st, 10th, 25th, 50th, 75th, 90th, and 99th percentile of the distribution, and use the relevant probit model to compute the predicted probability that each MP would have voted for reform.[22]

For each percentile of the distribution and each variable, Table 5.6 presents two sets of results: (i) the predicted share of English MPs who would have supported the bill had they been exposed to various levels of violent urban unrest, reform agitation, petitions, or political expediency, and (ii) the predicted number of pro-reform English MPs. For each estimate, we also report 95 percent confidence intervals to quantify the precision of the estimates. We recall that a minority of 229 English MPs (out of 466 present) actually voted for the bill (see Table 5.1). Table 5.6, column 1, shows the results for the proxy for the threat of revolution, *urban violent*. This counterfactual scenario shows that, had the MPs been exposed to violent urban unrest in the 75th percentile of the distribution rather than in the 25th, this would have persuaded (with 95 percent confidence) between eight and eleven more of them to vote for the Reform Bill and would almost have created a majority (49.81 percent) in favour of the reform amongst the English MPs. Table 5.6, columns 2 and 3, report the results for reform-related agitation and petitioning. For *reform agitation* and *petitions*, a move from the 25th percentile to the 75th percentile would have encouraged, respectively, three and ten more MPs to support the Reform Bill. It is, therefore, clear that urban violent unrest as a proxy for the threat of revolution, as well as peaceful reform-related agitation and petitioning, had a substantial effect on the outcome of the second reading and could have been pivotal.

Table 5.6, columns 4 and 5, evaluate the importance of the two (statistically significant) variables, *net seat gain* and *landed interest*, related to political expedience. From Table 5.6, column 4, we see that if all constituencies had been

[22] In Table C5.6 in the supplementary material appendix, we report the corresponding results for the other statistically significant variables *all protest*, *peaceful agitation*, *meetings*, and *gatherings*. The supplementary material appendix is available at www.oup.com/us/peacefulandviolentorigins

Table 5.6 Counterfactual analysis of the determinants of the MPs' votes

	Urban violent		Reform agitation		Petitions		Net seat gain		Landed interest	
Distribution	Predicted		Predicted		Predicted		Predicted		Predicted	
	Share of yes votes	Number	Share of yes votes	Number	Share of yes votes	Number	Share of yes votes	Number	Share of yes votes	Number
1st	47.68%	222	48.14%	224	45.61%	213	42.78%	199	47.08%	219
	[0.015]	{208; 236}	[0.014]	{211; 238}	[0.017]	{197; 228}	[0.032]	{170; 228}	[0.014]	{207; 232}
10th	47.68%	222	48.14%	224	47.50%	221	45.65%	213	47.08%	219
	[0.015]	{209; 236}	[0.014]	{211; 238}	[0.014]	{208; 234}	[0.020]	{195; 231}	[0.014]	{207; 232}
25th	47.70%	222	48.15%	224	47.50%	221	47.90%	223	47.08%	219
	[0.015]	{209; 236}	[0.014]	{211; 238}	[0.014]	{208; 234}	[0.013]	{211; 235}	[0.014]	{207; 232}
50th	47.75%	223	48.38%	225	48.47%	226	49.48%	231	47.08%	219
	[0.015]	{209; 236}	[0.014]	{212; 238}	[0.014]	{213; 239}	[0.013]	{218; 243}	[0.014]	{207; 232}
75th	49.81%	232	48.62%	227	49.47%	231	50.29%	234	47.08%	219
	[0.013]	{220; 244}	[0.014]	{214; 239}	[0.014]	{218; 243}	[0.015]	{220; 248}	[0.014]	{207; 232}
90th	51.30%	239	48.91%	228	50.50%	235	51.12%	238	59.03%	275
	[0.014]	{226; 252}	[0.014]	{215; 241}	[0.015]	{222; 249}	[0.018]	{222; 255}	[0.032]	{246; 304}
99th	82.16%	383	65.03%	303	54.89%	256	53.14%	248	59.03%	275
	[0.103]	{288; 477}	[0.070]	{240; 367}	[0.024]	{234; 278}	[0.028]	{222; 273}	[0.032]	{246; 304}

Note: This table reports results for a counterfactual analysis where we use the results in Table 5.4, column 3, (for *net seat gain* and *landed interest*) and Table 5.5, columns 4, 7, and 8 (for *urban violent, reform agitation*, and *petitions*). For each variable, we determine its value at the 1st, 10th, 25th, 50th, 75th, 90th, and 99th percentile of the respective distributions. Using the relevant probit estimate, we then calculate the predicted share of yes votes—i.e. the share of the 466 English MPs who would have voted for reform (standard errors for the predicted values are reported in square brackets) and the predicted number of yes votes (with 95 percent confidence intervals in curly brackets). The standard errors are calculated with the delta method.

located in a county that were to gain two extra seats (corresponding to the 75th percentile of the distribution of *net seat gain*), then a majority of 234 English MPs would have voted for the Reform Bill. Likewise, in Table 5.6, column 5, we see that had all constituencies enjoyed the benefit that the landed interest obtained from the new voting rules in the counties (corresponding to the 90th percentile of the distribution of *landed interest*), 275 of the English MPs would have voted in favour of the bill. Political expedience, thus, also had a substantial effect on the outcome of the vote.

In the second counterfactual scenario, we focus on the eighteen absent English MPs and analyse what would have happened to the outcome of the vote if they had attended the second reading and voted on 22 March 1831. From the biographies of individual MPs in Fisher (2009), we researched the reasons given for each MP's absence. We summarise the reasons in Table 5.7.[23] The two most frequent reasons were (i) poor health, and (ii) planned absence. To undertake the counterfactual calculation, we use the probit estimate from Table 5.4, column 3, to predict how the 18 MPs, given their personal characteristics and those of their constituencies, would have voted had they been present. The last column of Table 5.7 reports for each MP the predicted probability that he would have voted for the bill. Eight of the MPs were almost sure to vote yes with a predicted probability of doing so greater than 90 percent and five MPs were almost sure to vote no with a predicated probability of supporting the bill less than 10 percent. Of the remaining five absent MPs, one would in all likelihood have voted yes (with a predicted probability of 87 percent), while the other four would most likely have voted no with probabilities of voting yes between 18 and 38 percent. It, thus, appears that the absent MPs would have split equally between yes and no and that it, therefore, did not matter for the outcome of the vote that they did not attend. It is, however, interesting to observe that out of the nine potentially pro-reform absent MPs, seven were Whigs, as expected, but two were Tories: Bethell Walrond (1801–1876), with a 87 percent predicted probability of voting yes, and Charles Vere Ferrars Compton Townshend (1785–1853), with 98 percent probability. Conversely, one of the Whigs, William Henry Lytton Earle Bulwer, has a very low predicted probability of voting yes (only 2 percent).[24]

[23] We acknowledge that the reasons given in the bibliographical sources for the absence may contain some element of ex post rationalisation and should be interpreted with that in mind.

[24] Table C5.7 in the supplementary material appendix reports the reason why the four vacant seats were vacant. Table C5.8 in the supplementary material appendix reports a counterfactual analysis for the eighteen absent MPs similar to the one we reported in Table 5.6 for the MPs present. The supplementary material appendix is available at www.oup.com/us/peacefulandviolentorigins

Table 5.7 MPs absence from the House of Commons on 22 March 1831

Borough	County	MP	Affiliation	Occupation	Reason for absence	Prob. reform support
Brackley	Northamptonshire	Robert Haldane Bradshaw	Tory	Industrialist	On 22 November 1830, he was granted a month's leave because of ill health and was given another month on 10 February 1831.	0.08
Brackley	Northamptonshire	James Bradshaw	Tory	Army Officer	His father was ill (see above) and without any additional information, we speculate that he remained with him during this illness.	0.03
Derbyshire	Derbyshire	George Augustus Henry Cavendish	Whig	Landowner	He was apparently too ill to attend the House on 22 March 1831.	0.99
Dunwich	Suffolk	Frederick Barne	Tory	Army Officer	On 10 February 1831, he received a month's leave of absence on account of ill health and remained absent on 22 March 1831, even though the Reform Bill proposed Dunwich's disfranchisement.	0.21
Helstone	Cornwall	Samuel John Brooke Pechell	Whig	Army Officer	On 7 March 1831, he was excused from attending the Durham election committee because of illness and was absent from the division on the second reading of the Reform Bill.	0.91
Launceston	Cornwall	James Willoughby Gordon	Tory	Army Officer	In March 1831, he informed his patron, Lord Northumberland, who wished him to oppose the government's reform bill, that it was "quite impossible for me as the senior officer upon the King's staff to vote against His Majesty's government under any circumstances whatever", and that he could only promise to "keep away from the discussion". He was absent from the vote on 22 March 1831, and was then given 'notice to quit', and he eventually resigned his seat on 5 April 1831.	0.02

Midhurst	Sussex	George Smith	Whig	Banker	On 22 March 1831, he was ill but he made it known that he would have voted for the Reform Bill if present.	0.97
Newton	Lancashire	Thomas Legh	Tory	Landowner	On 14 February 1831, he was granted three weeks of leave, following his wife's death, and on 9 March 1831, another fortnight because of illness in his family. He did not vote on the second reading of the Reform Bill, which proposed Newton's disfranchisement.	0.30
Newtown	Hampshire	Hudson Gurney	Whig	Banker	He was plagued by a cold and did not vote. He, however, indicated two days later in a debate that he had actually voted in favour of the bill.	0.90
Pontefract	Yorkshire	Culling Eardley Smith	Whig	Landowner	On 7 March 1831, after serving on an election committee, he was granted a month's leave to attend to private business.	0.18
Sudbury	Suffolk	Bethell Walrond	Tory	Army Officer	On 16 March 1831, he was granted ten days of leave to attend the assizes.	0.87
Sussex	Sussex	Walter Burrell	Whig	Landowner	On 14 March 1831, after serving on an election committee, he was granted two weeks of leave to attend to private business.	0.38
Tamworth	Staffordshire	Charles Vere Ferrars Compton Town-shend	Tory	Landowner	No reason given as to his absence from the division on the second reading of the Reform Bill.	0.98
Thirsk	Yorkshire	Robert Frankland	Whig	Landowner	No reason given as to his absence from the division on the second reading of the Reform Bill.	0.99

continued

Table 5.7 *continued*

Borough	County	MP	Affiliation	Occupation	Reason for absence	Prob. reform support
Weobly	Herefordshire	Edward Thynne	Tory	Army Officer	An army officer on active service, he was returned in abstentia, rarely attended Parliament and let his younger brother Edward sit for the borough in April 1831.	0.05
Wilton	Wiltshire	William Henry Lytton Earle Bulwer	Whig	Army Officer	Bulwer was a Whig beholden to the Tory patron of Wilton, which was scheduled to lose one of its seats. This may have led him not to attend the second reading of the Reform Bill, after rumors began to circulate on 5 March that he had joined the ranks of the Tory opposition.	0.02
Winchelsea	Sussex	John Williams	Whig	Lawyer	On 22 March 1831, he was working on the legal circuit.	0.93
Yarmouth	Norfolk	Charles Edmund Rumbold	Whig	Army Officer	On 14 March 1831, he was excused because of illness, which also prevented him from voting on 22 March 1831.	0.94

Note: The table lists the MPs who did not attend the vote on 22 March 1831, along with their party affiliation and stated reason of absence, based on the bibliographic information in Fisher (2009). The last column (headed 'Prob. reform support') reports for each MP the counterfactual probability of voting for reform, obtained from the probit model in Table 5.4, column 3, given their personal characteristics and those of their constituencies.

5.4.4 Interpretation

We find strong statistical evidence that the MPs reacted to public expressions of reform support, as suggested by the social movement hypothesis. Our empirical analysis shows that two channels connected the MPs to pro-reform social movements and public opinion. The first channel was direct and targeted lobbying via petitions from the MPs' constituents about the reform question. The other channel was mass mobilisation in favour of reform expressed through public meetings, demonstrations, and gatherings. Information about mass mobilisation reached the MPs through their own participation in meetings and through frequent reports in the local and national press about meetings and demonstrations in their home county. It is clear from the debate in the House of Commons that such meetings made an impression on the MPs, and 'public support' was often used as an argument for reform. The Whig MP Thomas Denman (1779–1854), for example, appealed to 'a great meeting in the county of Nottingham where almost every respectable gentleman attended and where the resolution had been unanimously in favour of the measure [reform]' in his defense of the reform on 22 March 1831 (Hansard HC Deb, 22 March 1831, vol. 3, c719). Likewise, the Tory MP Robert Palmer (1793–1872) voted in favour of the reform in deference to his Berkshire constituents' strong support for the bill. He admitted in his contribution to the debate that his own had been the only dissenting voice at a meeting in his constituency, and he reiterated that the bill went further than he could personally endorse (Fisher 2009). Of course, not all MPs were convinced by such agitation, but it is clear that the MPs were aware of it; our statistical results indicate that social movement pressure worked on a sufficiently large number to make a difference. Petitions also came to the attention of the MPs, and they were frequently mentioned both by supporters and opponents of reform in the debate. Many opponents went to great lengths explaining why they would vote against the bill despite the wishes of their voters. Taken together, we conclude from the statistical and historical evidence that social movements and the force of lobbying, agitation, and public expressions of reform support were pivotal in pushing the Reform Bill over its second real hurdle. Interests outside of Parliament played a key role for the way the MPs inside the House of Commons voted on 22 March 1831.

In contrast, our 'horse race' tests suggest that the threat of revolution played a secondary role compared to social movement pressure and peaceful agitation. If anything, it was violent riots and demonstrations, in London and in other urban areas, rather than the rural Swing riots, that made an impression on the MPs elected in 1830. It is clear, nevertheless, from the transcripts of the seven days of debate that preceded the division on 22 March 1831 that many MPs did view the reform as a necessary means to avoid a revolution or, at least, were willing to use the specter of revolution rhetorically in the debates (Hamburger 1963). Lord John Russell, who had presented the first version of the bill to the House of Commons on 1 March 1831, had the opportunity to make the last substantive remarks on 22 March 1831. He used the example of the revolution in France in July 1830 to suggest that it could have been prevented by concessions to the people and that reform in Britain was now required to avoid a revolution. Similar views were expressed in the debate in the House of Lords in November 1830 when Lord Grey first announced that he intended to seek reform. William Pleydell-Bouverie, third Earl of Radnor (1779–1869), said 'that Parliamentary Reform was not merely expedient, but the only measure which could ensure the salvation of the country' (Hansard HL Deb, 22 November 1830, vol. 1, c604), a view also expressed by Grey himself in his speech to the House of Lords. This type of rhetoric notwithstanding, our statistical results suggest that the Reform Bill overcame the second roadblock on its way to the statute book, not so much because of fears of revolution, but thanks to social movements and the force of peaceful agitation and public expressions of reform support.

5.4.5 Omitted factors and indirect channels

Our statistical results show that social movement agitation and public opinion, political expedience, and, to a lesser extent, urban violent unrest directly influenced the MPs' support for the bill. We can plausibly rule out reverse causality since our sample of violent unrest, peaceful agitation, and petitions ends before the MPs voted on the reform, although for petitions there could be, as we discuss below, an anticipation effect. The main concern, therefore, is unobserved factors that could explain, at the same time, the spatial distribution of violent unrest or peaceful agitation and the MPs' position on the Reform Bill.[25] In this section, we evaluate the possibility of indirect channels and anticipation effects, and we conduct a placebo test to bolster the argument that the results are not due to unobserved omitted factors.

Direct and indirect influences on the MPs' votes: Tables 5.4 and 5.5 report estimates of the direct effect of violent unrest, peaceful social movement agitation, and political expedience on the MPs' votes. Support and opposition to the bill split, as noted above, along party lines, with the Whigs and Radicals being

[25] Table C5.9 in the supplementary material appendix shows that including an additional set of potentially confounding factors does not affect our results. The supplementary material appendix is available at www.oup.com/us/peacefulandviolentorigins

(mostly) in favour and the Tories being (mostly) against. The MPs who voted on the bill were elected in the 1830 General Election. Unlike the election in 1831, parliamentary reform was not yet a major issue when the polling period ended in September 1830. It did play, however, a role in the agitation in some constituencies: the Radical politician Henry Hunt stood unsuccessfully in Preston on a reform platform, and some of the successful candidates, including leading Whig politician Henry Brougham, were publicly committed to seek reform in the upcoming session (Brock (1973, Chap. 3); Tilly (1995, 324)). Moreover, some of the reform unions, included the influential Birmingham Political Union, organised their first mass meetings in early 1830. It is, therefore, possible that public agitation before and during the electoral campaign induced some voters and patrons in areas strongly affected by such agitation to elect candidates from a particular party who subsequently happened to vote in a particular way on the Reform Bill. If this were the case, public agitation exerted an indirect influence on the vote, and the evidence on the direct effect of agitation could reflect this.

To investigate whether public agitation and/or expectations of eventual gains and losses from a future parliamentary reform influenced the outcome of the 1830 General Election, we create the new dependent variable *Whig share in 1830*. It is equal to the share of seats in each (English) constituency won by the Whigs or Radicals—in other words, by the two parties which subsequently supported the Reform Bill. We also re-compute our measures of social movement agitation and violent unrest so that they only include events that happened before the polling period of the 1830 General Election started on 29 July 1830.

Table 5.8, columns 1 to 3, show the results from three linear regressions relating *Whig share in 1830* to our re-coded measures of agitation and unrest, as well as to the variables capturing political expedience and the set of control variables. We find that neither *violent unrest* nor *peaceful agitation* had any effect on the election outcome in 1830. With regard to political expedience, we see that *net seat gain* and *disenfranchised* are insignificant, and *landed interest* is only marginally significant at the 10 percent level. The variable *patron controlled* is, however, significantly and negatively related to the share of elected Whigs in 1830. The places that were controlled by patrons tended to elect Tories, as previously noted. Overall, these results reinforce our interpretation of the main results as evidence that extra-parliamentary pressure and agitation in its various forms had a direct effect on the vote choices of the MPs rather than on who got elected.

A related concern is that petitions could have been addressed primarily to MPs who were supporting the reform anyway. Since most Whig MPs voted for the reform, we would expect, if this concern is real, a positive correlation

Table 5.8 The effect of violent unrest and peaceful agitation on the share of Whigs and Radicals elected in the 1830 General Election: OLS estimates

	1	2	3	4
	Whig share in 1830			
All protest[a]	0.29 [0.38]			
Violent unrest[a]		8.12 [7.29]		
Peaceful agitation[a]			0.28 [0.39]	
Petitions[b]				0.54 [0.85]
Net seat gain	0.019 [0.10]	−0.0075 [0.11]	0.022 [0.10]	0.057 [0.095]
Landed interest	8.56 [4.77]*	8.43 [4.76]*	8.56 [4.77]*	8.39 [4.71]*
Disenfranchised	−8.28 [5.90]	−8.21 [5.92]	−8.27 [5.89]	−7.43 [6.53]
Patron controlled	−8.08 [3.46]**	−7.91 [3.48]**	−8.11 [3.45]**	−7.87 [3.37]**
Emp. Herfindahl index	−12.5 [25.4]	−11.1 [26.5]	−12.6 [25.4]	−10.9 [25.0]
Population density	0.22 [1.79]	0.57 [1.68]	0.23 [1.80]	0.20 [1.76]
Local newspapers	−0.019 [0.011]*	−0.023 [0.011]**	−0.019 [0.011]*	−0.022 [0.015]
Whig share in 1826	0.67 [0.046]***	0.67 [0.045]***	0.67 [0.046]***	0.67 [0.045]***
Adjusted R^2	0.55	0.55	0.55	0.55
Observations	244	244	244	244

Note: Linear regressions estimated with ordinary least squares (OLS). Constant not shown. Standard errors in parentheses are clustered at the county level. The sample is the 244 English constituencies.
[a]The variables are re-coded and accumulate participation in events before 29 July 1830.
[b]All but ten reform-related petitions were submitted after the 1830 election. * = Significant at the 10 percent level; ** = Significant at the 5 percent level; *** = Significant at the 1 percent level.

between the petitions for reform submitted (largely) after the 1830 General Election and the likelihood that a Whig (or Radical) candidate was elected in 1830. In Table 5.8, column 4, we report that the correlation between *petitions* and *Whig share in 1830* is insignificant, strongly suggesting that this was not the case.

Agitation and unrest in 1828–1831 and earlier reform attempts: To further check that our results are not driven by omitted factors correlated both with the geography of agitation and unrest and with the general pro-reform attitudes of the patrons, voters, and MPs in each constituency, we propose a falsification test. Its purpose is to assess whether agitation and unrest between 1828 and 1831 can predict the divisions (voting) in the House of Commons on two failed attempts at reform that took place before 1828. The attempts are the reform bill proposed by Thomas Brand, which was supported by 92 English MPs on 21 May 1810 (1807 Parliament), and the bill proposed by Lord John Russell, which was supported by 148 MPs on 25 April 1822 (1820 Parliament). Since social movement agitation and violent unrest happening between 1828 and 1831 had not yet happened, they should not predict whether the MPs in 1810 and 1822 voted for reform.[26]

To carry out the falsification test related to the failed attempts at reform in 1810 and 1822, we estimate probit models similar to that in equation 5.1 but with the two new dependent variables *yes vote 1810* and *yes vote 1822.* They are equal to 1 if the MP elected in a given constituency supported the reform bills of 1810 or 1822, respectively, and 0 otherwise. To match the control variables to the relevant time periods, we collect data on the party affiliations of the MPs who represented each English constituency in the 1807 and 1820 Parliaments, respectively. We also replace the *patronage index* with the indicator variable *uncontested elections* which equals 1 if there was no actual contest in the last seven general elections prior to the 1807 or 1822 General Election, respectively. We use information from the 1811 and 1821 Censuses of Great Britain to reconstruct *emp. Herfindahl index* and *population density.*

Table 5.9 shows the results. It is reassuring to observe that none of the variables related to violent unrest or to social movement agitation can predict support for reform amongst the MPs in 1810 and 1822. These results provide additional support for our interpretation that the estimated effect of 'pressure from below' on the second reading of the bill is causal rather than coincidental.

[26] We selected these two bills because they received the largest number of yes votes in the two decades before the Great Reform Act (see Chapter 3). The yes votes are reported in Hansard HC Deb, 21 May 1810, series 1, vol. 14, 123–164 and Hansard HC Deb, 5 April 1822, series 2, vol. 7, c139. For all the failed attempts at reform before 1832, only the votes in favour of reform were recorded. Therefore, our test can only be carried out for the two attempts in 1810 and 1822 which gathered a sufficiently large number of yes votes.

Table 5.9 Falsification tests. The effect of violent unrest and peaceful agitation in 1828–1831 on the MPs' votes on the failed reform bills in 1810 and 1822

	1	2	3	4	5	6
		Yes vote 1810			Yes vote 1822	
Violent unrest	0.013 (0.031)			−0.045 (0.059)		
Peaceful agitation		−0.0038 (0.0027)			−0.0053 (0.0035)	
Petitions			0.0052 (0.0061)			−0.0080 (0.011)
Net seat gain	0.0028 (0.0014)**	0.0035 (0.0017)**	0.0029 (0.0014)**	0.0060 (0.0018)***	0.0071 (0.0019)***	0.0058 (0.0018)***
Disenfranchised	−0.023 (0.035)	−0.021 (0.034)	−0.014 (0.039)	−0.018 (0.087)	−0.012 (0.088)	−0.030 (0.087)
Uncontested elections	−0.050 (0.027)*	−0.051 (0.026)*	−0.048 (0.026)*	0.069 (0.061)	0.069 (0.063)	0.061 (0.061)
Landed interest	0.036 (0.047)	0.029 (0.046)	0.039 (0.048)	0.092 (0.060)	0.089 (0.060)	0.090 (0.060)
Whig/Radical	0.33 (0.044)***	0.33 (0.042)***	0.32 (0.043)***	0.57 (0.042)***	0.57 (0.042)***	0.57 (0.042)***
Local newspapers	0.00015 (0.00015)	0.00029 (0.00014)**	0.00011 (0.00018)	0.00030 (0.00019)	0.00021 (0.00028)	0.00025 (0.00026)
Emp. Herf. Index	0.066 (0.14)	0.055 (0.13)	0.078 (0.14)	−0.18 (0.14)	−0.20 (0.14)	−0.20 (0.14)
Population density	0.0059 (0.014)	0.0082 (0.013)	0.0050 (0.014)	−0.020 (0.022)	−0.015 (0.021)	−0.017 (0.023)
Observations	486	486	486	487	487	487

Note: Probit estimates. Marginal effects evaluated at the mean of the explanatory variables. Constant not shown. Standard errors in parentheses are clustered at the county level. The sample is the English MPs. *Uncontested elections* is coded 1 if none of the seven previous elections had been contested, and 0 otherwise; *emp. Herf. index* and *population density* refer to the nearest census year. Only yes votes were recorded in the Hansard. MPs who did not vote are assumed to vote no.
* = Significant at the 10 percent level; ** = Significant at the 5 percent level; *** = Significant at the 1 percent level.

5.5 Conclusion

The division on 22 March 1831 was the first critical test of reform support in the House of Commons. It was far from a foregone conclusion that the Reform Bill would pass the second reading with a majority. In the end, it did, but with only one vote. Our empirical analysis of the way the MPs voted establishes that three forces played a role in tipping the scale in favour of the reform and helping the bill circumvent the second roadblock. We find that reform-related agitation and petitioning orchestrated by various social movements or political unions and violent unrest in urban areas could have induced eight to eleven MPs to vote yes rather than no. We also find that political expedience had a substantial effect on the outcome of the vote. This shows that different causal factors operated, and that elements of all the theories discussed in Chapter 2 came together to overcome opposition to parliamentary reform in the House of Commons in March 1831 and helped the Reform Bill pass the second roadblock.

The evidence presented in this chapter adds, more generally, to the understanding of the historical process of democratisation in two ways. First, in between the view that democratisation was an elite project devised for opportunistic reasons, and the view that democracy was unwillingly conceded by the elite to avoid a revolution, there is the third possibility. Social movements and peaceful protest and demonstrations, agitations, petitioning, and other public expressions of opinion might have influenced the views and attitudes of the elite politicians who contemplated reform without necessarily stoking fears of a violent revolution. This possibility has received too little attention in quantitative work on democratisation in the nineteenth century (with the notable exception of the pioneering work by Tilly (1995, 2007)). Building on the work by Tilly (1995), this chapter provides new evidence on the importance of social movement pressure in the 1830s. We are able to distinguish between peaceful agitation and violent unrest, and, thus, between social movement pressure and revolutionary threats. We find that peaceful agitation exerted an important influence on how the MPs voted, giving us reason to reassess the importance of social movements for democratic reform in a historical context.[27] The threat of revolution was stoked by urban (and not rural) social unrest but was less important than peaceful reform-related agitation for the result of the second reading vote.

Second, the chapter provides new evidence on the importance of political expedience. We follow the approach pioneered by Ziblatt (2008) and use the

[27] Social movements were arguable also instrumental in bringing about democratisation in several countries in South Asia, Eastern Europe, and Sub-Saharan Africa in the last thirty years (e.g. Bunce and Wolchik 2006; Chenoweth and Stephan 2011).

details of the seat redistribution embedded in the reform proposal to measure the expected gains and losses for individual MPs. Our statistical results show that MPs elected in borough constituencies located in counties that stood to gain representation, as well as those representing the counties and the landed interest, supported the bill. In addition, the debate in the House of Commons preceding the second reading provides many examples that are highly suggestive of self-interest at play. One example of this is the defense of the unreformed system that the Tory MP Philip Henry Stanhope, Viscount Mahon (1805–1875), who represented the 'rotten' borough of Wootton Basset, articulated in the House of Commons on 22 March 1831. He stressed how the nomination boroughs of Gatton and Old Sarum served the useful purpose of counterpoising the effect of more popular representation elsewhere and thus ensured the 'blending of several interests in forming a perfect whole' (Hansard HC Deb, 22 March 1831, series 2, vol. 3, c719). However, there was clearly a personal motive underlying such a principled stance against reform: the prospective loss of a seat. The fact that many other speakers in the debate went to great length to stress that they opposed the Reform Bill as a matter of principle and not because they would personally be affected adds, at the very least, to the suspicion that personal expedience played a role in the way that many MPs voted.

Chapter 6
A referendum on reform: the 1831 General Election

6.1 Introduction

We now turn our attention to the third roadblock that the Great Reform Act had to overcome to succeed. After the narrow victory in the House of Commons on 22 March 1831, and the subsequent defeats during the committee stage, Lord Grey had requested the King to call a general election in the hope of securing a solid mandate from the electors of the Unreformed Parliament to pursue reform.[1] The election in April–June 1831 was effectively a referendum on the bill. The election resulted in a solid Whig majority in the House of Commons, a majority which was necessary for the reform's ultimate success.

One of the leading theories of democratisation, discussed in Chapter 2, is the threat of revolution theory: democratic reforms can be a rational response by the ruling elite to a temporary threat of revolution (Acemoglu and Robinson 2000*b*). The key assumption is that the elite can credibly commit to democratic reform while they are expected to renege on policy concessions once the threat has passed. In practice, those who seek to overthrow the status quo in a violent revolution face many hurdles in mobilising and coordinating, and they do not pose a permanent threat to the elite (Tullock 1971). Widespread violent protests and rioting, however, constitute a credible signal to the elite that these hurdles have been temporarily overcome: those who riot could, either on their own or in conjunction with members of other groups, trigger more costly unrest, and possibly even a full-fledged revolution. This, in turn, may motivate the elite to implement democratic reforms to preempt such an escalation. The threat of revolution theory, therefore, predicts a causal chain running from observed riots and violent unrest to the elite's perceptions of the threat of revolution and the eventual adoption of democratic reform.

In Chapter 5, we tested the threat of revolution hypothesis in the context of the 22 March 1831 second reading in the House of Commons by correlating the scale of violent unrest that had happened near the MPs' constituencies to their vote on the Reform Bill. In this chapter, we explore a similar strategy but shift our

[1] This chapter is based on Aidt and Franck (2015).

Peaceful and Violent Origins of Voting Rights. Toke S. Aidt and Raphaël Franck, Oxford University Press.
 DOI: 10.1093/9780197679746.003.0006

attention from the MPs to those who elected them, and we go one step further: we isolate the causal effect of the threat of revolution on franchise extension by exploring the impact of plausibly exogenous variation in threat perceptions on constituency-level support for the reform amongst the voters and patrons of the Unreformed Parliament. The 1831 General Election offers a unique opportunity to test the threat of revolution hypothesis in this way. On the one hand, as we discussed in Chapters 3 and 4, parliamentary reform had become a 'party' question, with the Whigs and Radicals supporting the bill and the overwhelming majority of the Tories opposing it. We can, therefore, evaluate the support for parliamentary reform among voters and patrons by measuring the electoral success of the Whigs and Radicals relative to previous elections, held in 1826 and 1830. On the other hand, between August 1830 and the spring of 1831—that is, *between* the elections in 1830 and 1831—the uprising of agricultural labourers in the Swing riots caused an unprecedented spike in violent unrest across the English countryside (Hobsbawm and Rudé 1973; Tilly 1995). The rural aspect of the riots matters because the typical parliamentary constituency before 1832 was a small market town or sometimes simply a village embedded in the local agricultural economy. The Swing riots, therefore, gave the voters and patrons of the constituencies located in the affected areas first-hand experience with an uprising on an unprecedented scale. We quantify the scale of (local) riots at the constituency level by counting the number of Swing riots that happened within a 10-kilometre radius of each constituency.

Most importantly, the timing and geography of the Swing riots mean that they can be used to construct exogenous constituency-specific measures of threat perceptions. Firstly, the peak of the Swing riots occurred between the July–September 1830 General Election, which led to a change in government from the Tories to the Whigs, and the April–June 1831 General Election. We can, therefore, condition on the existing level of support for the Whig party in each constituency. This removes many factors that would otherwise confound the relationship between the Swing riots in the vicinity of a constituency and the electoral success of the Whigs in the 1831 election. Secondly, detailed analysis of the spatial and temporal distribution of the Swing riots demonstrates that they did not spread randomly after they broke out in Kent in August 1830 (Charlesworth 1979; Aidt, Leon-Ablan and Satchell 2022). Instead, they spread systematically along a route that closely followed the pre-existing road network, and the riot dynamics were driven by local social interaction effects: agricultural workers willing to revolt were encouraged to do so by observing others engaged in rioting but with diminishing strength as the distance from the epicentre of the riots increased.[2] This feature implies that we can use the travel-time

[2] Kuran (1989) provides a theory explaining why potential rioters are induced to riot. Individuals tend to hide their willingness to riot as long as they perceive that not many others are willing to join

distance between each constituency and Sevenoaks, the village in Kent where the first three Swing riots occurred on 3 August 1830, as an instrumental variable for the number of riots that happened in the vicinity of each constituency. In this way, we can isolate exogenous variation in threat perceptions. Our empirical strategy to test the threat of revolution hypothesis in the context of the 1831 General Election, therefore, is to relate the number of Swing riots that happened within a 10-kilometre radius of each constituency *due to diffusion of riots from neighbouring areas* to the share of seats won by the reform-friendly Whigs and Radicals in 1831, conditional on the share that they obtained in the previous election. Our results show that voters and patrons who in previous elections had not supported the Whigs and Radicals were led to vote for the candidates from these parties and thus indirectly for parliamentary reform after experiencing first-hand the violence of the Swing riots. Fear of revolution helped the Reform Bill overcome the third roadblock and helped the Whigs obtain the majority in the House of Commons that they needed.

6.2 The 1831 General Election and the Swing riots

6.2.1 A barometer of reform support

In the General Election held in April–June 1831, many Tories lost their seats, and the election result gave the Whigs the majority which they needed to pursue the reform. Figure 6.1 shows the shift in support for the Whigs between 1830 and 1831 across the 244 English constituencies. The Whigs (along with a few Radicals) held 210 of the 489 English seats in 1830; the 1831 election won them 66 additional seats (to 276) so that they gained control over 56 percent of the English seats. We use the party affiliation of the MP(s) elected in each constituency as a barometer of reform support amongst the voters and patrons in that location. We relate the shift towards the Whigs to the intensity of Swing riots that happened around each constituency between the two elections.

To fully understand the logic behind this strategy, three facts about the Unreformed Parliament must be emphasised. Firstly, one concern with our measure of reform support is that party affiliation may capture partisan divisions other than on the question of parliamentary reform, for example, on economic or religious issues. To evaluate this concern, we recall that the Whigs and the Tories were loose and shifting factions rather than political parties in the modern sense (Hill 1967; Jupp 1998), and both factions overwhelmingly belonged to an overlapping oligarchy of landowners, businessmen, lawyers, and career soldiers

in. A slight surge in the apparent size of the group of rioters, caused by events which are insignificant in and of themselves, can trigger a riot cascade.

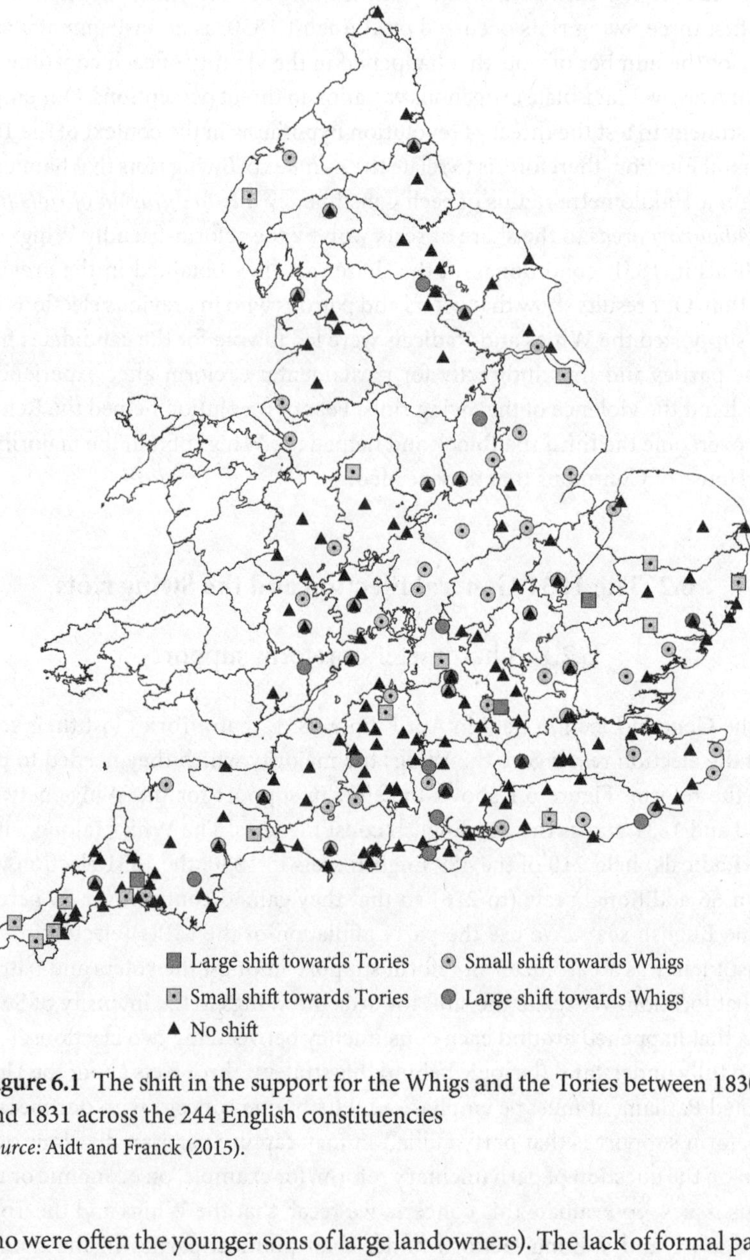

Figure 6.1 The shift in the support for the Whigs and the Tories between 1830 and 1831 across the 244 English constituencies
Source: Aidt and Franck (2015).

(who were often the younger sons of large landowners). The lack of formal party structures meant that political issues often cut across factions or united them. On the one hand, members of both factions were split on the questions of abolishing slavery, and on giving political and civil rights to Catholics. On the other hand, because of their common economic interests, Tories and Whigs agreed upon the necessity of protecting private property (Halévy 1923, Vol. 3, Part 1, Chap. 3). They also agreed that violent unrest should, as far as possible, be repressed by force, and this explains why the repression of the Swing riots carried out by the Whigs was tacitly supported by the Tories (Archer 2000; Stevenson 1992). In contrast, the divisions on the question of parliamentary reform closely followed party lines. The Whigs, in particular Lord Grey and the other Whig leaders in Parliament, favoured limited parliamentary reform. Long before the Swing riots, they were committed to give voting rights to the 'respectable' sections of society—that is, property owners—and to give representation to the expanding industrial cities and to other large towns. The Tory leadership, in contrast, did not support any measure of parliamentary reform.

Secondly, the geography of political representation in the Unreformed Parliament was strongly biased in favour of the countryside. With the exception of Liverpool, the large expanding commercial and industrial cities outside London were not represented. The voters in the county constituencies were mainly tenant farmers, and many landowners extended a dominant influence through patronage and employment. The typical borough constituency was a small market town which provided services to the surrounding agricultural economy. The borough voters were not just recruited from the local elite (e.g., in the corporation boroughs) but also from lower middle-class town dwellers (e.g. freemen and local ratepayers) and from relatively poor inhabitants (e.g. in boroughs with potwalloper franchise). A useful metaphor is to think of the parliamentary boroughs as small islands of representation scattered around the English countryside, as illustrated by the map of Essex in Figure 4.1 of Chapter 4.

Thirdly, the agricultural economy in Great Britain around 1830 consisted of three social strata: the large landowners, the tenant farmers, and the agricultural labourers. The tenant farmers rented relatively large pieces of land on long-term contracts from the large landowners and employed agricultural labourers on wage contracts, typically of short duration. The agricultural labourers did not own or rent land and were, therefore, not self-sufficient farmers. They did not possess the right to vote before 1832, and did not obtain it with the Great Reform Act. It was to this social stratum of casual agricultural workers that the Swing rioters belonged and much of their anger was directed at the other two strata.

6.2.2 The Swing riots

The Swing riots were named after the mythical avenger Captain Swing, whose signature could be found on many of the threatening letters received by tenant farmers, parsons (members of the clergy), and landowners, many of whom were parliamentary voters or patrons.[3] The rioters were landless agricultural labourers, and the riots were characterised by either a high degree of violence or threat of violence. Common tactics included arson, the burning of farm houses and haystacks, and the destruction of threshing machines owned by tenant farmers, as well as outright extortion of money and provisions from farmers, landowners, and parsons (Tilly 1995; Caprettini and Voth 2020).

Our empirical analysis is based on the assumption that the Swing riots were not an organised political movement with clear political aims related to parliamentary reform. This is important because this is what allows us to establish a link between the threat of revolution and change in reform support at the constituency level. If, in contrast, the riots had been systematically masterminded by national or local reform supporters, it would be harder to establish this link because riots would naturally tend to be concentrated in areas with strong underlying support for reform or in places where national political leaders would see a strategic advantage in organising them. The available historical evidence supports our assumption. First, the uncoordinated violence of the Swing riots contrasted with the tactics of the emerging trade unions in urban areas that combined targeted aggressive actions with peaceful strikes (Stevenson 1992). Second, the Swing riots were not fomented by the nascent Chartist movement or by organisations of middle-class activists (Halévy 1923, Vol. 3). Third, it is not even clear whether the meetings held by the radical politician William Cobbett in the southeast of England or by several radical orators in London after the outbreak of the Swing riots had any impact on the continuation of the violence (e.g. Halévy 1923, Vol. 3; Dyck 1992; Royle 2000, p. 85).[4] Finally, there was no union of agricultural labourers at that time which could have taken an active role in organising the riots.

The riots began with three disturbances in the village of Sevenoaks in Kent on 3 August 1830, peaked in intensity in November 1830, and ended in the spring of 1831 (Holland 2005). We observe from Figure 6.2, which shows the number of Swing riots by month in 1830 and 1831, that the riots occurred after the polling period for the 1830 election and before the polling period for the 1831 election. Figure 6.3 shows the spatial distribution of the riots. They spread from Kent to other counties, such as Sussex, Hampshire, and Wiltshire in the South and West, and engulfed East Anglia as well as parts of the Midlands. The

[3] Halévy (1923, vol. 3) relies on William Cobbett's publication, *The Political Register* (13 July 1833, 81, 72), to suggest that the word 'swing' refers to the swinging stick of the flail in agricultural parlance. Few authors of the Swing letters are known. Those who were identified include a straw plait manufacturer in Suffolk, a weaver in Norfolk, and a hostler in Hampshire. They independently wrote letters signed as Captain Swing (Archer 2000, 17).

[4] William Cobbett was brought to trial in July 1831 for publishing a libel to incite labourers to violence, but was acquitted (Briggs 1967, Chap. 7). However, the radical orator Richard Carlile was prosecuted for sedition and sentenced to two years in prison for issuing an 'Address to the Insurgent Labourers' (Royle 2000, 85).

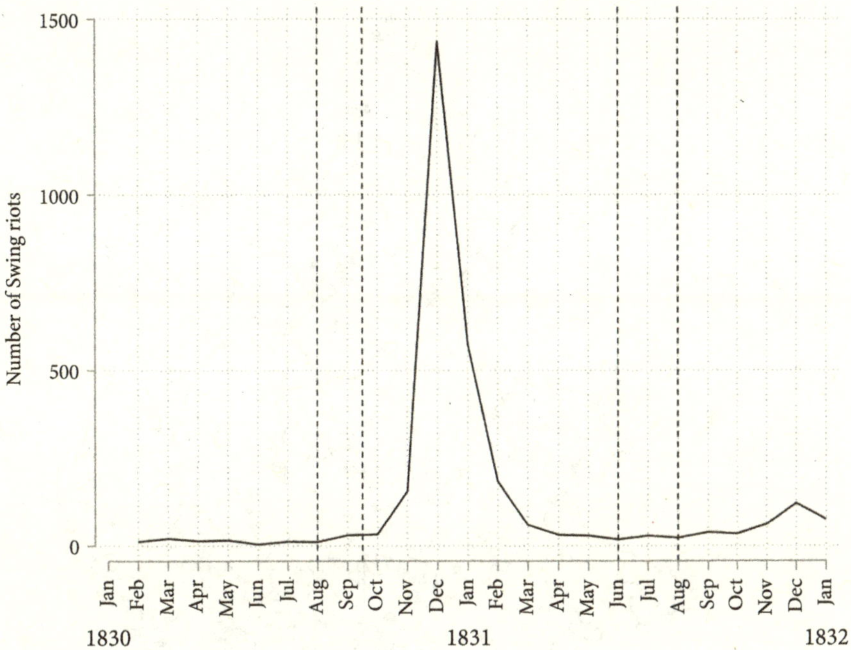

Figure 6.2 The number of Swing riots by month and the timing of the 1830 and 1831 General Elections

Note: The dotted vertical lines indicate the polling periods for the 1830 General Election (29 July to 1 September) and the 1831 General Election (26 April to 1 June), respectively.
Sources: Hobsbawm and Rudé (1973); Holland (2005).

North (e.g. Yorkshire) and the western part of the country (e.g. Cornwall and Devon) were relatively unaffected. Charlesworth (1979) was the first to document how the riots spread in a systematic manner by manually plotting many of them on maps. He contended that they spread along the road network and provoked new riots along the way as they did. While the road network clearly played a role, the econometric analysis of the diffusion of the riots reported in Aidt, Leon-Ablan, and Satchell (2022) shows that information about the riots mainly traveled through personal and trade networks while transport hubs (on the coach network) did not serve to amplify the diffusion. Their study also shows that arrest in an area did little to limit subsequent riots in that area. This makes it very unlikely that the Swing riots occurred primarily in areas where rioters expected to face little or no retaliation, especially given the historical patterns of riot repression in England (Bohstedt 2010; Stevenson 1992).[5] The spatial distribution was, instead, a result of local social interaction or imitation

[5] A local newspaper in Cornwall, *The Royal Cornwall Gazette*, published on 18 December 1830 a plea from a curate (a member of the clergy engaged as assistant to a parish priest) to stop the riots, which nonetheless included some veiled threats of punishments, but this did not stop the rioters.

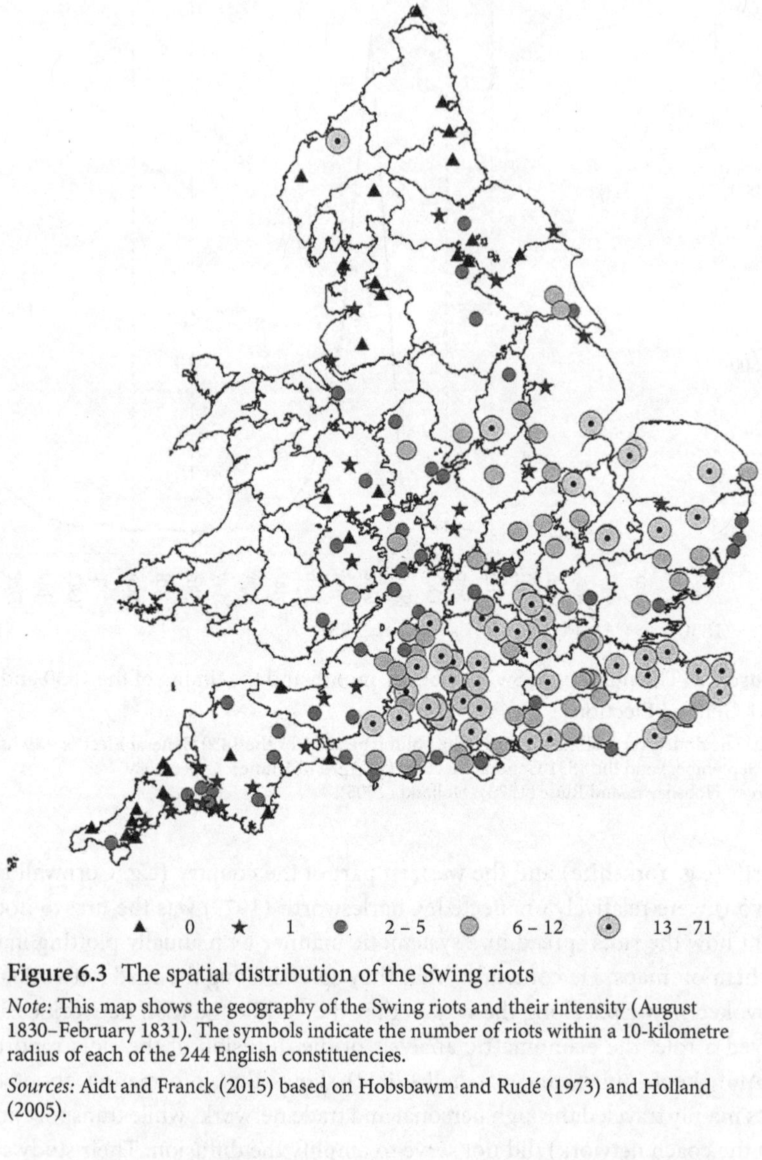

Figure 6.3 The spatial distribution of the Swing riots

Note: This map shows the geography of the Swing riots and their intensity (August 1830–February 1831). The symbols indicate the number of riots within a 10-kilometre radius of each of the 244 English constituencies.

Sources: Aidt and Franck (2015) based on Hobsbawm and Rudé (1973) and Holland (2005).

effects. Given the location of the 244 English constituencies (see Figure 6.3), it is apparent that the voters and patrons in some constituencies were more exposed to Swing riots in the surrounding countryside than others. Our empirical strategy takes advantage of this feature to construct constituency-specific

The Swing riots were eventually suppressed by troops under orders from Parliament and not by local militia, which were overwhelmed by the violence (Archer 2000).

measures of riot exposure that we can relate to the constituency-specific measure of support for the Whigs and Radicals amongst voters and patrons in the 1831 election.

6.2.3 Fear of revolution in 1830

The effect of the Swing riots must be viewed in a broader European context. First, since the 1789 French Revolution, the members of British elite had feared a 'democratic' revolution that would overthrow the monarchy and the aristocracy's hold on power. They dreaded the revolt of peasants and urban workers which 'Jacobins' and 'demagogues' would take control of (e.g. Jupp 1998, Clark 2000, Mitchell 2005).[6] In fact, the general mood of London in the autumn of 1830, as reported in the London newspapers studied by Tilly (1995), reflected a widespread concern regarding a potential joint uprising of the farm labourers and of the workers from the expanding industrial cities that would be led by radical politicians or community leaders. For instance, the Tory-leaning newspaper, *The Morning Post*, published on 1 February 1831, an anonymous letter arguing that Captain Swing was 'a Statesman of the first class' who would take advantage of the riots to implement the Radical agenda, and, in particular, introduce universal suffrage. It is reasonable to assume that first-hand experience of Swing riots would stoke such fears. Voters and patrons might have thought that a limited reform of the House of Commons could defuse the (perceived) threat to the established order by cutting any bond between radical leaders and the rural and urban poor.

Second, 1830 was a year of political upheavals in Europe. The Swing riots began in August 1830, but it is unlikely that the rioters knew about the 27–29 July 1830 revolution in France that overthrew King Charles X (see Halévy 1935, Gash 1956, Brock 1973). Even at the peak of the Swing riots in November 1830, it is unclear whether the rioters had learnt about the 1830 French revolution. However, by that time the members of the informed public around England certainly knew about it, and some (for example, in Preston) had seen tricolor flags (a symbol of Revolutionary France) paraded down the high street. As such, the news about the 1830 French revolution, and later on about the independence of Belgium from the Netherlands in November 1830, could have reinforced the impression that a revolution could also take place in England. It is against this background that we argue that first-hand exposure to the Swing riots influenced

[6] Even in 1830–1832, the British aristocracy remembered the 1780 Gordon riots in London and the damage that crowds could inflict when led by a skillful orator (De Castro 1926).

the voters and patrons' perceptions of a revolutionary threat and that local riots, therefore, can be used as a proxy for 'threat perceptions'.

6.2.4 Data

This section presents the data that we use to test the threat of revolution hypothesis in the context of the 1831 General Election. Table 6.1 reports descriptive statistics for the main variables.[7]

Support for parliamentary reform: We measure the electoral success of the Whigs and Radicals (henceforth, we use the term 'Whigs' to describe both groups) by the share of seats won by the Whigs in each of the 244 English constituencies in 1831 (*Whig share 1831*).

Local Swing riots: We geo-reference the location of the 2,818 Swing riots listed by Holland (2005), and construct two types of measures of local riots, which will be our main measures of the threat of revolution.[8] First, the variables *riots within R km* measure riots on the intensive margin. They record the number of Swing riots that happened within a radius of R kilometres from each constituency, where $R \in \{1, 10, 20, 30, 50\}$. In the baseline estimations, we employ the variable *riots within 10 km* and use the other radii as robustness checks. The mean and median of *riots within 10 km* are 9.4 and 5.5, respectively, and the spatial distribution is shown in Figure 6.3. The 10-kilometre radius includes the countryside and villages immediately outside the parliamentary borough towns and county seats. It is reasonable to assume that information about riots within such a small neighbourhood would reach voters and patrons, for example, via local markets and direct contact with individuals affected by the violence. Second, the indicator variable *riot treatment* measures riots at the extensive margin. It is equal to 1 if strictly more than one riot occurred within 10 kilometres of a constituency and 0 otherwise. Since there were thirty-five constituencies which were not exposed to any riots within a radius of 10 kilometres and another thirty-five which were exposed to just one, this cut-off implies that we, in practice, end up with 28 percent of the constituencies below the cut-off of one riot (which were then untreated to riots) and 72 percent above (which were treated to riots).

Characteristics of the constituencies: The elections in the constituencies could obviously be influenced by a host of local and national political, institutional, and economic factors other than the Swing riots. We need to account for them.

[7] The detailed sources are given in Section C6.1 in the supplementary material appendix, which also documents the variables used in the various falsification tests. The supplementary material appendix is available at www.oup.com/us/peacefulandviolentorigins

[8] Holland (2005) adds to the catalogue of 1,475 riots originally compiled by Hobsbawm and Rudé (1973, Appendix III).

Table 6.1 Descriptive statistics related to the 1831 General Election

	Obs.	Mean	Std. dev.	Min.	Max.
	Constituency-level variation				
Support for parliamentary reform					
Whig share 1831	244	56.6	44.7	0	100
Whig share 1830	244	42.9	37.9	0	100
Local Swing riots					
Riots with 1 km	244	0.84	1.84	0	11
Riots within 10 km	244	9.5	12.5	0	71
Riots within 20 km	244	33.4	38.8	0	234
Riots within 30 km	244	72.9	72.9	0	349
Riots within 50 km	244	193	168	0	614
Riots between 50 and 75 km	244	199	153	0	562
Riot treatment	244	0.71	0.45	0	1
Political controls					
Whig share 1826	244	39.2	39.4	0	100
(Whig share 1826)^2	244	3,087	3,892	0	10,000
Reform support in 1830	244	−0.03	0.55	−1	1
Institutional controls					
County constituency	244	0.16	0.37	0	1
University constituency	244	0.008	0.090	0	1
Narrow franchise	244	0.24	0.43	0	1
Patronage index	244	1.00	0.68	0	2
Employment structure controls					
Emp. fract. index	244	0.76	0.073	0.24	0.86
Agriculture (emp. share)	244	0.19	0.18	0	1
Trade (emp. share)	244	0.37	0.13	0	0.87
Professionals (emp. share)	244	0.054	0.026	0	0.14
Demographic and economic controls					
Population (in 1000s)	244	62.8	175	0.097	1,371
Population density	244	5.56	0.83	3.92	9.79
Thriving economy	244	0.17	0.38	0	1
Declining economy	244	0.21	0.41	0	1
Spatial controls					
Distance to urban centre (in days by foot)	244	30.9	15.2	0	72.8
Connection to London	244	2.27	2.41	0.68	20.4
Market integration	244	22.4	107.2	3.81	1,424
Cereal area	244	0.48	0.50	0	1
Dairy area	244	0.30	0.46	0	1
Instrumental variable					
Distance to Sevenoaks (in days by foot)	244	7.7	4.2	0.30	19.4
Variables for Placebo tests in Table 6.6					
Whig vote share 1835	115	0.55	0.21	0	1
Share of MPs' votes for 1867 reform bill	186	0.0026	0.027	0	0.34
Variables for tests in Table 6.8					
Petitions against reform	244	0.26	0.60	0	4

continued

Table 6.1 *continued*

	Obs.	Mean	Std. dev.	Min.	Max.
Petitions for reform	244	1.69	2.50	0	31
Petitions against slavery	244	2.47	3.33	0	20
Petitions against Catholic relief	244	1.30	2.16	0	18
Petitions for Catholic relief	244	0.62	1.14	0	8
		County-level variation			
Variables for placebo tests in Table 6.6					
Food Riots 1800–1818	244	10.8	9.81	0	39
Labour Riots 1793–1822	244	1.49	4.08	0	18
Variables for tests in Table 6.8					
Share of harsh sentences	244	23.1	27.2	0	100
Special commission	244	0.21	0.41	0	1
Growth in Poor Law expenses (%)	241	706	323	258	1,580

Note: For the variables with county-level variation, we attribute the county average to each constituency within that county.

First, the Swing riots occurred between the 1830 and 1831 elections. To quantify the general support for the Whigs in a constituency prior to these events, we code the variable *Whig share 1826*. It measures the share of seats won by the Whigs in each constituency in the 1826 General Election.[9] This is a useful proxy for many unobserved constituency-specific determinants of support for the Whigs. Using a similar logic, we make use of information on the division in the House of Commons on Lord Russell's (failed) bill to give direct representation to Birmingham, Leeds, and Manchester to control for the general attitude towards parliamentary reform in each constituency prior to the Swing riots. The bill was second read and defeated on 23 February 1830 in the House of Commons, almost half a year before the Swing riots started. We construct the variable *reform support 1830* as the difference between the shares of the MPs from each constituency who supported and opposed the bill.[10]

Second, under the Unreformed Parliament, the rules which defined who held the right to vote varied, as discussed in Chapter 4, across the 244 English constituencies. We code three dummy variables to capture some of these differences: *county constituency* and *university constituency* capture if the constituency was a county or university constituency, respectively, and *narrow franchise* is equal to 1 for the boroughs with the smallest number of voters (often less than a dozen) and 0 for those with a relatively large electorate. To account for patronage and electoral corruption, we construct on a scale from 0 to 2 the variable *patronage*

[9] We use the 1826 rather than the 1830 General Election to make sure that the Swing riots could not have affected the outcome of the election. In practice, it makes no difference.

[10] Hansard HC Deb, 23 February 1830, series 1, vol. 22, c915.

index based on the information in Table 4.2 on aristocratic influence and information on contested elections from Cannon (1973, Appendix 3). The index is equal to 0 if the constituency was neither controlled by a patron nor singled out as one of the boroughs to be disenfranchised by the Reform Bill and held at least one contested election between 1802 and 1831. It takes the value 1 if the constituency was wholly or partly controlled by a local patron or by the Treasury, or if it was one of the boroughs to be disenfranchised, or if no contested election was held between 1802 and 1831. The index is equal to 2 if a constituency was both controlled by a patron and considered to be 'rotten'.

Third, as suggested by modernisation theory (Lipset 1960), the economic conditions in the constituencies could have influenced the voters' attitude to reform. We use information from the 1831 Population Census of Great Britain to estimate occupation shares.[11] We distinguish between three main categories of employment: *agriculture (emp. share)* measures the share of tenant farmers and agricultural labourers; *trade (emp. share)* measures the share of workers employed in trade and industry or as artisans; *professionals (emp. share)* measures the share of doctors, lawyers, and other educated individuals, and can be interpreted as a proxy for the size of the middle class. The largest omitted category consists of domestic servants. We use the shares to construct an employment fractionalisation index (*emp. fract. index*) defined as 1 minus the Herfindahl index of employment. These variables give a snapshot of the economic structure in the constituencies in 1831. Moreover, to capture the dynamics of economic change in the years prior to the 1831 General Election, we use the admittedly incomplete, information recorded by Philbin (1965) on medium-term economic trends in each of the constituencies to construct two indicator variables, *thriving economy* and *declining economy*. The omitted group is the constituencies which followed the general economic trend of the period. Finally, we also control for the population (in 1,000s) of each constituency (*population*) and for the number of inhabitants per house (*population density*).

6.3 Empirical framework

Our empirical strategy is to assess whether spatial variation in the Swing riots that occurred in the neighbourhood of each of the 244 English constituencies affected the electoral success of the Whigs in the 1831 General Election. We employ two complementary strategies to help establish a causal link between

[11] The Census reports these data at the constituency level for the counties, but not for the boroughs. For the latter, we use the closest geographical unit to approximate, which is usually the parish or the town.

local exposure to riots and reform support: namely, a matching and an instrumental variable approach.

The starting point, however, is to estimate a linear regression model with ordinary least squares:

$$(\textit{Whig share } 1831)_i = \gamma_0 + f[(\textit{Whig share } 1826)_i] + \gamma_1(\textit{riots within } 10\ km)_i + \mathbf{X}_i\gamma_2 + \varepsilon_i, \quad (6.1)$$

where the dependent variable is the share of seats in constituency i won by Whigs in 1831, *riots within 10 km* is the baseline measure of local Swing riots, **X** is a vector of control variables, and ε is a disturbance term. We control flexibly for past Whig support in the constituency by including a polynomial function (f) of *Whig share 1826*.[12] We report standard errors that correct for spatial correlation in the error structure (Conley 1999). The main empirical challenge is to account for the possibility that numerous unobserved aspects of the economic and political environment in the constituencies could be correlated with factors which both affected the electoral success of the Whigs and the number of riots in specific areas. Even with the most comprehensive set of controls, 'selection on observables' is likely to fail, and the least squares estimate of γ_1 in equation 6.1 will be biased. The direction of the bias is, however, not clear. If riots were more widespread in places where voters and patrons were more willing to support the Whigs for reasons which we do not observe, then the bias would be positive, but if they were more widespread in Tory-leaning (anti-reform) places, it would be negative. Moreover, attenuation bias drives the coefficient estimate towards zero. To assess the size of any omitted variable bias, we use the approach of Altonji et al. (2005) and Oster (2019) to bound it.

6.3.1 Matching approach

Based on the coding of the binary variable *riot treatment*, we divide the constituencies into 172 treated constituencies with strictly more than one riot within a radius of 10 kilometres and 70 control constituencies with either no or just one riot within that radius.[13] The two subsamples are, on average, similar in terms of past Whig shares and reform support as well as in terms of their economic, demographic, and employment-related characteristics. The only significant difference between the two is that *patronage index* is higher in the control group.[14] This is because many of the small, declining, corrupt constituencies established

[12] A special case of equation 6.1 is a regression model where the dependent variable is the change in the Whig share between 1826 and 1831. Equation 6.1 is preferable because it is more flexible.

[13] The two university constituencies both belong to the treatment group. This makes it impossible to find a good match, and we exclude them from the sample.

[14] See Table C6.1 in the supplementary material appendix. The supplementary material appendix is available at www.oup.com/us/peacefulandviolentorigins

in the Middle Ages were in Cornwall, which was relatively unaffected by the Swing riots.

The aim of the matching strategy is to estimate the impact of the local Swing riots on Whig support amongst those constituencies which were exposed to riots, that is, the average effect of the treatment on the treated (ATT). This requires that two conditions be met. First, Whig support in the control constituencies is independent of the Swing riots, given the vector of observable factors used to match treatment and control constituencies ('selection on observables'). Second, each treated constituency has a counterpart amongst the control constituencies with similar observable characteristics ('common support'). The choice of these observable factors, thus, involves a trade-off: more variables make the 'selection on observables' assumption more plausible, but make it harder to ensure common support. Since the observable factors discussed in Section 6.2.4 are likely to simultaneously affect the exposure to the local Swing riots and Whig support, while being predetermined at the time of the riots, we match on all rather than on a subset of these observable factors. We use the nearest-neighbour covariate matching estimators, developed by Abadie and Imbens (2006) and Abadie et al. (2004), and the propensity score matching estimators, developed by Rosenbaum and Rubin (1983). The propensity score matching estimators are implemented with a variety of different matching algorithms (nearest neighbour, radius, kernel, or stratification). These algorithms tackle the trade-off between the quality (bias) and the quantity (efficiency) of matches in different ways.

6.3.2 Instrumental variable approach

To relax the 'selection on observables' assumption, which is required for causal inference using ordinary least squares and matching, we also estimate equation 6.1 with instrumental variable (IV) estimators. Our instrument is motivated by the studies of Charlesworth (1979) and Aidt, Leon-Ablan and Satchell (2022) that analyse the geography and dynamics of the Swing riots. By mapping some of the riots, Charlesworth (1979) shows that after they started in Kent in August 1830, they spread systematically along the main road network. This diffusion pattern suggests that the farm labourers who were ready to protest against poor economic conditions learned about rioting elsewhere through direct observation or verbal reports by individuals travelling through the affected areas, and not through newspapers or nationally orchestrated political agitation. The importance of local social interactions and local information hubs is confirmed by the spatial econometrics analysis in Aidt, Leon-Ablan and Satchell (2022) and Aidt and Leon-Ablan (2022). This contagion dynamics is plausibly exogenous to the geographical pattern of reform support because it is defined by physical geography and by the pre-existing road network.

We use the distance between the starting point of the riots and each constituency to instrument for the number of Swing riots that eventually occurred in the neighbourhood of each of them. We consider the starting point to be the village of Sevenoaks in Kent, where the first three Swing riots are said to have taken place on 3 August 1830 (Holland 2005).[15] To enable accurate calculations of travel-time distances along the road network between Sevenoaks and the centroid of each constituency, we digitalise John Cary's map of England in the early 1830s and measure our instrument *distance to Sevenoaks* in days of travel by foot at the average speed of 30 kilometres per day.[16]

To generate the required exogenous variation in local riots, the instrument should satisfy the independence condition and the exclusion restriction, and, in addition, it should be strongly correlated with *riots within 10 km*. The independence condition is that the travel-time distance between a constituency and Sevenoaks cannot be a function of the Whig success (or lack thereof) in the 1831 General Election in that constituency. This condition is likely to be satisfied because the road network, and, hence, the travel-time distance to Sevenoaks, cannot respond to the electoral success of specific candidates in particular places in the short run.[17] The exclusion restriction requires that the instrument only operates through a single known causal channel, which is in our case the number of Swing riots in the neighbourhood of a constituency. The condition may, however, fail for at least three reasons. First, *distance to Sevenoaks* could be correlated with unobserved time-invariant aspects of the political geography that also determine shifts in the electoral success of the Whigs in 1831. Below we present placebo tests related to the 1830 General Election that suggest that this is unlikely to be the case. Second, between August 1830 and April 1831, the English constituencies could have been affected by unobserved region-specific shocks. These shocks could have induced systematic shifts in the electoral support for the Whigs that were correlated with the spatial distribution of the Swing riots. While we cannot entirely rule out this possibility, we stress that we are unaware of any historical evidence suggesting the presence of such asymmetric shocks.[18] The two most likely transmission

[15] The results are not sensitive to the location in Kent which we use as the starting point for the Swing riots.

[16] John Cary published the first accurate map of England in 1793 (Cary 1793). We use an updated version from the early 1830s. The average speed estimate is based on the assumption that an individual can walk at a speed of 5 kilometres per hour for six hours a day.

[17] By 1820, England already had a dense network of roads that connected the 40 counties (Albert 1972). The major turnpike roads were maintained by private trusts, while local roads were maintained by local government authorities (e.g. Aidt et al. 2010).

[18] For instance, it is unlikely that weather shocks and/or trade shocks only affected the areas hit by the Swing riots and which subsequently experienced the rise in the share of Whigs elected. This is because the English market was, unlike the French octroi system (Franck et al. 2014), not segmented

channels for asymmetric economic shocks are the geography of agricultural production and spatial differences in market integration. There were three different agricultural regions in England in the 1830s, and the Swing riots were concentrated in the cereal-producing region while the regions with dairy and extensive (sheep) farming were less affected. To control for these agricultural production patterns, we define two indicator variables based on Clapham (1952) that single out the cereal-producing southeastern part of the country (*cereal area*) and the dairy-producing southwestern part (*dairy area*), while the northern part with extensive farming constitutes the omitted category. To proxy for spatial differences in market integration, we construct the variable *market integration*. It measures the travel distance between any given constituency and the 243 other constituencies weighted by population. Third, the instrument could pick up a constituency's connection to London or to other major towns. In the early 1830s, London was England's largest urban centre and information hub, where the major daily national newspapers as well as many weekly and quarterly newspapers were published. The surrounding countryside was linked to London through trade and finance. The economic and informational connections to the capital were naturally stronger for the constituencies closer to London and in the constituencies where the circulation of local weekly newspapers would help disseminate information from London. To control for such links, we build the constituency-specific variable *connection to London*. This variable isolates each constituency's geographic distance from Sevenoaks from its geographical, economic, and informational connections to London. Along similar lines, the relative proximity of a constituency to regional urban centres could have potentially affected the electoral support of the Whigs, just as its connection to London might have. To control for this possibility, we identify the thirteen largest towns (by population) in 1831 and code the variable *distance to urban centres* as the distance in travel days from each constituency to the nearest of these towns.[19]

by internal trade barriers. In fact, the historical evidence suggests that English markets were well integrated by 1820 (e.g. Buchinsky and Polak 1993; Szostak 1991). Moreover, the historical evidence suggests that wheat prices were high in 1829, 1830, and 1831 throughout England, and not only in Kent where the riots started (Rostow 1948, 124–125). Furthermore, it does not appear that the economic depression of the late 1820s was harsher in the southeast of England than in the North, or that the economic conditions in Cornwall in the Southwest were relatively better than those of Kent in the Southeast. Finally, to invalidate the exclusion restriction, the trade and/or weather shocks would have to be concentrated within the short time window between August 1830 and April 1831.

[19] See supplementary material appendix Section C6.2 for details on how these variables are constructed. The supplementary material appendix is available at www.oup.com/us/peacefuland violentorigins

6.4 Results

6.4.1 Ordinary least squares results

Table 6.2 presents the baseline estimates of the effect of *riots within 10 km* on the share of seats won by Whigs in the 1831 General Election.[20] We report ordinary least squares estimates with standard errors that correct for spatial correlation for a radius of 50 kilometres (and for the sake of comparison, also report White robust standard errors for *riots within 10 km*).[21] Column 1 shows a specification without any control variables, while columns 2 to 5 progressively add more controls. Column 6 reports a specification which is tested down using a general-to-specific strategy. Across all the specifications, the point estimate on *riots within 10 km* is statistically significant. The point estimate on *riots within 10 km* decreases from 0.57 in column 1 to 0.37 in column 2 when we control flexibly for *Whig share 1826* and for *reform support 1830*, and it reaches values between 0.42 and 0.47 as we add additional controls. Overall, the point estimate is remarkably stable. The university constituencies and those with a high *patronage index* returned a lower share of Whigs, while the county constituencies returned a higher share (columns 5 and 6). The two indicator variables accounting for the general economic trends are marginally significant, but only the negative correlation between the economic decline of a constituency and Whig support is robust to the general-to-specific strategy. The occupational variables are insignificant, both individually and as a group, as are *population* and *population density*.

Column 5 reports our preferred specification, which includes all the control variables. The point estimate on *riots within 10 km* indicates that exposure to one additional riot within a radius of 10 kilometres from a constituency increased the share of Whigs elected in that constituency by 0.47 percentage points relative to past Whig support. This implies that the share of Whigs elected in a constituency in the top quartile of the riots distribution (exposed to at least twelve riots) was 5.2 percentage points higher than in a constituency in the bottom quartile (exposed to at most one riot). To put these results into perspective, we observe that the shares of Whigs elected in 1830 and 1831 were 42.9 and 56.6 percent, respectively. For a constituency that moved from the bottom to the top quartile in the riot distribution, the ordinary least squares estimate, therefore,

[20] As an alternative, we can also estimate a probit model where the unit of analysis is a seat rather than a constituency and the outcome variable is a dummy variable equal to 1 if the seat was won by a Whig in 1831 (see Table C6.2 in the supplementary material appendix). The supplementary material appendix is available at www.oup.com/us/peacefulandviolentorigins

[21] The dependent variable is a share, and we also estimate equation 6.1 with the fractional estimator of Papke and Wooldridge (1996). Table C6.3 in the supplementary material appendix shows that the results are qualitatively similar.

implies that the share of Whigs elected increased to 48.1 percent because of the riots. This explains about half of the actual increase between 1830 and 1831.

Table 6.2 Local Swing riots and the outcome of the 1831 election: baseline results

	1	2	3	4	5	6
	Whig share 1831 (%)					
	Least squares					
Riots within 10 km	0.57	0.37	0.44	0.47	0.47	0.44
	(0.32)*	(0.22)*	(0.18)**	(0.18)**	(0.18)**	(0.18)**
	[0.25]**	[0.19]*	[0.18]**	[0.18]**	[0.19]**	[0.18]**
Whig share 1826		0.87	0.32	0.35	0.38	0.38
		(0.19)***	(0.19)	(0.20)*	(0.20)*	(0.071)***
(Whig share 1826)^2		-0.0045	0.00055	0.00035	-6.8e-06	
		(0.0019)**	(0.0020)	(0.0020)	(0.0020)	
Reform support 1830		12.0	12.1	11.2	12.1	12.6
		(5.60)**	(4.97)**	(5.09)**	(5.14)**	(4.77)**
County constituency			33.0	37.2	35.2	31.6
			(5.14)***	(6.50)***	(7.04)***	(4.68)***
University constituency			-60.8	-58.1	-58.1	-61.8
			(9.39)***	(10.7)***	(8.60)***	(10.50)***
Narrow franchise			-3.35	-2.85	-3.62	
			(5.62)	(5.39)	(5.26)	
Patronage index			-17.0	-13.5	-12.2	-15.3
			(3.42)***	(3.94)***	(3.86)***	(3.52)***
Emp. fract. index				7.52	7.83	
				(30.9)	(29.49)	
Agriculture (emp. share)				-28.4	-27.2	
				(27.5)	(27.0)	
Trade (emp. share)				11.4	14.0	
				(30.9)	(31.1)	
Professionals (emp. share)				-143	-119	
				(120)	(120)	
Population					0.00028	
					(0.009)	
Population density					0.15	
					(2.68)	
Thriving economy					-10.1	
					(5.91)*	
Declining economy					-10.6	-10.3
					(5.86)*	(5.72)*

continued

Table 6.2 *continued*

	1	2	3	4	5	6
	Whig share 1831 (%)					
Selection ratio	n.a.	0.67	2.26	2.54	2.56	2.59
Adjusted R^2	0.021	0.27	0.44	0.44	0.45	0.45
Obs. (constituencies)	244	244	244	244	244	244

Note: The table reports ordinary least squares estimates associating local Swing riots to the outcome of the 1831 General Election (constant terms not shown). We report spatial (Conley 1999) standard errors (50-kilometres radius) in parentheses and White robust standard errors in brackets. The selection ratio (Altonji et al. 2005; Oster 2019) indicates how large the selection on unobserved factors must be relative to the selection on the observed factors included in each specification for the point estimate on *riots within 10 km* to entirely result from an omitted variables bias. The regression in column 6 is tested down using a general-to-specific strategy that progressively drops variables that are insignificant. * = Significant at the 10 percent level; ** = Significant at the 5 percent level; *** = Significant at the 1 percent level.

We can use the estimation strategy developed by Altonji et al. (2005) and Oster (2019) to evaluate the extent of selection bias. At the bottom of the table, we report the selection ratio, which is defined as the ratio of standardised selection on unobservables to observables under the assumption that the Swing riots did not influence the outcome of the 1831 General Election. We see that it varies between 0.67 in the specification in column 2 that only conditions on past Whig and reform support to 2.56 in our preferred specification in column 5. This means that the normalised shift in the distribution of the unobservable factors would have to be about two and half times as large as the shift in the observable factors to fully explain the effect of the Swing riots that is reported in Table 6.2 as a manifestation of selection bias.

Table 6.3, panel A, examines the robustness of the baseline results in two ways. Firstly, we assess the impact of riots within a radius of 1, 10, 30, and 50 kilometres of each constituency. Secondly, we report standard errors that allow for spatial correlation in the error structure for constituencies located within a radius of 20, 100, or 200 kilometres of each other. We observe that the Swing riots exerted a positive significant effect on the share of Whigs elected in 1831 for all radii between 1 and 50 kilometres. The standardised beta coefficients reported below the point estimates suggest that a one standard deviation increase in one of the *riots within R km* variables raises *Whig share 1831* by 0.10–0.13 standard deviations. The largest effect is for *riots within 10 km*, and we observe a slight decline as the radius is expanded beyond 10 kilometres. Column 6 reports a regression that relates the number of riots that took place between 50 and 75 kilometres from a constituency (*riots between 50 and 75 km*) to *Whig share 1831*. Consistent with the hypothesis that the voters and patrons

Table 6.3 Local Swing riots and the outcome of the 1831 and 1830 elections. Alternative measures of local Swing riots and spatial correlation

	1	2	3	4	5	6
Panel A			**Whig share 1831 (%)** Least squares			
Riots within 1 km	2.76					
Riots within 10 km		0.47				
Riots within 20 km			0.14			
Riots within 30 km				0.066		
Riots within 50 km					0.028	
Riots between 50 and 75 km						0.021
Beta coefficient	0.11	0.13	0.12	0.11	0.11	0.07
Spatial std. errors, 20 km	⟨0.99⟩***	⟨0.20⟩**	⟨0.060⟩**	⟨0.030⟩**	⟨0.013⟩**	⟨0.016⟩
Spatial std. errors, 50 km	(1.02)***	(0.18)**	(0.058)**	(0.028)**	(0.013)**	(0.017)
Spatial std. errors, 100 km	{1.13}**	{0.17}***	{0.059}**	{0.029}**	{0.013}**	{0.019}
Spatial std. errors, 200 km	[1.12]**	[0.17]***	[0.061]**	[0.032]**	[0.014]**	[0.020]
White robust std. errors	[0.97]***	[0.19]**	[0.058]**	[0.030]**	[0.014]**	[0.017]
Adjusted R^2	0.44	0.45	0.44	0.44	0.44	0.43
Panel B (Placebo test)			**Whig share 1830 (%)** Least squares			
Riots within 1 km	0.59					
Riots within 10 km		0.11				
Riots within 20 km			0.014			
Riots within 30 km				−0.0010		
Riots within 50 km					−0.0069	
Riots between 50 and 75 km						−0.011
Beta coefficient	0.03	0.04	0.01	−0.002	−0.03	−0.04
Spatial std. errors, 50 km	(1.02)	(0.11)	(0.042)	(0.025)	(0.010)	(0.011)
White robust std. errors	[0.96]	[0.11]	[0.038]	[0.022]	[0.010]	[0.012]
Adjusted R^2	0.56	0.56	0.56	0.55	0.56	0.56
Difference test (*p*-value)	0.06	0.03	0.02	0.02	0.007	n.a.
Baseline controls included	YES	YES	YES	YES	YES	YES
Obs. (constituencies)	244	244	244	244	244	244

Note: Panel A reports ordinary least squares estimates associating local Swing riots within various radii from the constituency to the outcome of the 1831 General Election. We report spatial Conley (1999) standard errors for four different radii (20 kilometres, 50 kilometres, 100 kilometres, and 200 kilometres) and White robust standard errors. Panel B reports the corresponding results for the placebo test related to the outcome of the 1830 General Election. The difference test is a chi-square test where the null hypothesis is that the coefficient on the *riots within R km* variable in panel A is statistically different from the corresponding coefficient in panel B (Gelman and Stern 2006). In both panels, the controls from column 5 in Table 6.2 are included (the coefficient in column 2 in panel A is, therefore, the coefficient from column 5 in Table 6.2). The standardised beta coefficients show how many standard deviations the dependent variable will change per standard deviation increase of each of the *riots within R km* variables. * = Significant at the 10 percent level; ** = Significant at the 5 percent level; *** = Significant at the 1 percent level.

reacted to the local Swing riots and not to second-hand reports about riots far away from their constituency, we find that this variable is insignificant. Finally, it makes little difference to the size of the standard errors whether we allow for spatial correlation in the error structure within a radius of 20, 50, 100, or 200 kilometres.

Table 6.3, panel B, reports the results of the main placebo test. It investigates whether the *riots within R km* variables are related to the Whig electoral success in the 1830 election. This election took place *before* the Swing riots began, and there should not, therefore, be any such relationship unless our measures of riots are correlated with unobserved constituency-specific determinants of Whig electoral success. It is reassuring to observe that there is not any significant relationship, irrespective of the radius which we use to assess local riots. Moreover, using the approach of Gelman and Stern (2006) to test the difference between the significant coefficients of *riots within R km* in panel A and the corresponding insignificant ones in panel B is statistically significant, we find that it is.[22]

6.4.2 Matching estimates

Table 6.4, panel A, reports a selection of covariate and propensity score matching estimates of the sample average treatment effect of the treated (ATT) of the Swing riots on the outcome of the 1831 General Election.[23] The ATT estimates are corrected for the finite sample bias caused by non-exact matches. We restrict the sample to the constituencies that belong to the intersection of the propensity scores of the control and treatment groups (two-sided common support).[24] This reduces the sample to 163 treated constituencies which were exposed to strictly more than one riot, and 65 control constituencies which were exposed to less than that number.

The covariate matching estimates reported in columns 1 and 2 are significant at the 5 percent level. The specification shown in column 2 requires exact matches on the two variables, *Whig share 1826* and *reform support 1830*, that summarise many of the unobserved determinants of support for the Whigs and for reform in each constituency. We observe that this increases the ATT estimate from 11.1 to 13.8. Columns 3 to 6 report propensity score matching

[22] Table C6.4 in the supplementary material appendix reports the complete results. The supplementary material appendix is available at www.oup.com/us/peacefulandviolentorigins

[23] Tables C6.5 to C6.12 in the supplementary material appendix report the complete results.

[24] This is a stronger assumption than what is needed for the estimation of the ATT. However, if we only impose a one-sided common support restriction (which limits the matches to be in the support of the propensity score for the treatment group), we include in the analysis many treated constituencies which are very unlikely to be untreated given their characteristics. This is not desirable since these constituencies are hard to match.

Table 6.4 Local Swing riots and the outcome of the 1831 and 1830 elections: matching estimates

	1	2	3	4	5	6
	Covariate matching		**Propensity score matching**			
	Nearest neighbour	**Nearest neighbour w. overweighting**[a]	**Nearest neighbour**	**Radius (r=0.05)**	**Kernel**[b] **(bw= 0.02)**	**Stratification**[c]
Panel A			Whig share 1831 (%)			
ATT (bias corrected)	11.1	13.9	15.0	16.0	14.2	14.2
Bootstrapped std. errors			(7.57)**	(7.12)**	(6.92)**	(6.84)**
Analytic std. errors	[5.35]**	[5.92]**	[8.82]*	[6.97]**	n.a.	[6.62]**
Panel B (placebo test)			Whig share 1830 (%)			
ATT (bias corrected)	1.8	1.2	6.2	4.4	5.2	1.6
Bootstrapped std. errors			(5.73)	(5.67)	(4.73)	(5.25)
Analytic std. errors	[4.28]	[4.03]	[7.31]	[5.81]	n.a.	[5.16]
Treated constituencies	163	163	163	163	163	163
Control constituencies	65	65	43	63	65	65
Obs. (constituencies)	228	228	206	226	228	228
Common support	Yes	Yes	Yes	Yes	Yes	Yes
Balancing test passed[d]	n.a.	n.a.	Yes	Yes	Yes	Yes

Note: Panel A reports the covariate and propensity score matching estimates of the average treatment effect of the treated (ATT) on the outcome of the 1831 General Election. Panel B reports the corresponding placebo estimates for the outcome of the 1830 General Election. The treatment variable *riot treatment* is a dummy variable equal to 1 if the number of riots within 10 kilometres of the constituency is strictly greater than 1, and 0 otherwise. The vector of matching variables includes the variables listed in Table 6.2, column 5, except that the two university constituencies are excluded since they both belong to the treatment group. The ATT estimates are corrected for the finite sample bias caused by non-exact matches. We report analytic heteroskedasticity-consistent standard errors in square brackets and bootstrapped standard errors in parentheses (1,000 iterations). We apply the minima-maxima rule and restrict the sample to the overlap between the support of the propensity score of the treated and non-treated constituencies (two-sided common support). The range of overlap is [0.38;0.92]. The propensity score and covariate matching (inverse variance method with replacement) estimations are implemented with the STATA procedures developed by Becker and Ichino (2002) and Abadie et al. (2004), respectively.

[a] We require perfect matches on *Whig share 1826* and *reform support 1830.*

[b] The Epanechnikov kernel.

[c] The stratification method compares within five blocks, where the covariates are balanced the average outcome for the treatment and control constituencies. Each block is weighted with the fraction of treatment constituencies within the block.

[d] The balancing test assesses whether the matching variables differ between the treatment and control constituencies, within blocks where the propensity scores of the two groups of constituencies do not differ. * = Significant at the 10 percent level; ** = Significant at the 5 percent level; *** = Significant at the 1 percent level.

estimates using the nearest neighbour, the radius, the Epanechnikov kernel, or the stratification matching algorithm. We note that all the specifications pass the balancing test at the 5 percent level of significance. This indicates that the control and treatment constituencies are on average similar in all their observable characteristics within the blocks where their propensity score does not differ (Dehejia and Wahba 2002). The propensity score matching estimates lie in the range from 14.2 to 16.0 and are, therefore, not sensitive to the choice of the matching algorithm. To evaluate if these matching estimates are contaminated by systematic, unobserved differences in the determinants of Whig electoral success in the control and treatment constituencies, we report in Table 6.4, panel B, a placebo test which investigates if *riot treatment* can explain the outcome of the 1830 General Election. We observe that this is not the case.

Overall, the matching estimates suggest that the local Swing riots increased the share of Whigs elected in 1831 by about 14 percentage points in the constituencies which were 'treated' to more than one riot. This corresponds to an 11 percentage point increase in the average share of Whigs returned in the 1831 General Election—that is, roughly three quarters of the difference between the share of Whigs elected in 1830 (42.9 percent) and 1831 (56.6 percent). The lack of a 'sharp' cut-off between the control and treatment constituencies implies that these estimates should be understood as lower bound estimates for the treatment effect of the Swing riots. This is because the presence in the treated group of constituencies that were barely exposed to more than one riot within a neighbourhood of 10 kilometres attenuates the strength of the treatment.

To gauge the importance of the choice for the cut-off, we carry out two robustness checks. First, we repeat all the matching estimations under the restriction that the treated group consists of the constituencies in the top 50 percentile of the spatial distribution of riots while we retain as the control group the bottom quartile. The constituencies in this new treated group were exposed to at least six riots within a radius of 10 kilometres. We find that the covariate and propensity matching estimates are slightly larger than the estimates in Table 6.4 and that they remain precisely estimated despite the smaller sample. Second, we implement a randomisation inference procedure to account for potentially strong spatial patterns in the assignment to 'treatment' in our data and the relatively small sample size (Barrios et al. 2012; Rosenbaum 2002, 2010). This yields ATT estimates that are close to 20 percentage points and remain statistically significant at the 5 percent level.[25]

[25] Tables C6.7, C6.10, and C6.11 in the supplementary material appendix report these results. The supplementary material appendix is available at www.oup.com/us/peacefulandviolentorigins

6.4.3 Reduced form and instrumental variable estimates

Table 6.5, columns 1 to 3, show the estimates of the reduced form relationship between *distance to Sevenoaks* and *Whig share 1831*. We report ordinary least squares estimates with spatial standard errors (and White robust standard errors for comparison). Column 1 does not include any control variables, while column 2 includes the control variables from column 5 in Table 6.2 as well as the five spatial controls (*distance to urban centre*, *connection to London*, *market integration*, *cereal area*, and *dairy area*). Column 3, specifically, excludes all the constituencies in Kent—the county where the Swing riots started. All the results indicate that the share of Whigs elected in 1831 falls as the distance to Sevenoaks increases. In particular, the point estimate in column 2 suggests that one extra travel day from Sevenoaks reduces *Whig share 1831* by 2.60 percentage points. Since the average of *distance to Sevenoaks* is 7.7 travel days, the average decrease in *Whig share 1831* is about 20 percentage points.

Table 6.6 reports a summary of the instrumental variable estimates.[26] The assumption underlying these estimates is that the effect of *distance to Sevenoaks* on the outcome of the 1831 General Election operates only through its effect on the geography of the Swing riots. Panel A, columns 1 to 3, show two-stage least squares (2SLS) estimates of the (instrumented) impact of *riots within 10 km* on *Whig share 1831*. We report generalised method of moments (GMM) standard errors adjusted for spatial correlation (Conley 1999) and for comparison, 2SLS robust standard errors. Panel B shows a summary of the first-stage regression results, while panel C shows, for each column, the ordinary least squares estimate corresponding to the instrumental variable estimate in panel A.[27]

The first-stage relationship between the instrumental variable *distance to Sevenoaks* and *riots within 10 km* in panel B is negative, as expected. The coefficient associated with *distance to Sevenoaks* is significant at the 1 percent level in all the specifications. The Kleibergen-Paap F statistic for weak identification is equal to 15.2 in our preferred specification in column 2 but just below 10 in the specification that excludes Kent. To remove any concern regarding weak identification, we report in panel A, below the 2SLS robust standard errors, the *p*-value associated with the Anderson-Rubin test of significance which is robust to weak instruments.

In the second-stage results in panel A, all the estimates of the effect of *riots within 10 km* are significant at the 5 percent level when we correct the standard

[26] The full results are reported in Tables C6.13 to C6.16 in the supplementary material appendix. The supplementary material appendix is available at www.oup.com/us/peacefulandviolentorigins

[27] The ordinary least square estimate of the coefficient on *riots within 10 km* in the specification in column 2, which conditions on the five spatial controls, is almost identical to the baseline estimate reported in Table 6.2, column 5. None of the spatial controls are significant in the baseline models reported in Table 6.2.

Table 6.5 Distance to Sevenoaks and the outcome of the 1831 and 1830 elections: reduced form estimates

	1	2	3
Panel A		Whig share 1831 (%)	
		Least squares	
Distance to Sevenoaks	−1.89	−2.60	−2.60
Spatial std. errors[a]	(0.84)**	(0.78)***	(0.86)***
White robust std. errors	[0.67]***	[0.81]***	[0.87]***
Adjusted R^2	0.03	0.44	0.43
Panel B (placebo test)		Whig share 1830 (%)	
		Least squares	
Distance to Sevenoaks	−0.84	0.39	0.46
Spatial std. errors[a]	(0.60)	(0.75)	(0.79)
White robust std. errors	[0.57]	[0.75]	[0.80]
Adjusted R^2	0.005	0.55	0.55
Baseline controls included[b]	No	Yes	Yes
Spatial controls included[c]	No	Yes	Yes
Kent included	Yes	Yes	No
Observations	244	244	235

Note: Panel A reports reduced form ordinary least squares estimates of the effect of *distance to Sevenoaks* on *Whig share 1831*. Panel B reports the corresponding placebo estimates with *Whig share 1830* as the outcome variable. In column 3, we exclude the constituencies in Kent.
[a]Spatial (Conley 1999) standard errors (50-kilometres radius).
[b]The controls are those from Table 6.2, column 5.
[c]The spatial controls are *distance to urban centre, connection to London, market integration, cereal area*, and *dairy area*. * = Significant at the 10 percent level; ** = Significant at the 5 percent level; *** = Significant at the 1 percent level.

errors for spatial correlation and at the 1 percent level when we do not. The point estimate in the specification without any control variables (column 1) is 1.32. Adding the baseline and spatial controls (column 2) increases the point estimate to 2.53, while the point estimate obtained when Kent is excluded is 3.48 (column 3). These 2SLS estimates are, therefore, about five times larger than the corresponding ordinary least squares estimates reported in panel C of Table 6.6. This suggests that the bias in the least squares estimate is negative. This could be because riots happened to be concentrated around constituencies where, for reasons unobserved to us, the voters and patrons favoured the Tory Party, or because attenuation bias is more important that any (positive) selection bias. However, these 2SLS estimates are not unreasonably large. The share of Whigs elected in a constituency in the top quartile of the riot distribution is about 28 percentage points higher than in a constituency in the bottom quartile. This estimate suggests that the Swing riots contributed to the creation of the Whig

Table 6.6 Local Swing riots and the outcome of the 1831 and 1830 elections: instrumental variable estimates

	1	2	3
Panel A	Whig share 1831 (%)		
	Second stage		
	2SLS	2SLS	2SLS
Riots within 10 km	1.32	2.53	3.48
Spatial GMM std. errors[a]	(0.60)**	(1.08)**	(1.60)**
2SLS robust std. errors	[0.46]***	[0.87]***	[1.32]***
Anderson-Rubin p-values[e]	0.006	0.002	0.003
Panel B	Riots within 10 km instrumented		
	First stage		
Distance to Sevenoaks	−1.43	−1.03	−0.75
White robust std. error	⟨0.17⟩***	⟨0.26⟩***	⟨0.24⟩***
Partial R^2 on excl. instrument	0.23	0.05	0.03
Kleibergen-Paap F statistic	74.3***	15.2***	9.9***
Panel C	Whig share 1831 (%)		
	Least squares		
Riots within 10 km	0.57	0.50	0.52
Spatial std. errors[b]	(0.32)*	(0.19)**	(0.25)**
White robust std. errors	[0.25]**	[0.21]**	[0.29]*
Panel D (Placebo test)	Whig share 1830 (%)		
	Second stage		
	2SLS	2SLS	2SLS
Riots within 10 km	0.59	−0.38	−0.61
Spatial GMM std. errors[a]	(0.43)	(0.75)	(1.11)
2SLS robust std. errors	[0.39]	[0.71]	[1.05]
Anderson-Rubin p-values[e]	0.14	0.60	0.56
Baseline controls included[c]	No	Yes	Yes
Spatial controls included[d]	No	Yes	Yes
Kent included	Yes	Yes	No
Observations	244	244	235

Note: Panel A reports two-stage least squares (2SLS) estimates of the effect of local Swing riots on *Whig share 1831*. Panel B summarises the first-stage estimates for the 2SLS procedure. Panel C reports the ordinary least squares estimates corresponding to the instrumental variable estimates in Panel A. Panel D reports the placebo second-stage estimates related to the outcome of the 1830 General Election. The instrument is *distance to Sevenoaks* (the village in Kent where the riots began).

[a]Spatial Conley (1999) GMM standard errors (50-kilometres radius).

[b]Spatial Conley (1999) standard errors (50-kilometres radius).

[c]The controls are those from Table 6.2, column 5.

[d]The spatial controls are *distance to urban centre, connection to London, market integration, cereal area*, and *dairy area*.

[e]The Anderson-Rubin test of significance of *riots within 10 km* is robust to weak instruments.

* = Significant at the 10 percent level; ** = Significant at the 5 percent level;
*** = Significant at the 1 percent level.

majority in the House of Commons. We return to the question regarding the actual size of this effect in Section 6.4.5.

The instrumental variable estimates can only be given a causal interpretation if *distance to Sevenoaks* does not affect the electoral success of the Whigs through any other channel than the Swing riots that happened in the vicinity of a constituency. This exclusion restriction cannot be tested directly, and it is a concern that the spatial instrument may be correlated with distance to many other things than the riots. The five spatial controls included in the instrumental variable estimations aim at addressing this concern and are highly significant in the first-stage regressions.[28] We can go one step further and assess the validity of the exclusion restriction indirectly through falsification tests. If *distance to Sevenoaks* affected the support for the Whigs in different geographical locations through other spatial channels than the geography of the Swing riots, we would expect to find a significant reduced form relationship between *distance to Sevenoaks* and the outcome of the 1830 election, which took place before the Swing riots. Similarly, we would expect to find significant correlations between local Swing riots instrumented by *distance to Sevenoaks* and the outcome of the 1830 election. We re-estimate the reduced form and instrumental variable models with the dependent variable *Whig share 1830*. We find no statistical significant relationship in any of these placebo tests (see panel B of Table 6.5 and panel D of Table 6.6). We also investigate if *distance to Sevenoaks* is correlated with the economic characteristics of the constituencies. Conditional on the five spatial controls, we find no correlation between *distance to Sevenoaks* and demographics, occupational structure, and medium-run economic trends, except that constituencies closer to Sevenoaks tended to be more densely populated.[29] This is consistent with the identifying assumption that *distance to Sevenoaks* did not affect the electoral support for the Whigs through other channels than the Swing riots.

[28] See Table C6.14 in the supplementary material appendix. The supplementary material appendix is available at www.oup.com/us/peacefulandviolentorigins. Table C6.17 in the supplementary material appendix presents a robustness check that reports instrumental variable and reduced form estimates where we include variables coding the latitude and longitude of each constituency as additional control variables. Unlike the other spatial control variables, latitude and longitude are not correlated with *riots within 10 km* (or any of the other Swing riot variables). However, they are highly correlated with *distance to Sevenoaks* and along with the other spatial controls, latitude and longitude can explain 84 percent of the variation in the instrument. As a result, *distance to Sevenoaks* becomes a weak instrument for *riots within 10 km* (the Kleibergen-Paap F statistic is equal to 2.78) in specifications with these variables included. Inference must, therefore, be based on a weak instrument robust test statistic. We note that the *p*-value associated with the Anderson-Rubin (weak instrument robust) test of significance of *riots within 10 km* is below 0.01. The problem of weak identification can be alleviated by considering a larger radius around each constituency. In specifications with *riots within 20* km and *riots within 30* km, the Kleibergen-Paap F statistic is equal to 6.05 and 10.9, respectively, and in both cases, the second-stage estimate is statistically significant irrespective of how the standard errors are calculated.

[29] Table C6.18 in the supplementary material appendix reports the results.

6.4.4 Further falsification tests

In this section, we discuss additional falsification tests aimed at alleviating concerns about confounding factors.[30] The first of these tests extends the placebo test related to the outcome of the 1830 General Election discussed above and investigates if the local Swing riots can predict other election outcomes before and after the Great Reform Act. If Swing riots observed directly by voters and patrons truly caused the shift in the electoral fortunes of the Whigs, there should be no such connection. Table 6.7, columns 1 and 2, show that *riots within 10 km* is uncorrelated with the election outcome in 1826 and in 1835. Along similar lines, there should not be any systematic relationship between local Swing riots in 1830–1831 and constituency-level support for the Second Reform Act in 1867. We test this with data from Moser and Reeves (2014) on the parliamentary divisions associated with the Second Reform Act. Table 6.7, column 3, shows that there is no relationship between Swing riots in the neighbourhood of a constituency (*riots with 10 km*) and the voting behaviour of the MPs elected in that constituency in 1867.

Another way to look for evidence of confounding factors is to test if riots that pre-date the Swing riots can predict the outcome of the 1831 election. If they can, it would suggest that it was not the Swing riots per se and the fear of revolution that they instilled in voters and patrons that caused the Whig victory in 1831 but something else related to the general propensity for violent unrest in an area. To conduct this test, we collect information on the spatial patterns of food and rural labour riots between 1793 and 1822 from Charlesworth (1983) and Bohstedt (2010). We re-estimate equation 6.1 with these measures of pre-Swing riots in place of *riots within 10 km.* Table 6.7, column 4, shows that they cannot predict the 1831 election result. We also use the pre–Swing riots data to test for a link between the spatial distribution of riots in the past and the Swing riots. Such a link might be seen as evidence that riots tend to happen around specific constituencies and might, therefore, be correlated with constituency-specific confounding factors. Table 6.7, column 5, shows that the raw correlations between pre-Swing food and labour riots and *riots within 10 km* are significant, but that these relationships disappear once we control for observable spatial factors such as agricultural areas (column 6).[31]

Overall, these tests are inconsistent with the view that our results are driven by unobserved constituency-specific characteristics.

[30] We discuss these tests in detail in Section C6.3 of the supplementary material appendix. Tables C6.19 to C6.24 in the supplementary material appendix report the full results. The supplementary material appendix is available at www.oup.com/us/peacefulandviolentorigins

[31] Using these data on pre-Swing riots, we also test if riots that occurred in the neighbourhood of the constituencies in the lead-up to each of the seven elections between 1802 and 1826 had an effect on the share of Whigs elected in those elections. We find no evidence of this.

Table 6.7 Local Swing riots and the outcome of the 1831 election: additional placebo tests

	1	2	3	4	5	6
	Whig share 1826	Whig vote share 1835	Share of votes for 1867 reform bill	Whig share 1831	Riots within 10 km	Riots within 10 km
Riots within 10 km	0.16	0.00044	−0.00013			
Spatial std. errors[a]	(0.12)	(0.001)	(0.00014)			
White std. errors	[0.12]	[0.001]	[0.00015]			
Food Riots 1800-1818				0.082	−0.30	0.039
Clustered std. errors[b]				[0.21]	[0.097]***	[0.088]
White std. errors				(0.24)	(0.048)***	(0.052)
Labour Riots 1793–1822				−0.25	0.38	−0.14
Clustered std. errors[b]				[0.49]	[0.22]*	[0.20]
White std. errors				(0.43)	(0.15)**	(0.17)
Baseline controls	Yes[c]	Yes[d]	Yes[d]	Yes[c]	No	No
Spatial controls[e]	No	No	No	No	No	Yes
Distance to Sevenoaks	No	No	No	No	No	Yes
Obs. (constituencies)	244	97	164	244	244	244

Note: Table 6.7, columns 1 and 2, report the ordinary least square results associating *riots within 10 km* to the share of Whig MPs elected in the 1826 General Election and to the share of votes obtained by Whig candidates in the 1835 General Election, respectively. Column 3 reports the ordinary least squares results associating *riots within 10km* to the cumulative number of votes in support of Benjamin Disraeli's (1804–1881) 1867 (successful) reform bill at the committee stage from the MPs elected in a given constituency as a proportion of the total votes that could have been cast by MPs from that constituency. Column 4 reports the ordinary least squares results associating labour and food riots between 1793 and 1882 (recorded at the county level) to the outcome of the 1831 General Election. Columns 5 and 6 report ordinary least squares results associating labour and food riots between 1793 and 1822 (recorded at the county level) to *riots within 10 km.*

[a]Spatial (Conley 1999) standard errors (50-kilometres radius).

[b]Clustered at the county level.

[c]In columns 1 and 4, the controls are those from column 5 in Table 6.2.

[d]In columns 2 and 3, we control for *county constituency, population, population density, employment shares,* and *emp. fract. index.* In column 3, the demographic controls are from the 1861 Population Census of Great Britain instead of the 1831 Population Census, and we control for *liberal seat share* and for *conservative seat share.* In column 2, we control for the Whig vote share in the 1832 General Election.

[e]The spatial controls are *distance to urban centre, connection to London, market integration, cereal area,* and *dairy area.*

* = Significant at the 10 percent level;

** = Significant at the 5 percent level; *** = Significant at the 1 percent level.

6.4.5 Heterogeneity and local average treatment effects

Above we interpreted the instrumental variable estimate (of 2.53) as the average treatment effect (ATE)—that is, as having identified the population parameter of interest—of local Swing riots on Whig support. This interpretation is only valid if the effect of the instrument is the same for all constituencies—that is, if its effect is homogeneous. If the instrument affects units differently, then the instrumental variable estimate will be a local average treatment effect (LATE) that estimates the ATE effect of the units that are, in fact, affected by the instrument. For example, suppose that *distance to Sevenoaks* only affects Swing riots in constituencies in location X and not elsewhere. In that case, the instrumental variable estimate will estimate the effect of an extra riot caused by the diffusion of riots into location X on the support for the Whigs in *that* location. The effect in location X may, of course, be very different from the effect of the diffusion of riots into other places that were not affected by the instrument and, thus, may not be representative of the treatment effect across the entire population of constituencies.

Under the assumption of mean independence required for a single instrument to be valid, any function of that instrument is also a valid instrument. Adding functions of the original instrument to the first stage will not affect the second-stage point estimates (much) if the effect of the instrument is homogeneous across the constituencies, as it should identify the same population parameter (Angrist et al. 2000; Heckman et al. 2006). However, if there is a substantial difference, then there is important unmodeled heterogeneity in the way the instrument affects the various constituencies. Dieterle and Snell (2016) propose a diagnostic test for such unmodeled first-stage heterogeneity. The test involves including the square of the original instrument as a 'second' instrument and analysing the second-stage estimate of the parameter of interest. In particular, an overidentification test can be used to test whether the linear-homogeneous-effects model is appropriate. A rejection of the null means that the specifications with one or two instruments, respectively, lead to statistically different estimates of the second-stage parameter of interest. This, in turn, implies that the ATE interpretation of the instrumental variable estimate is invalid under the mean independence assumption and that it should be given a LATE interpretation instead.

Table 6.8 reports the results of this specification test. The first column reproduces the baseline 2SLS estimate from Table 6.6, column 2, with *distance to Sevenoaks* as the only instrument. Columns 2 to 4 report specifications where the first stage also includes the square of *distance to Sevenoaks*. In all cases,

Table 6.8 Local Swing riots and the outcome of the 1831 election. Specification tests with transformations of the instrument

	1	2	3	4
		Whig share 1831		
Riots within 10 km	2.53	1.67	1.91	1.98
Robust std. errors	[0.87]***	[0.72]**	[0.91]**	
Spatial std. errors[a]	(1.08)**			(1.10)*
Anderson-Rubin test (*p*-value)[b]	0.0020	0.0070		
Number of IVs	1	2	2	2
Estimation method	2SLS	2SLS	LIML	GMM
Overidentification test (*p*-value)		0.063	0.073	0.24
Kleibergen-Paap F statistic	15.2	8.42		
Obs. (constituencies)	244	244	244	244

Note: In the specification with one instrument, the first stage is linear in *distance to Sevenoaks*; in the specification with two instruments, the first stage, in addition, includes the square of *distance to Sevenoaks.* The controls included in all specifications (but now shown) are those from Table 6.6, panels A and B, column 2, and include all the baseline and spatial controls.
[a]Spatial (Conley 1999) GMM standard errors (50-kilometres radius).
[b]The Anderson-Rubin test of significance of *riots within 10 km* is robust to weak instruments.
* = Significant at the 10 percent level;
** = Significant at the 5 percent level;
*** = Significant at the 1 percent level.

the second-stage estimate of the coefficient on *riots within 10 km* is positive and statistically significant. Most importantly, the *p*-value associated with the overidentification test (a Hansen J-test) is between 0.063 and 0.24 depending on which estimator is used. In all cases we, therefore, fail to reject the null of independence at the 5 percent level and in the specification with the spatial GMM estimator also at the 10 percent level. The 2SLS and the GMM estimates with two instruments are 1.67 and 1.98, respectively, and, therefore, 33 and 22 percent smaller than the baseline estimate of 2.53. The Kleibergen-Paap F statistic falls below 10, however, in the specification with two instruments (column 2). This raises the possibility of downwards bias (towards the ordinary least squares estimate) due to weak instruments. In column 3, we report results with the limited information maximum likelihood (LIML) estimator. In small samples, the 2SLS estimate with weak instruments will be biased towards the least squares estimate while the LIML is median-unbiased. As such, a comparison of the two can indicate if the reduction in the 2SLS estimate (in column 2) is partly due to the weakening of the instruments. We find that the LIML point estimate is 1.91, which is 13 percent higher than the 2SLS estimate in column 2, suggesting that, in part, it is.

These specification tests are, by no means, alarming, but they do not unambiguously rule out the presence of unmodeled heterogeneity in the first stage, and, therefore, caution against interpreting the baseline instrumental variable estimate of 2.53 as the average treatment effect. It is, however, important to investigate further the nature of such heterogeneity before re-interpreting the estimate as a local average treatment effect. To do this, we follow Dieterle and Snell (2016) and order the sample of 244 constituencies by increasing distance to Sevenoaks. We then estimate the 2SLS model with *distance to Sevenoaks* as the sole instrument for each ordered quartile separately. Figure 6.4 depicts the resulting 2SLS point estimates of the coefficient on *riots within 10 km* along with 90 percent confidence intervals for each quartile. It shows that the point estimates are large and positive in the two upper quartiles but insignificant in the first two quartiles. The instrument is, however, weak in the three first quartiles.[32] Substantively, this suggests that the instrument primarily affected constituencies at least seven days of travel by foot away from the origin of the riots (Sevenoaks). This is consistent with the logic underlying our instrument. Recall that *distance to Sevenoaks* isolates the social dynamics of the riots. That is, the instrumental variable estimate captures the increase in Whig support in a constituency caused by local Swing riots that were induced by diffusion of riots into its neighbourhood rather than by local structural factors. The pattern that we observe in Figure 6.4 is very much consistent with this theoretical argument. The constituencies close to Sevenoaks in Kent, Sussex, or Essex had a history of Swing-type agricultural riots, while such events were rarer further away. Thus, the diffusion of Swing riots into constituencies far away from the starting point is likely to have come as a major surprise for the voters in those areas and made them update their perceptions of the threat of revolution more strongly than voters in constituencies closer to the epicentre who had experienced Swing-type riots before.

In sum, if we interpret the baseline instrumental variable estimate of 2.53 as a local average treatment effect that primarily captures what is happening in the 122 constituencies in the two upper quartiles of the 'distance to Sevenoaks' distribution, then the impact of riots on the Whig victory is obviously smaller than what is suggested by the average treatment effect interpretation. Comparing two constituencies located in the bottom and top quartile of the subpopulation of the 122 constituencies that 'complied', the instrumental variable estimate of 2.53 implies that the share of Whigs elected in the later would be 12.7 percentage points higher than in the former.[33] This is roughly twice the effect implied by

[32] Given that the instrument *distance to Sevenoaks* is weak in these subsamples, we should use the Anderson-Rubin Wald test to assess significance. This test rejects significance in the first and second quartile, but not in the third.

[33] This calculation restricts the sample to the subset of 122 constituencies in the third and forth quartiles of the 'distance to Sevenoaks' distribution. Within that sample, a constituency in the bottom quarter of the *riots within 10* km distribution experienced no riots while a constituency in the top quarter experienced at least five riots, making the share of Whigs elected in the later relative to the former 12.7 (= 2.53 × (5 – 0)) percentage points higher.

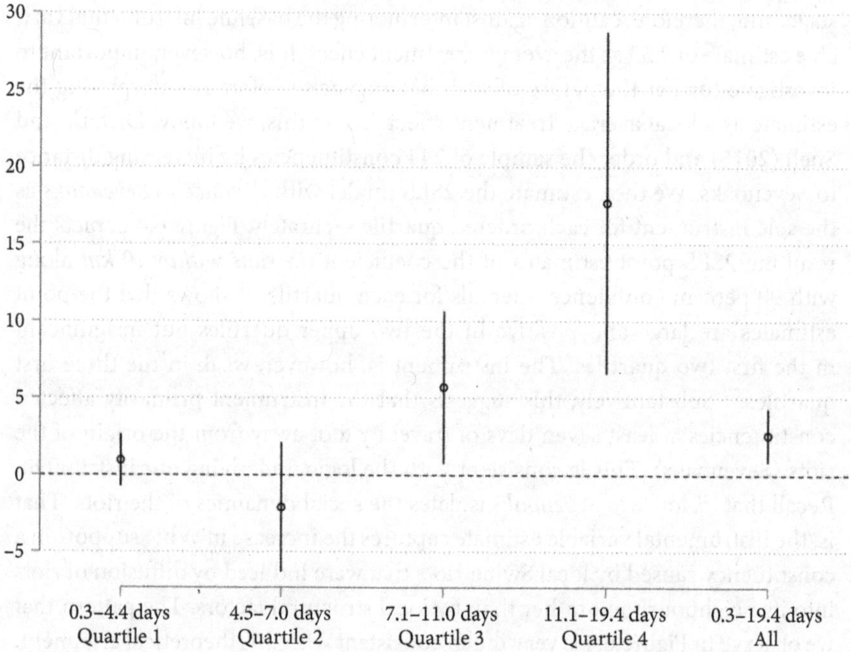

Figure 6.4 Heterogeneous treatment effects: the instrumental variable estimate of the effect of local Swing riots on Whig support in the 1831 election by quartile

Note: The figure depicts the estimated coefficient (the dots) on *riots within 10 km* from separate 2SLS regressions in subsamples defined by the four quartiles of the sample ordered by increasing distance to Sevenoaks, along with the baseline instrumental variable estimate (reported to the far right). The lines indicate 90 percent confidence intervals. In each case, the first-stage specification is linear in the instrument (*distance to Sevenoaks*). Carlisle is excluded as an extreme outlier in the fourth quartile. The x-axis indicates the range of distances in travel days included in each quartile subsample. It is not possible to include the control for the different agricultural areas consistently in the subsample regressions but, otherwise, all the baseline and spatial controls are included.

the ordinary least squares estimate (5.2 percentage points) but less than half the size of the average treatment effect interpretation of the instrumental variable estimate (28 percentage points). To put these estimates into perspective, recall that the Whigs had 210 of the 489 (English) seats in 1830 and increased that by 66 in 1831 to 276. To get a majority in England, the Whigs needed to win just thirty-five seats. The ordinary least squares estimate suggests that the Swing riots helped them win twenty-six seats (489 × 0.052). The LATE interpretation of the instrumental variable estimate suggests that the riots helped them win seats in only half the constituencies, which implies a gain of 31 seats (489 × 0.127/2), while the ATE interpretation suggests a much larger gain of 137 seats (489 × 0.28). Either way the quantitative effect of the Swing riots was substantial.

6.4.6 Alternative explanations of the Whig victory in 1831

Our empirical analysis suggests that the Whig victory in 1831 was helped along by the Swing riots and the fear of revolution that observing the riots first hand instilled in the electors and patrons of the Unreformed Parliament. The historical literature, however, points to alternative explanations for the Whig victory in 1831, and it is important to evaluate them explicitly. To do this, we collect quantitative data related to each of them and augment equation 6.1 with additional control variables. This allows us to test the relevance of the alternatives directly and to evaluate if the effect of local Swing riots is diminished in the augmented regression models.[34] Table 6.9 reports the main results.

The first alternative explanation for the Whig victory in 1831 is that administrative reforms in the pre-reform years weakened the Tories' ability to control seats (Morrison 2011). While it is true that Lord Liverpool undertook reforms after 1815 to make the English administration more efficient and less corrupt (e.g. Jupp (1998, Chap. 1) or Mokyr (2009, 425–426)), this had little effect on the number of seats in the House of Commons that were actually controlled by the Treasury (and, thus, by the Tory governments that ruled between 1807 and 1830). This number stayed within the range from twenty-five to thirty seats between 1750 and 1832 (Namier and Brooke (1964, Vol. 1, 54–57), Thorne (1986, Vol. 1, 46–56), Philbin (1965)). A simple test of Morrison (2011)'s conjecture is to assume that the Tories lost hold of the fourteen English constituencies (twenty-eight seats) which were controlled by the Treasury in 1830 and then to re-estimate equation 6.1 on the reduced sample that excludes these constituencies. If the conjecture is true and we confound the effect of the administrative reforms with that of the Swing riots, the coefficient on *riots within 10 km* should become insignificant. Table 6.9, column 1, shows that this is not the case.

A second alternative explanation is that the Whig victory in 1831 was caused by mobilisation of religious networks, of anti-slavery advocates, or of pro-reform political associations. The basis for this conjecture is that pressure groups became more and more effective at organising successful campaigns to influence the House of Commons in the years after 1815, and as we saw in Chapter 5, played an important role in persuading the MPs in the House of Commons to support the Reform Bill in the critical second reading in March 1831. A long similar lines, the mobilisation of dissenters and Catholics in the 1820s contributed to the adoption of the Catholic Relief Act in 1829 (10 Geo. 4. c. 7), which gave the members of these religious minorities substantial political rights (Machin 1964; Jupp 1998, 366–376). Likewise, the London Society for Mitigating and Gradually Abolishing the State of Slavery throughout the

[34] Section C6.4 in the supplementary material appendix details the alternatives. The supplementary material appendix is available at www.oup.com/us/peacefulandviolentorigins

Table 6.9 Local Swing riots and the outcome of the 1831 election: alternative explanations for the Whig victory

	1	2	3	4	5
			Whig share 1831		
			Least squares		
Riots within 10 km	0.37	0.46	0.52	0.49	0.51
	(0.18)**	(0.18)**	(0.17)***	{0.19}**	{0.17}***
	[0.19]*	[0.19]**	[0.18]***	(0.17)***	(0.16)***
Petitions against Catholic relief		1.44	2.15	2.19	2.14
		(1.24)	(1.18)*	{1.31}	{1.33}
Petitions for Catholic relief		0.82	2.35	2.85	2.26
		(2.21)	(2.29)	{2.52}	{2.33}
Petitions against slavery		0.27	0.61	0.62	0.64
		(0.93)	(0.92)	{1.00}	{1.00}
Petitions against reform			−8.02	−7.76	−7.83
			(3.37)**	{4.50}*	{4.39}*
Petitions for reform			−1.30	−0.32	−1.30
			(0.95)	{1.84}	{1.03}
Growth in Poor Law expenses				0.0081	
				{0.0050}	
Special commission					−11.5
					{5.27}**
Share of harsh sentences					0.18
					{0.068}**
F-test for added group[a]	n.a.	0.87	4.00**	n.a.	4.35**
Baseline controls included[b]	Yes	Yes	Yes	Yes	Yes
With Treasury boroughs	No	Yes	Yes	Yes	Yes
Adjusted R^2	0.44	0.45	0.46	0.47	0.46
Obs. (constituencies)	230	244	244	241	244

Note: The table reports alternative estimates associating *riots within 10 km* to the outcome of the 1831 General Election to account for the presence of Treasury boroughs, petitions for and against Catholic relief, petitions against slavery, petitions for and against parliamentary reform, growth in Poor Law expenses, and the level of repression. For *riots within 10 km*, we report in columns 1 to 3 spatial (Conley 1999) standard errors (50-kilometres radius) in parentheses and White robust standard errors in square brackets; in columns 4 and 5, where *growth in Poor Law expenses, share of harsh sentences,* and *special commission* are measured at the county level, the standard errors in curly brackets are clustered at the county level while those in parentheses are spatial standard errors (50-kilometres radius). In column 1, we exclude the fourteen boroughs (twenty-eight seats) that were controlled by the Treasury around 1830 according to Philbin (1965). In column 4, three constituencies (London, Monmouth, and Monmouthshire) are excluded because Gonner (1912, Appendix B) does not report their Poor Law expenses.

[a]The null hypothesis is that the coefficients of the variables added in the column are all 0.

[b]The baseline control variables are those reported in Table 6.2, column 5.

* = Significant at the 10 percent level;

** = Significant at the 5 percent level;

*** = Significant at the 1 percent level.

British Dominions, along with its 230 local groups, had a large impact on the anti-slavery debate in the late 1820s and early 1830s. A common tactic of these pressure groups was to send petitions to Parliament calling for the abolition of slavery or ending discriminatory legislation against Catholics (Leys 1955; Knights 2010). These petitions are recorded in the *Journal of the House of Commons.* Based on words searches for the names of the constituencies in the index of petitions, we can quantify how many petitions related to religious issues or to the anti-slavery campaign originated from each of them between 1828 and 1831 (Journal of the House of Commons, 1828-1831, vol. 83–86). We use these counts as proxies for civic mobilisation at the constituency level for other purposes than reform agitation. Table 6.9, columns 2, reports a regression where we add three constituency-specific measures of petitions: *petitions for Catholic relief*, *petition against Catholic relief*, and *petition against slavery.* These three variables are insignificant, individually and jointly, and the point estimate on *riots within 10 km* is similar to the baseline estimate in Table 6.2, column 5. This result is, perhaps, to be expected since Catholic relief and the abolition of slavery were issues which cut across, and not between, political factions. Variations in local mobilisation on these questions are, therefore, unlikely causes of the Whig victory in 1831.[35] In contrast, the attitude to parliamentary reform closely followed, as discussed in Chapter 4, party lines, and it is, therefore, possible that the mobilisation of political associations could account for the Whig victory in 1831. We use constituency-level petition data related to the reform question to test this conjecture. Table 6.9, column 3, shows that the number of petitions against reform is negative correlated with Whig share 1831, while the number of petitions in favour of reform is insignificant. The point estimate on *riots within 10 km* is a little larger than in the baseline and significant at the 1 percent level. This, on the one hand, suggests that anti-reform mobilisation was correlated with Tory electoral success. On the other hand, the effect of local Swing riots is larger and more precisely estimated than in the baseline. This also serves as evidence against the conjecture that local reform agitators played a systematic role in organising Swing riots.

A third alternative explanation is that local variations in Poor Law expenditures simultaneously determined the intensity of the Swing riots and the Whig

[35] In addition to the petition data related to Catholic relief, we also use the 1851 Census of Religious Worship (PP, 1852–1853, vol. 89, LXXXIX.1 (1690)) to construct alternative constituency-specific proxies for the density of religious networks. We match these data to the constituencies of the Unreformed Parliament by attributing the return for the census district with the name of the constituency to that constituency. In Table C6.25, column 2, in the supplementary material appendix, we find a positive correlation between the presence of a Catholic church and the share of Whigs elected in 1831, and note that the point estimate on *riots within 10* km is larger and more precisely estimated than in the baseline. The supplementary material appendix is available at www.oup.com/us/peacefulandviolentorigins

success in 1831. This could have been the case since responding to systematic underemployment and preventing disorder were among the objectives of the Poor Law system (e.g. Blaug (1963), Marshall (1985), Boyer (1990), and the related discussion in Greif and Iyigun (2013)). To test the hypothesis that higher Poor Law expenses might be systematically correlated with the ideological leaning of the voters in the constituencies, we use data from Gonner (1912, Appendix B) on the growth in Poor Law expenses between 1750 and 1813 in each county. Table 6.9, column 4 shows that the variable *growth in Poor Law expenditures* is insignificant and that there is no substantial change in the size or significance of the point estimate on *riots within 10 km.*

A fourth alternative explanation is that the Whig victory was a consequence of the Whig government's effective repression of the Swing riots: it convinced voters and patrons that the Whigs could be trusted to protect private property rights and preserve social order in spite of their commitment to parliamentary reform. To investigate this possibility, we take advantage of variations in the harshness with which the disturbances were repressed in different counties (Hobsbawm and Rudé 1973, Appendix II). Table 6.9, column 5, shows that these differences have an ambiguous impact on the share of Whigs elected in 1831. On the one hand, the share of harsh sentences handed out to convicted rioters has a positive and significant impact on the Whig success. On the other hand, the establishment of a special commission in a county to swiftly try rioters has a negative and significant effect. More importantly, however, controlling for these variables does not affect the size or significance of the point estimate on *riots within 10 km.*

Overall, these results show that some of the alternatives have explanatory power for the Whig electoral success in 1831 but none of them weaken the effect of the local Swing riots.

6.5 Conclusion

This chapter shows that the violence of the Swing riots helped the the reform-friendly Whigs obtained a majority of seats in the House of Commons in the 1831 General Election. Without such a majority, the reform process would almost surely have come to a stop, or, at least, been delayed. Our estimates suggest that the share of Whigs elected was between 5.2 percentage points (the ordinary least squares estimate) and 28 percentage points (the ATE interpretation of the instrumental variable estimate) higher in constituencies that were exposed to many Swing riots. The local average treatment effect (LATE) interpretation puts the effect of the riots somewhere in the middle at 12.7 percentage points. To win a majority in England and Wales, the Whigs needed to gain thirty-five seats. The ordinary least squares estimate implies winning 21 seats, while the LATE estimate (operating only on the 122 constituencies in the two upper quartiles) implies winning 31 seats. It is clear that exposure to the Swing riots played an important role in securing the Whig majority, even if the riots were not sufficient on their own. These results are robust to different identification strategies, and their credibility is strengthened through falsification tests.

Our interpretation of these results is that the voters and patrons shifted their allegiance towards the Whigs in the wake of the Swing riots that they had observed first-hand in the immediate neighbourhood of their constituency because they feared that the rioters could become useful allies for the segments of the population that supported far-reaching political changes. Such fears could, on the one hand, have been stoked by the fact that radical orators took up the Swing riots in their London lectures at the Blackfriars Rotunda (Royle 2000, 85). On the other hand, the Blackfriars Rotunda radicals' opposition to the Reform Bill—they wanted universal suffrage and secret ballot—highlights the tension between their National Union of the Working Classes and middle-class-dominated reform unions (such as the Birmingham Political Union) that supported the bill. This tension created an opening for splitting the reform movement by enabling Grey to push his reform through (LoPatin 1999, Chap. 2). Consequently, by returning a Whig (rather than a Tory) in 1831, the voters and patrons knew that they were helping the Whig leadership build the required majority to pass the Reform Bill. Although it was clear that the Swing rioters themselves would not obtain voting rights if the bill succeeded, the limited extension of the franchise and the redistribution of seats sought by the Whig leadership would be sufficient to appease upper-class and middle-class reformers who might otherwise have taken advantage of agricultural riots to initiate a revolution. In short, we argue that the local Swing riots observed first-hand by voters and patrons made the prospect of revolution tangible in their minds, and convinced them that the extension of the franchise to a limited section of the population and redistribution of seats were necessary; they reacted by backing reform-friendly Whig candidates in the 1831 election; this gave the Whig leaders, who were already committed to parliamentary reform prior to the Swing riots, the majority they needed to move the reform process forward. Taken together, the evidence from this juncture in the Great Reform Act's journey to become a reality is, therefore, consistent with the threat of revolution hypothesis. Fears of revolution helped the reform overcome the third major roadblock.

Chapter 7
The battle with the lords: voting on reform in the House of Lords

7.1 Introduction

The result of the 1831 General Election had secured a solid pro-reform majority in the House of Commons. However, for the Reform Bill to become law, the Whigs needed to get it through the anti-reform, Tory-dominated House of Lords. This chapter seeks to understand how the bill overcame the final roadblocks between October 1831 and June 1832: to break the stalemate between the two houses of Parliament and to obtain a majority amongst the lords.

The study of the Reform Bill in the House of Lords engages with the democratisation puzzle in a new and novel way. The lords and the MPs all belonged to the elite, but the two subgroups' incentives with respect to constitutional reform were arguably different, and they faced fundamentally different constraints. As we discussed in Chapter 5, the MPs were partly accountable to the pre-reform electors, and they would be directly affected by the Reform Bill. In contrast, the lords were unaccountable to the electorate, and the constitutional status of the House of Lords was not directly threatened by the bill. As such, we can test the three hypotheses laid out in Chapter 2, related to the threat of revolution, to social movement agitation, and to political expedience, in a different environment. We ask if any of the mechanisms highlighted by the three hypotheses influenced the way the unelected lords voted on the Reform Bill and, if so, whether their reactions were similar to, or different from, those of the elected MPs in the House of Commons.

Notwithstanding self-interest and ideological considerations, the lords were caught between two forces. On the one hand, they observed the increase in social unrest and reform agitation, including the spike in unrest during the Days of May. On the other hand, the Whig government repeatedly tried to extract a credible promise from King William IV that he would create, if needed, enough new pro-reform Whig lords to create a majority in favour of the bill in the House of Lords. In other words, the majority group of Tory lords faced a threat from below in the form of social violence, revolution, and agitation while, at the same time, they faced a threat from above that, if realised, could eliminate their majority in the House of Lords for many years to come. A central question that we try

Peaceful and Violent Origins of Voting Rights. Toke S. Aidt and Raphaël Franck, Oxford University Press.
 DOI: 10.1093/9780197679746.003.0007

to answer in the chapter is why the Tory lords ultimately accepted the Reform Bill. Did they fear a revolution? Were they responsive to reform arguments? Or did they fear the threat from above that the King would eliminate their control of the House of Lords?

7.2 The Reform Bill in the House of Lords

The lords rejected the Reform Bill in its entirety three times and introduced numerous committee-stage amendments aimed at undermining it before it was finally accepted on 4 June 1832 after the King made a credible promise to create enough new pro-reform (Whig) lords to engineer a majority should the House of Lords continue to vote it down.

The Whig government presented the second version of the bill to the House of Lords on 22 September 1831, and the second reading took place during the night between 7 and 8 October 1831. The anti-reform opposition won the vote by 199 to 158 votes. The Reform Bill was dismissed and sent back to the House of Commons where Lord Grey's Cabinet had to put together a new, third version and to try to get that through the House of Lords.

The rejection by the lords encouraged peaceful pressure on the lords from 'below' and triggered social unrest. The future Chartist leader Francis Place held a well-attended pro-reform meeting on 12 October 1831, just one week after the one he had organised during the debate in the House of Lords. Riots took place in various parts of the country. They culminated in the Bristol riots at the end of October 1831. The lords residing in the affected areas would have observed these events first-hand, while others saw them reported in the newspapers. The twenty Tory-leaning bishops who had opposed the bill were targeted and, in some cases, threatened with violence.

Nonetheless, most Tory lords were not interested in a compromise. Despite the efforts of Dudley Ryder, first Earl of Harrowby (1762–1847), who sought to rally moderate opponents of the bill, most lords accepted the judgement of their leader, the Duke of Wellington, that popular support for the Reform Bill outside Parliament would wane if the peers were to persist in their opposition. This was a miscalculation, as unrest continued. On 6 November 1831, the situation was so serious that Lord Grey decided to recall the Commons from recess in order to issue a declaration against the military organisation of political unions.

In this volatile political environment, Lord John Russell presented the third version of the Reform Bill in the House of Commons on 12 December 1831. It passed without much opposition. However, despite the bill being modified to appease Tory peers Lord Grey and the members of his Cabinet remained concerned by the strength of the anticipated opposition to the revised bill in the House of Lords. To win over reluctant peers, Lord Grey followed a two-pronged strategy. On the one hand, he and his Cabinet orchestrated a systematic attempt to win over Tory peers whom they considered willing to compromise. On the other hand, they threatened the Tories with the creation of new Whig lords. It was estimated that about fifty new Whig peers would be sufficient to ensure the passage of the bill, but this was an aberrant measure for many members of the Cabinet, even for Grey himself at first. Nonetheless, through a formal demand from the Cabinet on 13 January 1832, Lord Grey ultimately asked the King to create new (Whig) peers if need be. Two days later, William IV reluctantly agreed to the Cabinet's proposal. However, the King's insistence that any list of new peers would be limited to the eldest sons of existing lords, relatives of heirs to the peerage, or, as a last resort, to Scottish and Irish peers undermined the credibility of the implied threat.

The second reading in the House of Lords began on 9 April 1832. This time, the debate was less intense. The members of Grey's Cabinet were by now confident that they could win the vote, although they were wary because the King had, in the end, refused to commit to create new peers in the eventuality of a defeat. In the vote on 13 April 1832, 184 peers supported the bill and 175 voted against it.[1]

At the following committee stage, however, Tory peers sought to postpone discussion of the clauses related to the disenfranchisement of the small boroughs in Schedules A and B. Lord Grey refused to accept this, as it had the potential to undermine the very principle of the Bill. But on 7 May 1832, when the postponement motion was brought to a vote in the House of Lords, the lords voted in its favour by 151 to 116, defeating the government.

Following the defeat, Grey's Cabinet resigned. Two days later, William IV accepted the resignation and immediately asked John Copley, first Baron Lyndhurst (1772–1863) (who was a judge and considered to be 'above politics') to seek someone among the Tories who could form a Tory Cabinet that would be willing to undertake *some* measure of reform. On 10 May 1832, the leading Tory politician in the Commons, Robert Peel, refused. Without Peel's support, the King understood that it was impossible to find anyone, including Wellington, to lead a Tory government that would undertake reform. On 18 May, the King reinstated Lord Grey and his Cabinet, and he made a firm commitment to the necessity of creating a sufficiently large number of Whig peers in the House of Lords for the bill to obtain a majority, if needed.

All these parliamentary dealings took place in an atmosphere of heightened social unrest and heated reform-related agitation, subsequently referred

[1] The actual vote took place on 14 April 1832 at 6.30 a.m., but we follow the convention to date the vote by the last day of debate, that is, 13 April. We do the same with the other votes.

to as the Days of May. Pro-reform agitation, stirred in part by radical politicians such as Thomas Attwood and Francis Place, led to a spike in pro-reform meetings, demonstrations, and riots, as well as to a boom in petitions against Wellington and the Tories. This agitation sent a strong signal that the Reform Bill enjoyed substantial popular support outside Parliament and created the impression of a serious threat from below. Clearly, some politicians did fear a potential violent uprising at the time. In his memoirs, Lord John Russell, for example, wrote about the Days of May: 'This was indeed a moment of peril. It was the only time during my political life in which I have felt uneasy as to the result' (Russell 1875, 102-103).

After the return of Lord Grey to power and with a credible threat from the King that he would accept the creation of new pro-reform Whig lords if the Reform Bill was rejected again, it went very quickly through the various legislative stages in the House of Lords. The vote on the third reading took place on 4 June 1832. The Bill was supported by 106 peers. Many Tories, who had previously voted against, did not take part in the vote. Only 22 hardliners voted against. The Reform Bill had then garnered majority support in both Houses, and the King gave it royal assent on 7 June 1832: the Great Reform Act had overcome the last roadblocks.

7.3 Data

The tests of the three hypothesises—the threat of revolution, the social movement, and the political expedience hypothesis—focus on the two votes on the second and third version of the Reform Bill in the House of Lords that took place respectively on 7 October 1831 and 13 April 1832, and on the vote on the postponement amendment on 7 May 1832. For the final (third) reading on 4 June 1832, only a qualitative analysis is possible. This is because Hansard only lists the names of the 22 hardliners who opposed reform to the very end and not those of the 106 peers who voted for the Reform Bill.

Before we turn to the formal statistical analysis, it is useful to look at the raw vote data. The top panels of Tables 7.1, 7.2, and 7.3 report vote counts for all lords (including Scottish and Irish peers). The middle and the bottom panels in each table break the vote results down for the English peers[2] and the bishops, respectively, which is the sample used in the empirical analysis.[3] For each vote,

[2] In line with the rules of the House of Lords, we consider that English lords held a peerage of England, of Great Britain, or of the United Kingdom.

[3] We do not have data on social unrest and social movement mobilisation in Scotland and Ireland and are forced to exclude from the analysis peers who held a Scottish or an Irish peerage unless they also held a peerage of England, of Great Britain, or of the United Kingdom.

Table 7.1 The votes for and against the Reform Bill in the House of Lords on 7 October 1831

	All	Tory	Whig	Other	Tory	Whig	Other	Tory	Whig	Other
		All			Present			Proxy		
All peers										
Against	199	171	6	22	129	4	17	42	2	5
For	158	2	119	37	2	98	30	0	21	7
Total	357	173	125	59	131	102	47	42	23	12
Peerage of England, Great Britain, and United Kingdom (incl. Royal Family)										
Against	145	124	5	16	100	3	13	24	2	3
For	137	2	103	32	2	84	26	0	19	6
Total	282	126	108	48	102	87	39	24	21	9
Bishops										
Against	20	20	0	0	11	0	0	9	0	0
For	2	0	2	0	0	1	0	0	1	0
Total	22	20	2	0	11	1	0	9	1	0

Source: Hansard HL Deb, 7 October 1831, series 2, vol. 8, c339–344.

Table 7.2 The votes for and against the Reform Bill in the House of Lords on 13 April 1832

	All	Tory	Whig	Other	Tory	Whig	Other	Tory	Whig	Other
		All			Present			Proxy		
	All peers									
Against	175	147	5	23	106	3	19	41	2	4
For	184	18	122	44	18	83	27	0	39	17
Total	359	165	127	67	124	86	46	41	41	21
	Peerage of England, Great Britain, and United Kingdom (incl. Royal Family)									
Against	129	108	4	17	83	2	15	25	2	2
For	151	13	102	36	13	69	22	0	33	14
Total	279	121	105	53	96	71	37	25	34	16
	Bishops									
Against	13	13	0	0	10	0	0	3	0	0
For	13	5	5	3	5	3	2	0	2	1
Total	26	18	5	3	15	3	2	3	2	1

Source: Hansard HL Deb, 13 April 1832, series 2, vol. 12, c453–455.

Table 7.3 The votes for and against the Reform Bill in the House of Lords on 7 May 1832

	All	Tory	Whig	Other	Tory	Whig	Other	Tory	Whig	Other
		All			Present			Proxy		
	All peers									
Against	154	126	6	22	126	6	22	0	0	0
For	122	2	89	31	2	89	31	0	0	0
Total	276	128	95	53	128	95	53	0	0	0
	Peerage of England, Great Britain, and United Kingdom (incl. Royal Family)									
Against	114	93	5	16	93	5	16	0	0	0
For	106	2	77	27	2	77	27	0	0	0
Total	220	95	82	43	95	82	43	0	0	0
	Bishops									
Against	16	14	0	2	14	0	2	0	0	0
For	4	0	3	1	0	3	1	0	0	0
Total	20	14	3	3	14	3	3	0	0	0

Note: Henry Beresford, third Marquess of Waterford (1811–1859), also known as Earl or Lord Tyrone, only took part in the third vote on 7 May 1832 because he was born on 26 April 1811. Although he had succeeded to the marquessate at the death of his father in 1826 at age 15, he was only allowed to sit in the House of Lords after turning 21 years old on 26 April 1832.

Source: Hansard HL Deb, 7 May 1832, series 2, vol. 12, c725–728.

we report vote counts by party affiliation (Tory, Whig, or other (independent)) and further distinguish between peers who were present and those who voted by proxy.[4] Many Tory lords were, for ideological reasons, against reform while Whig or independent lords were more likely to be supportive. These ideological differences are clearly reflected in the voting pattern of the English peers. The voting behaviour of the bishops shows more volatility: the majority voted against in October 1831 and in May 1832, but the bishops were equally split in April 1832.

To test the threat of revolution and the social movement hypotheses, we return to the data on public agitation and social unrest collected by Horn and Tilly (1988) and Tilly (1995). As in Chapter 5, we make a distinction between events that were peaceful and related to social movement mobilisation and agitation, and those that were violent and related to the threat of revolution. Amongst peaceful events, we make a further distinction between meetings (pre-announced and orderly) and gatherings (more spontaneous demonstrations). We also single out peaceful events that were directly related to the reform question. Amongst violent protest, we distinguish between violent protest in rural areas and in urban areas. Rather than aggregating the data to the county level as in our analysis of the MPs' vote in Chapter 5, we geo-reference each event to the parish level outside London and to the street level in London. This enables us to code the number of people who participated in events that happened around the residence(s) of each lord or bishop. For this purpose, we record the address of the main residences of each lord using the information in Lodge (1832). All the peers had a country home outside London which was their primary place of residence.[5] Most of them also had a residence in London. For each lord, we first identify the events of the various types that took place within a radius of either 10 kilometres of their country home or within 1 kilometre of their London home (if they possessed one) and then compute the number of participants. For those peers without a home in London, we assign to them a value of zero for all types of (London) events.

For each of the three votes, we accumulate these data from 1 January 1828 to the date of the vote. This means that, for each vote, we only associate events that had actually happened at the time of the vote near the home of each lord. We refer to these variables with the notation 'TYPE HOME' where TYPE refers to the type of event (all (types), violent, peaceful, gatherings, meetings, reform, or violent urban) and HOME refers to either 'country home' or 'London home'. We

[4] We code party affiliation using information from Lodge (1832), Dod and Dod (1832), Namier and Brooke (1964), Stooks Smith (1973), Thorne (1986), and Fisher (2009). We also draw on these sources to code variables (introduced below) related to the lords' army and political careers.

[5] For some peers, Lodge (1832) lists two or even three country homes in different regions. We use the primary home in the analysis.

use these lord- and vote-specific measures of violent unrest to test the threat of revolution hypothesis and the various measures of peaceful agitation to test the social mobilisation hypothesis.

The maps in Figures 7.1 and 7.2 show the distribution of the number of people participating in peaceful (panels A) and violent (panels B) events that took place between 1 January 1828 and 7 May 1832 around the respective homes of the lords. These maps enable us to make two general observations. First, depending on the location of their country home, the lords were exposed to very different levels of both peaceful agitation and violent unrest within a radius of 10 kilometres. Second, most of the London homes of the lords cluster in the Mayfair area, and therefore many lords would have been exposed to very similar levels of peaceful agitation and violent unrest with a radius of 1 kilometre.

To test the political expedience hypothesis, we use information from Sack (1980) to determine the number of nomination borough seats each lord controlled in 1830–1832, many of which stood to be disenfranchised by the Reform Bill. The variable *nomination 1830–1832* records the number of nomination boroughs controlled by each lord, ranging from zero to nine. The hypothesis is that lords with more nomination boroughs at stake had a particular material reason to oppose the reform.

Our statistical analysis controls for various personal characteristics of the lords which could have had an impact on how they voted. We code a dummy variable *army career* equal to 1 if the lord had an army career and 0 otherwise. Having an army career would distinguish a lord from many others who, besides being large landowners, rarely had any independent employment experience. We compute the variables *years in House of Lords* and *years in House of Commons* related to the political career of each lord. They record the number of years a lord had sat in the House of Lords by 1830, and, if applicable, how many years he had sat in the House of Commons before becoming a peer. The variable *years in House of Lords* controls for generational differences in reform attitude between lords who had recently been appointed and those with a longer history of service. The variable *years in House of Commons* controls for the possibility that the reform attitude of those lords who had personal experience with the House of Commons may be different from those without.

The most important of the personal characteristics is, however, party affiliation. It is clear from Tables 7.1 to 7.3 that this is a very strong predictor of how a lord would vote. We define the dummy variable *Tory* as being equal to 1 if the lord or bishop was a Tory and to 0 if he was a Whig or was independent. Table 7.4, panel A, reports statistical tests for mean differences between Tory and Whig lords with respect to their personal characteristics and circumstances. We see that there were some differences with respect to years served in the House of Lords and to control over nomination boroughs: the Tory lords

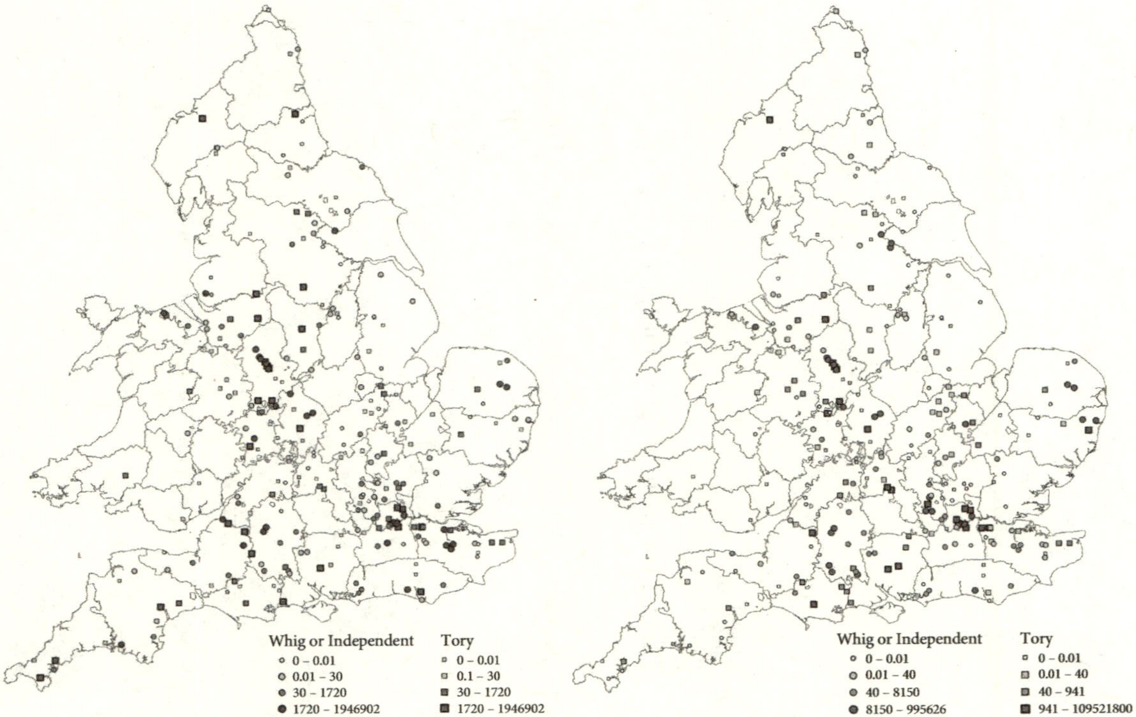

(A) Peaceful agitation

(B) Violent unrest

Figure 7.1 The spatial distribution of the number of participants in violent unrest and peaceful agitation within a radius of 10 kilometres of the country homes of the lords between 1 January 1828 and 7 May 1832

Source: Own construction using data from Horn and Tilly (1988).

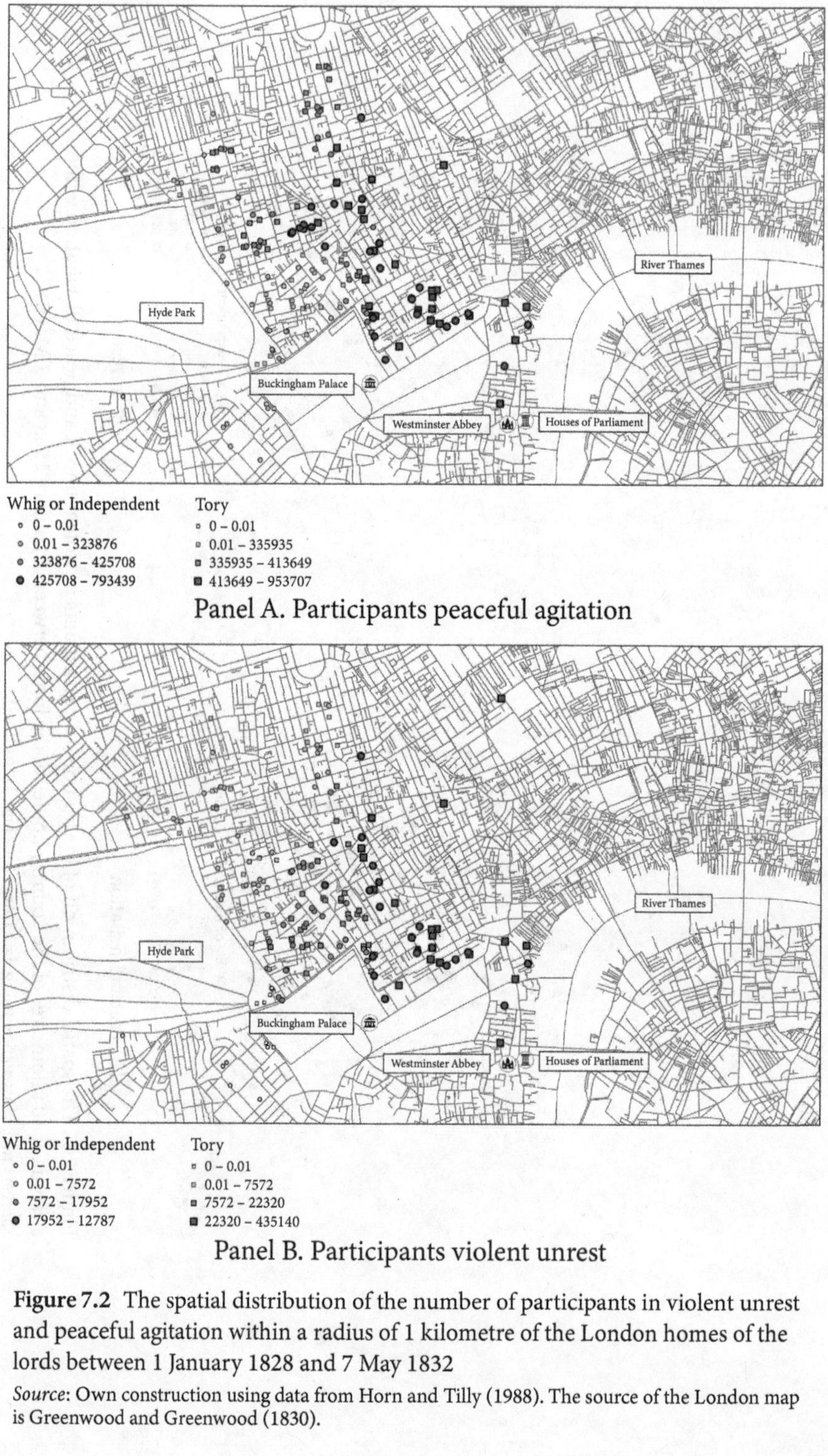

Figure 7.2 The spatial distribution of the number of participants in violent unrest and peaceful agitation within a radius of 1 kilometre of the London homes of the lords between 1 January 1828 and 7 May 1832

Source: Own construction using data from Horn and Tilly (1988). The source of the London map is Greenwood and Greenwood (1830).

Table 7.4 Test of means differences by party affiliation of the lords

	Tory		Whig		
	Mean	**Std. dev.**	**Mean**	**Std. dev.**	***p*-value**
Panel A: Characteristics of the lords					
Army career	0.13	[0.03]	0.18	[0.03]	0.350
Years in House of Lords	2.43	[0.03]	2.73	[0.03]	0.011
Years in House of Commons	1.36	[0.10]	1.36	[0.07]	0.996
Nomination 1830–1832	0.24	[0.12]	0.38	[0.11]	0.051
Panel B: Participation in protest (10,000s)					
All country home	4.05	[2.58]	3.85	[2.28]	0.953
All London home	24.58	[2.34]	26.65	[2.19]	0.522
Violent country home	0.97	[0.89]	1.03	[0.79]	0.966
Violent London home	1.27	[0.23]	1.94	[0.40]	0.180
Peaceful country home	3.07	[1.74]	2.82	[1.53]	0.913
Peaceful London home	23.31	[2.23]	24.71	[2.01]	0.641

Note: We divide the sample of the 253 peers from the English, British, and United Kingdom peerage into those who identify with the Tory party and those who identify with the Whig party, respectively, excluding bishops and independent peers. The table reports means and standard deviation (in square brackets) for these subsamples. The last column reports the *p*-value associated with a t-test of the null hypothesis that the means of the two subsamples are different. The unrest and agitation data cover the period from 1 January 1828 to 7 May 1832.

Source: Definitions and sources of the variables are in the text.

were 'newcomers' (reflecting the fact that many had been appointed on the recommendation of successive Tory governments since the turn of the century) and were less likely to control seats in the House of Commons. With respect to exposure to violent unrest or peaceful agitation, Table 7.4, panel B, shows that there was no systematic differences: anti-reform Tory and pro-reform Whig lords were exposed to similar levels of violence and social movement agitation. Table 7.5 reports descriptive statistics for the main variables used in the analysis.[6]

7.4 Empirical strategy

The dependent variables in our analysis are the votes cast by the English lords and bishops who were present and voted on 7 October 1831, 13 April 1831, and 7 May 1832, respectively. For each peer and vote, we create the dummy variable *against reform*, which takes the value 1 if the peer opposed reform by voting against the bill on 7 October 1831 or on 13 April 1832 or by voting for the

[6] Table C7.1 in the supplementary appendix reports descriptive statistics for the protest events disaggregated by type. The supplementary material appendix is available at www.oup.com/us/peacefulandviolentorigins

Table 7.5 Descriptive statistics: the House of Lords

	Obs.	Mean	Std. Dev.	Min.	Max.
Votes					
Against reform (7 October 1831)	322	0.55	0.50	0	1
Against reform (13 April 1832)	325	0.47	0.50	0	1
Against reform (7 May 1832)	252	0.55	0.50	0	1
Change in reform opposition[a]	322	0.16	0.37	0	1
Characteristics of the lords					
Tory	342	0.48	0.50	0	1
Army career	342	0.17	0.37	0	1
Years in House of Lords	342	16.87	12.88	0	58
Years in House of Commons	342	5.93	9.24	0	56
Political Expedience					
Nomination 1830–1832	342	0.58	1.33	0	9
Participants in violent unrest and peaceful agitation (10,000s)					
From 1 January 1828 to 7 October 1831					
All country home	342	0.86	4.23	0	41.47
All London home	342	2.52	3.23	0	12.99
Violent country home	342	0.07	0.41	0	5.03
Violent London home	342	0.26	0.36	0	1.43
Peaceful country home	342	0.79	3.94	0	36.50
Peaceful London home	342	2.26	2.90	0	11.88

From 1 January 1828 to 13 April 1831					
All country home	342	3.15	23.42	0	304.10
All London home	342	23.13	25.42	0	98.66
Violent country home	342	0.76	8.07	0	109.52
Violent London home	342	1.47	3.65	0	43.51
Peaceful country home	342	2.39	15.79	0	194.58
Peaceful London home	342	21.65	23.69	0	95.37
From 1 January 1828 to 7 May 1832					
All country home	342	3.19	23.43	0	304.21
All London home	342	23.13	25.43	0	98.66
Violent country home	342	0.76	8.07	0	109.52
Violent London home	342	1.47	3.65	0	43.51
Peaceful country home	342	2.43	15.81	0	194.69
Peaceful London home	342	21.65	23.69	0	95.37

Note: [a]Change from reform opposition (voting against the Reform Bill) on 7 Oct 1831 to abstention in the vote on 7 May 1832.
Source: Definitions and sources of the variables are in the text.

amendment to postpone discussion of the disenfranchisement clauses on 7 May 1832, respectively. We then estimate, separately for each of the three votes, a probit model that relates the measures of violent unrest, peaceful agitation, and political expedience to whether a peer voted against reform or not:

$$Prob(against\ reform_k = 1) = \Phi(\delta_0 + \mathbf{threat}_k\delta_1 + \mathbf{movement}_k\delta_2 + \delta_3 expedience_k + \mathbf{X}_k\delta_4), \quad (7.1)$$

where Φ is the distribution function of the standard normal distribution, *against reform* is equal to 1 if lord k voted against reform, and 0 if he supported it. The vector **threat** combines the various measures of violent unrest (e.g. violent unrest, urban violence); the vector **movement** collects the variables that proxy for social movement agitation (e.g. peaceful agitation, meetings, gatherings); the variable *expedience* accounts for the number of nomination (rotten) boroughs that a peer controlled. The vector **X** controls for the lord's political affiliation, his occupation, as well as for the number of years he sat in the House of Lords and, if applicable, in the House of Commons.

Attendance in the House of Lords was not mandatory and some lords attended very rarely. Many lords were not present in the House for the votes we consider and did not even vote by proxy. Thus, we cannot know how they would have voted had they been present. It is unlikely that absent lords were ignorant about when the votes would approximately take place and missed them at random. As with the MPs analysed in Chapter 5, we need to consider selection bias induced by non-random participation in the votes. For this purpose, we estimate a Heckman-probit model where we use the distance from a lord's country residence to London and the lord's age to estimate a selection equation which is similar to equation 5.2.

7.5 Evidence on the three hypotheses

7.5.1 Voting on reform

Table 7.6 reports the main results obtained by estimating equation 7.1 on the data from the three votes in the House of Lords for which a full record of who voted for and against exist. For each vote, we report three specifications: one for all types of unrest and agitation combined, one for violent unrest, and one for peaceful agitation as measured by the number of people involved in events either around a lord's country home or around his London home. All probit models include the proxy for political expedience (*nomination 1830–1832*) and the control variables, including the party affiliation dummy variable and variables related to political experience and occupation. We report marginal effects evaluated at the mean of the explanatory variables.

Let us start with the evidence related to the threat of revolution and the social movement hypothesis, respectively. Table 7.6 shows that the probability of voting against reform is increasing in the number of people involved in all types of unrest and agitation around a lord's country home in all three votes, with the point estimates being significant at the 1 to 5 percent level. Quantitatively, if the number of participants in the neighbourhood of a lord's country home were to increase by one standard deviation (by 40,100 until 7 October 1831, by 221,500 until 13 April 1832, and by 221,600 until 7 May 1832), then the probability of voting against the bill would increase by 6.42 percentage points on 7 October 1831 (column 1), by 79.74 percentage points on 13 April 1832 (column 4), and by 68.70 percentage points on 7 May 1832 (column 7). In contrast, the number of people involved in events that happened around a lord's London home did not have any effect.

When we distinguish between violent unrest and peaceful agitation, we find that it was exposure to violence around a lord's country home that made it more likely that he would vote against reform in the first two votes. However, in the amendment vote on 7 May 1832 that triggered the Days of May, it was peaceful agitation, again around the lord's country home, that hardened opposition to the bill.[7]

Figure 7.3, panels A and B, graphs the coefficients from (unreported) probit models that distinguish between three types of peaceful agitation (meetings, gatherings, and reform-related agitation) and between violent urban and rural unrest. They show that gatherings and reform-related agitation near the country home of a peer increased opposition to the bill in all votes, while violent urban protests had the same effect on the 7 October 1831 vote. Reform-related agitation near a peer's London home increased reform opposition in relation to the 13 April vote, but the effect is quantitatively small. The imprecise results related to events around the London home of a lord may indicate that as large landowners, most of them were primarily influenced by what happened in the countryside and in nearby provincial market towns rather than by what happened around their London home. It is, of course, also possible that the variation which we pick up with the 1-kilometre circles around the London homes is too noisy.[8]

[7] Table C7.2 in the supplementary material appendix reports the corresponding results for the number of events. The results are qualitatively similar but less precisely estimated. The supplementary material appendix is available at www.oup.com/us/peacefulandviolentorigins

[8] An alternative interpretation is that the lords, who would most likely all read the same London newspapers, did not pay particular attention to events near their home, but rather took note of what happened in London more generally.

Table 7.6 The determinants of the probability that a lord voted against reform in the three votes: probit estimates

	1	2	3	4	5	6	7	8	9
	Against Reform								
	7 October 1831			13 April 1832			7 May 1832		
All country home	0.016 (0.0058)***			0.0036 (0.00098)***			0.0031 (0.0010)***		
All London home	−0.0085 (0.012)			0.0021 (0.0015)			−0.00075 (0.0017)		
Violent country home		0.20 (0.063)***			0.014 (0.0024)***			0.020 (0.091)	
Violent London home		−0.090 (0.12)			0.012 (0.013)			0.013 (0.013)	
Peaceful country home			0.016 (0.0063)**			0.0047 (0.0016)***			0.0041 (0.0017)**
Peaceful London home			−0.0091 (0.014)			0.0022 (0.0016)			−0.0011 (0.0018)
Nomination 1830–1832	0.12 (0.089)	0.12 (0.089)	0.12 (0.090)	0.081 (0.080)	0.087 (0.077)	0.082 (0.080)	0.22 (0.085)**	0.20 (0.086)**	0.22 (0.086)**
Tory	0.88 (0.028)***	0.88 (0.028)***	0.88 (0.028)***	0.77 (0.037)***	0.76 (0.037)***	0.77 (0.037)***	0.82 (0.036)***	0.81 (0.064)***	0.82 (0.036)***

Army career	−0.028	−0.034	−0.028	−0.018	−0.027	−0.017	−0.020	−0.028	−0.021
	(0.13)	(0.13)	(0.13)	(0.099)	(0.098)	(0.099)	(0.10)	(0.10)	(0.10)
Years in House of Lords	0.027	0.032	0.027	0.041	0.045	0.040	−0.027	−0.027	−0.025
	(0.039)	(0.039)	(0.039)	(0.042)	(0.041)	(0.042)	(0.043)	(0.041)	(0.043)
Years in House of Commons	−0.084	−0.082	−0.085	−0.038	−0.031	−0.038	−0.040	−0.040	−0.040
	(0.040)**	(0.040)**	(0.040)**	(0.030)	(0.030)	(0.030)	(0.036)	(0.034)	(0.037)
Observations	322	322	322	325	325	325	252	252	252

Note: The variables related to violent unrest and peaceful agitation refer to the number of people involved in events around each lord's country or London home. In columns 1–3, these data are aggregated from 1 January 1828 to 7 October 1831; in columns 4–6, these data are aggregated from 1 January 1828 to 13 April 1832; in columns 7–9, these data are aggregated from 1 January 1828 to 7 May 1832. Marginal effects evaluated at the mean of the explanatory variables are shown. Constant not shown. Heteroskedasticity-robust standard errors are reported in brackets. * = Significant at the 10 percent level; ** = Significant at the 5 percent level; *** = Significant at the 1 percent level.

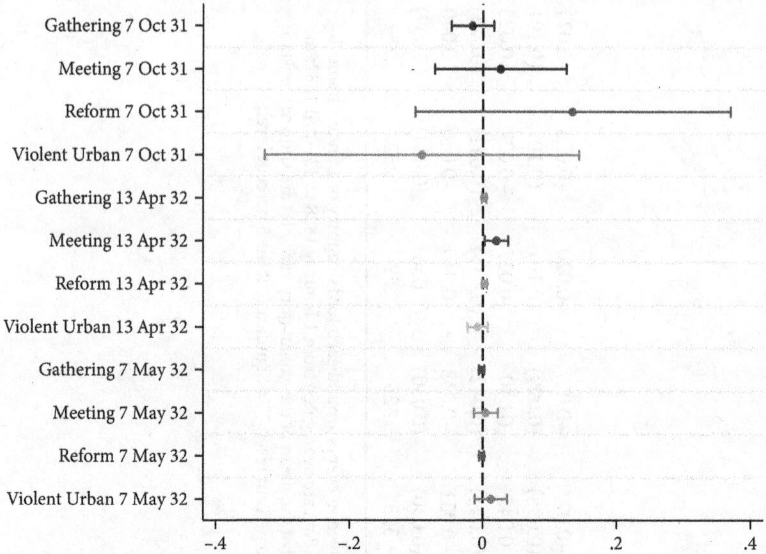

Panel A. Participants in events within 10 kilometres of country home

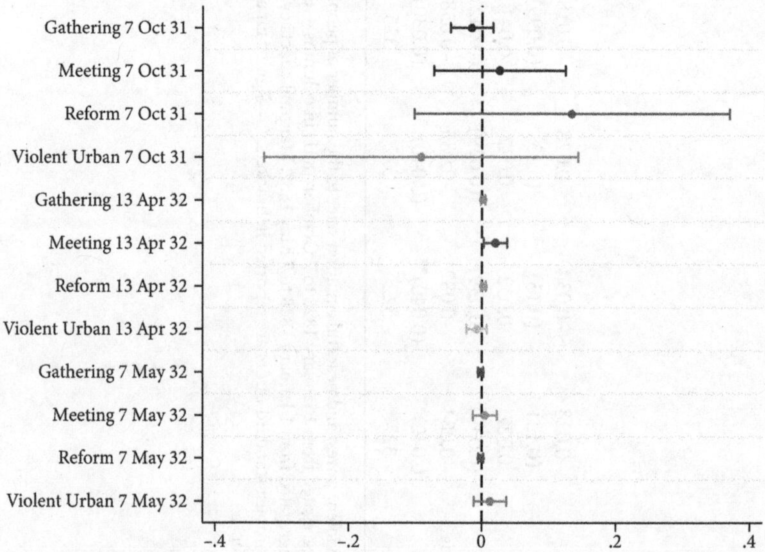

Panel B. Participants in events within 1 kilometre of London home

Figure 7.3 Probit estimates of the effect of different types of peaceful agitation or violent unrest around a lord's country or London home on the probability that a lord voted against reform in the three votes

Note: The circles indicate the marginal effect, evaluated at the mean, associated with a one unit increase in the explanatory variable indicated on the y-axis. These are estimated with probit models similar to those reported in Table 7.6. The explanatory variables refer to the number of people involved in events around either the country or London home of a peer. Panel A shows results for unrest and agitation that happened within 10 kilometres of the country home; panel B shows results for unrest and agitation within 1 kilometre of the London home.

Overall, the results from the statistical analysis indicate that the lords were *hardened* in their stance against reform both by peaceful agitation, including agitation specifically related to the reform question, and by violent unrest that occurred in the neighbourhood of their country home. This is inconsistent with both the social movement and the threat of revolution hypothesis. Moreover, it stands in sharp contrast to the reactions of the MPs in the House of Commons documented in Chapter 5. The MPs who were exposed to peaceful agitation around the constituency they represented were more likely to vote in favour of reform in the critical second reading vote in the Commons on 22 March 1831. The MPs also reacted to violent unrest by backing reform, but to a lesser extent. Conversely, the unelected lords were neither persuaded by expressions of popular support for reform, nor by fears of social violence. This difference in the reactions to unrest and agitation by the MPs and the lords suggests that constitutional rules, especially with respect to electoral accountability, can shape the response of politicians to extra-parliamentary reform pressures. While politicians who are elected respond positively to pressure from below, those who are not directly elected tend to harden their opposition to change.

With regard to the political expedience hypothesis, we observed from Table 7.6 that the lords who controlled nomination boroughs in 1830–1832, many of which would be disenfranchised by the Reform Bill, were significantly more likely (at the 5 percent level) to oppose reform in the last vote on 7 May 1832. Political expedience, thus, motivated some lords, in particular towards the end of the legislative process in a vote that was focused on the question of seat redistribution. In Chapter 5, we documented that this was also the case for some of the MPs in the House of Commons. This suggests that self-interest played a role for both elite groups.

The probit models reported in Table 7.6 include four control variables: *Tory*, *army career*, *years in House of Lords*, and *years in House of Commons*. Unsurprisingly, we find that Tory lords were much more likely to oppose reform than Whig and independent lords in all the votes. This reflects the general opposition to reform amongst the Tories.[9] In addition, lords who had previously served for many years in the House of Commons where less likely to vote against reform, in particular in the first vote on 7 October 1831. One possible reason for this is that lords who had, before elevation, served in the House of Commons for many years behaved more like the MPs and were more attuned to social movement demands and agitation from outside Parliament. This would be consistent with the social movement hypothesis. Conversely, the fact that the variable *years*

[9] In additional estimations (not reported), we find that interactions between the various measures of unrest and agitation around a lord's country home and the Tory dummy variable never are significant. In other words, the Tories and Whigs did not react differently to peaceful agitation and violent unrest.

in House of Lords is insignificant in all three votes indicates that political generations did not matter for the opposition to the bill: 'Pitt's lords' (lords appointed on the recommendation of Pitt the Younger around the turn of the century) did not try to block reform to any larger extent than other lords, in line with the conjecture of Turberville (1958, 51–52). Finally, peers with an army career were not more or less likely to oppose reform than those without.

7.5.2 Attendance and selection effects

Many lords did not attend the votes, and attendance might not have been random. To investigate if the results reported above are subject to selection bias, we re-estimate equation 7.1 with the Heckman-probit estimator that accounts for self-selection. Table C7.3 in the supplementary material appendix reports the results while Table C7.4 in the supplementary material appendix records information about the lords who were absent from all three votes.

In the selection equation, we find that the age of the lord is not a good predictor of participation, most likely because the peers were old on average. However, distance to London from the country home of a lord has the expected sign, and is significant in all but one specification: a long travel distance from the country home to London would, therefore, be one reason why some lords did not attend specific votes. In Chapter 5, we found the opposite for the MPs in the House of Commons, that is, that it was age and not travel distance that deterred participation. Importantly, the Heckman correction has very minor effects on the outcome equation 7.1. It does, therefore, not appear that selection bias is a major concern in practice.

7.5.3 Change in voting behaviour across votes

Another way to analyse support and opposition to the Reform Bill among the lords is to track their voting record over time and ask why some of them changed their mind. As a matter of fact, only one peer who voted against reform on 7 October 1831 (as part of the majority) changed his mind and voted for reform (as part of the minority) on 7 May 1832: Henry Peyto-Verney, sixteenth Baron Willoughby de Broke and de jure twenty-fourth Baron Latimer (1773-1852). He was a Tory from an old aristocratic family (the creation of the peerage by writ dating back to 1492). Conversely, three peers voted for reform on 7 October 1831, but opposed the amendment on 7 May 1832: Charles Rose Ellis (1771–1845), George Granville Leveson-Gower, Earl Gower (1758–1833), and Peter Robert Drummond-Burrell (1782–1865). All three sat in the House of

Commons before joining the House of Lords; however, they came from different backgrounds. Charles Rose Ellis was heir to a family fortune that included a plantation in Jamaica and owed his peerage to his lifelong friendship with George Canning. Therefore, as a liberal Canningite Tory, it is maybe not surprising that he flip-flopped around the question of parliamentary reform. George Granville Leveson-Gower and Peter Robert Drummond-Burrell were both heirs to aristocratic families. They had been loosely affiliated with the Whigs when they sat in the House of Commons, but they might have disliked some of the more 'radical' policies of the Whig leadership. If anything, Drummond-Burrell's allegiance evolved enough in the wake of the Great Reform Act for him to ultimately side with the Tories (Olney 1973, 19). These changes of heart are obviously too few for any meaningful statistical analysis.

What we can do instead is to focus on the 177 English peers who opposed the Reform Bill in the first vote on 7 October 1831 and investigate statistically why 49 of them decided to abstain in the vote on 7 May 1832 related to postponing the discussion of the schedules.[10] For the forty-nine peers who did so, we interpret this move as a softening of their opposition, and we ask whether violent unrest and peaceful agitation from outside Parliament can explain this shift. In so doing, we provide a test of the social movement and the threat of revolution hypotheses that condition on unobserved (fixed) individual characteristics.[11]

Table 7.7 reports the results of this analysis. First, for events near a lord's country home, we find an asymmetry: the number of people involved in peaceful agitation does not explain the switch, while involvement in violent agitation does have an effect (albeit only significant at the 10 percent level). The coefficient is, however, negative: more violent unrest around the country home hardened opposition.[12]

Second, for events around a lord's London home, it is the other way around: peaceful agitation but not violent unrest had an effect (Table 7.7, column 3). This is corroborated by the fact that all types of peaceful agitation (gatherings, meetings, and reform-related agitation) have a significant effect on the likelihood that a lord would abstain on 7 May 1832 (Table 7.7, columns 4 to 6). However, all these point estimates are negative, not positive. In other words, if there were

[10] Along with the peers who abstained, we include Peyto-Verney who opposed the Reform Bill on 7 October 1831 and voted for the amendment on 7 May 1832.

[11] We chose to compare the results of the first vote on the entire bill on 7 October 1831 to those on the amendment on 7 May 1831 and not to those on the vote on the entire bill on 13 April 1832 for two reasons. First, it seems more natural to compare the first and last vote on reform in the House of Lords. Arguably, the defeat of the government on the amendment was a major setback for reform, leading to the resignation of Lord Grey. Second, fewer lords switched sides between 7 October 1831 and 13 April 1832.

[12] In additional (unreported) regressions, we find that the results remain the same if we consider all the peers who voted on 7 October 1831 and/or if we only code events that happened between 7 October 1831 and 7 May 1832.

Table 7.7 The impact of violent unrest and peaceful agitation on the probability that a lord would change his mind between 7 October 1831 and 7 May 1832: probit estimates

	1	2	3	4	5	6	7
	From reform opposition on 7 October 1831 to abstention on 7 May 1832						
All country home	−0.0012 (0.00084)						
All London home	−0.0038 (0.0014)***						
Violent country home		−0.0042 (0.0024)*					
Violent London home		−0.0079 (0.0083)					
Peaceful country home			−0.0016 (0.0013)				
Peaceful London home			−0.0042 (0.0015)***				
Gatherings country home				−0.0026 (0.0017)			
Gatherings London home				−0.0042 (0.0017)**			
Meetings country home					−0.0025 (0.0061)		
Meetings London home					−0.032 (0.0089)***		

Reform country home						−0.0019	
						(0.0016)	
Reform London home						−0.0048	
						(0.0017)***	
Violent Urban country home							−0.0043
							(0.0024)*
Violent Urban London home							−0.0079
							(0.0083)
Observations	177	177	177	177	177	177	177

Note: Marginal effects evaluated at the mean of the explanatory variables are shown. Heteroskedasticity-robust standard errors are reported in brackets. The violent unrest and peaceful agitation variables are aggregated between 1 January 1828 and 7 May 1832. All estimations include the controls reported in Table 7.6, including party affiliation. * = Significant at the 10 percent level; ** = Significant at the 5 percent level; *** = Significant at the 1 percent level.

more peaceful agitation of any type near a reform-unfriendly peer's London home, then he would be less likely to abstain in the later vote, that is, he would harden rather than soften his opposition to the Reform Bill. Taken together, these results are, therefore, additional evidence against the social movement and the threat of revolution hypothesis.

7.5.4 The final vote on 4 June 1832

On 4 June 1832, the Reform Bill was subject to the final vote in the House of Lords. It was supported by a majority of 106 against 22. Table 7.8 records the personal characteristics of these twenty-two hardliner lords who opposed reform to the end. Most of them came from aristocratic families (only three had been raised to the peerage), twelve were members of the House of Commons before their elevation to the Lords, and all but three were Tories. Importantly, eight of them controlled nomination boroughs and therefore stood to lose influence in the House of Commons. It is plausible that they viewed any reform that involved redistribution of seats as a potential attack on their privileges and on their influence in the lower House, as suggested by the political expedience hypothesis.

7.6 William IV and the threat from above

If the lords were not influenced by peaceful agitation and violent unrest, it raises the question as to why they eventually withdraw their opposition to the Reform Bill: did they give in to pressure from above rather than to threats or agitation from below? The historical evidence suggests that William IV's personal intervention in the reform process was the pivotal reason that they relented.

William IV was the third son of George III and had ascended to the throne a few months before the reform process started in 1830. Judging from the writings of his contemporaries and later biographies (see Fitzgerald (1884), Allen (1960), Ziegler (1971), and specifically Somerset (1980) for the iconography), he appears to have been politically inexperienced and was certainly less skillful than many of the leading politicians of his reign. Importantly, he was not fundamentally in opposition to the Whig government or to the reform project, as is evident from his willingness to dissolve Parliament at the request of Lord Grey in March 1831 and to contemplate the idea of creating pro-reform (Whig) lords.

As we saw above, following Wellington's refusal to form a government on 15 May 1832, William IV called on Lord Grey to return to government. In his

Table 7.8 The twenty-two lords who voted against the Reform Bill on 4 June 1832

Name	Title	Birth year	Politics	Peerage	Occupation	MP in the House of Commons	Years in House of Commons	Entered the House of Lords in	First in Family Raised to the Peerage	Family Raised to Peerage in	Nomination 1830-32
Bexley	Baron	1766	Tory	English	Lawyer	Yes	27	1823	Yes	1823	0
Carrington	Baron	1752	Tory	Irish	Banker	Yes	18	1797	Yes	1796	2
Carteret	Baron	1770	Tory	English	Born Pol.	Yes	22	1826	No	1784	0
Clanbrassill	Baron (Earl Of Roden)	1788	Tory	Irish	Born Pol.	Yes	14	1820	No	1665	1
Dartmouth	Earl	1784	Tory	English	Born Pol.	Yes	1	1810	No	1682	1
Delamere	Baron	1767	Tory	English	Landowner	Yes	16	1821	No	1821	0
Doneraile	Viscount	1786	Tory	Irish	Landowner	No	–	1819	No	1776	0
Ellenborough	Baron	1790	Tory	English	Born Pol.	Yes	5	1818	No	1802	6
Gage (Viscount Gage)	Baron/ Viscount	1791	Tory	Irish	Born Pol.	No	–	1812	No	1622	0
Gordon	Viscount (Earl of Aberdeen)	1784	Tory	Scottish	Born Pol.	No	–	1801	No	1642	2

continued

Table 7.8 *continued*

Name	Title	Birth year	Politics	Peerage	Occupation	MP in the House of Commons	Years in House of Commons	Entered the House of Lords in	First in Family Raised to the Peerage	Family Raised to Peerage in	Nomination 1830-32
Grantley	Baron	1796	Tory	English	Born Pol.	No	–	1822	No	1782	0
Guildford	Earl	1772	Unaffiliated	English	Clergyman	No	–	1827	No	1683	0
Malmesbury	Earl	1778	Tory	English	Born Pol.	Yes	13	1820	No	1788	4
Mansfield	Earl	1777	Tory	Scottish	Lawyer	No	–	1798	No	1605	0
Monson	Baron	1809	Unaffiliated	English	Born Pol.	No	–	1830	No	1611	0
Newcastle	Duke	1785	Tory	English	Born Pol.	Yes	–	1806	No	1572	0
Poulett	Earl	1783	Tory	English	Landowner	No	–	1819	No	1627	0
Powis	Earl	1754	Tory	Irish	Born Pol.	Yes	20	1794	No	1762	1
Rolle	Baron	1756	Tory	English	Born Pol.	Yes	16	1796	Yes	1796	0
Strathallan	Earl	1767	Tory	Scottish	Merchant	Yes	12	1824	No	1686	5
Westmorland	Earl	1759	Tory	English	Born Pol.	No	–	1774	No	1624	0
Willoughby De Eresby	Baron	1782	Whig	English	Born Pol.	Yes	8	1820	No	1313	0

Note: The Baron of Clanbrassill was also known as Earl of Roden, while the Viscount Gordon was also known as the Earl of Aberdeen. The Viscount Gage was also a baron in the peerage of Great Britain. The term 'born pol.' refers to individuals who were either appointed (via a nomination seat) or elected (in an open seat) to the House of Commons or who took up a seat in the House of Lords as soon as they became of age.

Sources: Hansard HL Deb, 4 June 1832, series 2, vol. 13, c373, Lodge (1832), Dod and Dod (1832), Namier and Brooke (1964), Stooks Smith (1973), Thorne (1986), and Fisher (2009).

acceptance reply, Lord Grey wrote that he considered the creation of a sufficient number of peers necessary for the Reform Bill to pass. On 18 May, accompanied by Brougham, Grey met the King at Windsor Castle. At the end of the meeting, Brougham asked the King to put his promise to create peers in writing, something that William IV, unlike in January 1832 when the issue of creation had first come up, finally agreed to do (Brougham (1871, Vol. 3, 199–201) Allen (1960, 151), Ziegler (1971, 219–220)). On top of that, the King had, the day before, instructed his private secretary, Sir Herbert Taylor (1775–1839), to send a letter in his name to a dozen peers, including Wellington, asking them to withdraw their opposition to the Reform Bill. This letter, along with the written commitment, convinced many Tory lords that the King would create peers if they kept on opposing reform. Since they did not wish to lose their majority in the House of Lords, many Tory peers chose not to attend the third reading of the Reform Bill on 4 June 1832, knowing that the bill would then pass.

The evidence, therefore, suggests that the Tory lords were not swayed by the threat from below but reacted to a threat from above. These interactions between the Whig Cabinet, the two Houses of Parliament, and the King can be seen as manifestations of constitutional bargaining within the King-Parliament template of Congleton (2011). An influential faction within the political elite, who wanted to preserve the status quo, was locked into an equilibrium relationship with another faction that wanted to overturn it and reallocate policymaking authority. Without a shock to the initial equilibrium, the status quo would prevail because there were no deals to be made that would benefit all factions. Viewed in this way, the rise in social unrest in the spring of 1832 can be interpreted as the shock that allowed a new constitutional bargain to be reached. The King wanted to calm tensions and agreed to create sufficient new lords. This, in turn, created space for a new bargain between the Whigs and the Tories whereby the Tory lords accepted a reformed House of Commons in return for preserving policymaking authority in the House of Lords.

7.7 Conclusion

The behaviour of the lords stands in sharp contrast to that of the MPs, which we analysed in Chapter 5. The way the lords voted cannot be explained by the social movement or the threat of revolution hypothesis. Neither peaceful agitation, be it in the form of gatherings or meetings, nor violent unrest enticed the lords to support reform. In fact, it made them more likely to vote against. Clearly, the lords did not respond with acquiescence to pressure from below. In contrast, we find some evidence supporting the political expedience hypothesis in that lords who controlled nomination boroughs, which were singled out to be disenfranchised by the Reform Bill, were more like to oppose the bill.

Overall, our statistical analysis is in line with the historiographical narrative and suggests that the lords were not moved by threats of social unrest and revolution or convinced by agitation from social movements (Brock 1973; Cannon 1973). They were instead swayed by political expediency and by a credible threat from the King that he would create enough new pro-reform Whig lords to carry the bill in the House of Lords if the peers did not accept the reform. Thus, it was only when they were faced with a credible threat of a sweeping creation of peers that they abandoned their steadfast opposition to it. Insofar as the House of Lords continued to have a major influence on legislation years later, many peers served in the Cabinet long after 1832, and it was possible for a Prime Minister to govern from the House of Lords as late as in 1902, it might be said that their political judgement was sound.

Chapter 8
Conclusion

This book emphasises the process aspect of democratic reform. Rather than treating reform as one discrete event, it argues that much can be learned about the causes of democratisation by focusing on sub-events within the reform process. In the case of the Great Reform Act of 1832, this perspective shows that different causal forces played pivotal roles at different points in the Reform Bill's journey through the Unreformed British Parliament. In short, this book offers new insights into the root causes of democratisation and shows, through detailed econometric analysis of rich micro-political data, how theoretically relevant factors play a crucial role in particular instances and not in others and helped the reformers navigate numerous roadblocks.

Our empirical analysis shows that bottom-up theories, whereby the elite only reluctantly agree to share power with groups whose goals they oppose, explain important aspects of the reform process. The threat of revolution hypothesis offers a convincing explanation for the electoral victory of the pro-reform Whigs in the 1831 General Election (roadblock 3): the direct exposition of the voters of the Unreformed Parliament to violent riots around their constituencies increased their fear of revolution and induced them to act on that by electing reform-friendly MPs. In contrast, the threat of revolution hypothesis does not provide a convincing account for how the other roadblocks were overcome.

The other bottom-up theory of democratisation—the social movement hypothesis—whereby peaceful agitation, lobbying, and mass mobilisation in support of reform originating from social movements and groups outside the ruling elite convince politicians to democratise, can, however, help explain how the Reform Bill overcame the second roadblock. At the start of the reform process, the reformers needed to garner majority support in the House of Commons. Social movement agitation played a pivotal role in securing the one-vote majority in the critical vote in March 1831 as our analysis suggests that a critical number of MPs responded positively to peaceful means of reform agitation.

The bottom-up theories of democratisation cannot, however, explain how the reform process overcame the other roadblocks: the Duke of Wellington's resignation which enabled Charles Grey to become Prime Minister and form a pro-reform government (roadblock 1), the stalemate in the House of Lords leading to Grey's resignation and the Days of May (roadblock 4), and the final promise by King William IV to Grey that he would create new pro-reform peers

Peaceful and Violent Origins of Voting Rights. Toke S. Aidt and Raphaël Franck, Oxford University Press.
 DOI: 10.1093/9780197679746.003.0008

leading to the surrender of the lords (roadblock 5). In fact, our empirical analysis establishes that the peers in the House of Lords were not swayed in their opposition to reform by pressure from below, neither in the form of pro-reform social movement agitation, nor in the form of violent social unrest and threats of revolution.

The fall of the first roadblock, which began the reform process, can best be thought of as a random shock to the political system which was not directly related to the reform question. The split in the Tory party around Catholic emancipation ultimately triggered Wellington's downfall, and it is unlikely that any of the Tories tried (and failed) to prevent the fall *because* they foresaw that it would lead to reform of Parliament. Nonetheless, the downfall enabled Grey to take office and pursue parliamentary reform. Our analysis of the fourth and fifth roadblocks, related to getting the Reform Bill through the House of Lords, vindicates one of the top-down theories of democratisation. It can be interpreted as an instance of constitutional bargaining between various members of the elite (Congleton 2011). The social unrest during the Days of May had created new opportunities for constitutional bargaining between the King and the lords, primarily because William IV, in the volatile atmosphere, finally committed to eliminate the Tory majority in the House of Lords if the lords kept on opposing the bill. With that threat hanging in the air, many reform-opposing Tory lords decided to strike a bargain: accept the reform of the House of Commons in return for keeping control of the House of Lords.

Our empirical analysis does not provide any clear-cut evidence on other strands of top-down democratisation theories. Grey's reform agenda, and that of the Whigs more generally, was to change the franchise rules in order to deal with the worst cases of electoral corruption and the unbalanced distribution of seats. However, our analysis does not indicate that the reform process was driven by the prospect of long-term electoral advantage, by Pareto-improvement schemes to provide public goods, or by the exchange of political rights for tax payments. We nonetheless find clear evidence that both the MPs in the House of Commons and the peers in the House of Lords were motivated by political expedience and self-interest. While this is consistent with the general notion of top-down democratisation, it does not speak to specific top-down theories.

Seen in this perspective, the book provides new insights into the causal drivers of democratisation which enhance our understanding of the relative importance of competing theories. Whether the Great Reform Act by itself was a major step towards democracy in Britain and whether it deserves the adjective 'great' is an open question. In hindsight, it is, of course, easy to dismiss claims made by some peers that the Reform Bill would entirely overthrow British society and lead to the abolition of private property rights. For instance, in March 1833, the Duke of Wellington told his friend John Wilson Croker (1780–1857), a former Tory MP and first secretary to the Admiralty, that

> The operation of the Reform Bill, though it would probably be slow, was nevertheless sure. The old aristocratical interest has great stamina, and will hold together a long while, but seeing how it has yielded before this shock when in its entire strength, what is it to do in a succession of shocks, each of which will give fresh powers to the democracy? (Croker 1884, Vol. 2, 11)

It is also clear that the Great Reform Act did not lead to a full extension of the franchise, as only about five percent of the total population was able to vote in 1833, the ballot remained open, and many areas were left without parliamentary representation. It took at least six more reforms before elections could be considered free and fair and for women to obtain voting rights.

A useful way to provide a longer-term perspective on the 'greatness' of the Great Reform Act is to compare it to each subsequent reform of the House of Commons in 1867, 1872, 1884–1885, 1918, and 1928. Figure 8.1 plots two

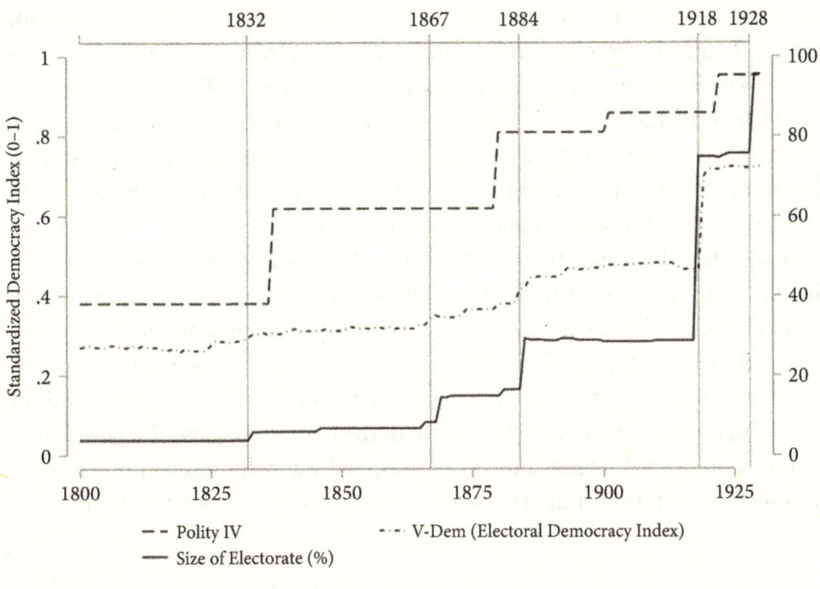

Figure 8.1 The Great Reform Act in perspective: democracy indices for Britain, 1800–1930

Note: The figure shows on the left-hand y-axis, the Polity IV index, re-coded to range from 0 (hereditary monarchy) to 1 (consolidated democracy), and the V-Dem Electoral Democracy index, which codes five components of electoral democracy: freedom of association, suffrage, clean elections, elected executive, and freedom of expression and alternative sources of information on a scale from 0 to 1. The percentage of the adult population (aged twenty and above) that could vote is measured on the right-hand y-axis. The Polity IV and the V-Dem Electoral Democracy indices refer to Great Britain while the voter data are for England and Wales only.

Sources: Marshall and Gurr (2020), Coppedge et al. (2023) and Flora et al. (1983).

commonly used indices of democracy—the Polity IV index and the V-Dem Electoral Democracy index—along with the evolution of the size of the electorate, measured as the percentage of the adult population with the right to vote in parliamentary elections, between 1800 and 1930.

These indices capture important components of democracy but emphasise different aspects. The Polity IV index focuses on five aspects of political authority patterns: (i) competitiveness of executive recruitment, (ii) openness of executive recruitment, (iii) executive constraints, (iv) regulation of participation, and (v) competitiveness of participation. When the Great Reform Act is measured by the Polity IV index, it stands out as the key event in Britain's journey to democracy. The index exhibits a large upwards shift a few years after the Reform Bill in 1837 and smaller improvements in 1880, 1901, and 1922. The large improvement in 1837 can be directly traced to the 1832 reform insofar as it improved institutionalised procedures regarding the transfer of executive power and the competitiveness of parliamentary elections. In contrast, the Polity IV index does not register any 'jumps' around the second and third Reform Acts.

Instead, the V-Dem Electoral Democracy index codes freedom of association, suffrage, clean elections, elected executive, as well as freedom of expression and alternative sources of information. It singles out the fourth Reform Act in 1918 as the key event and shows very little upwards movement around the three other reform bills. A similar picture emerges if we focus on the size of the electorate: its increase is the smallest after the Great Reform Act and becomes progressively larger for each of the subsequent reform bills until 1918.

How 'great', then, was the Great Reform Act? This book suggests that the answer to this question critically depends on the aspect of democracy one considers. Arguably, the Great Reform Act was mostly 'great' because it was the first in a sequence of reforms of the British political system. It opened the door for reform of the municipal corporations and the Poor Laws in the second half of the 1830s, for the Factory Act, the repeal of the Corn Laws, and the permanent introduction of the income tax in the 1840s, and was followed by the sequence of subsequent reforms of the House of Commons. It got the snowball rolling.

Historical printed sources

Census of Great Britain, 1801 (PP 1801–1802, vol. 6, VI.1 (9))
Census of Great Britain 1811 (PP 1812, vol. 11, XI.547 (317))
Census of Great Britain 1821 (PP 1822, vol. 15, XV.1 (502))
Census of Great Britain 1831 (PP 1833, vol. 36–38, XXXVI.1, XXXVII.1, XXXVIII.1 (149))
Census of Religious Worship 1851 (PP, 1852–1853, vol. 89, LXXXIX.1 (1690))
Cobbett's Parliamentary History (Bodleian Libraries, University of Oxford)
House of Commons Hansard (HC), Parliamentary Debates, printed by T. C. Hansard (1803–1831)
House of Lords Hansard (HL), Parliamentary Debates, printed by T. C. Hansard (1803–1831)
House of Commons Parliamentary Papers (PP), with references given in the text
Journal of the House of Commons (JHC), with references given in the text.

Newspapers

Morning Chronicle (London, England)
The Morning Post (London, England)
The Examiner (London, England)
The Political Register (London, England)
The Times (London, England)
The Royal Cornwall Gazette (Cornwall, England)

A note on the book cover

The book cover is a satirical print titled 'The reformers' attack on the old rotten tree; or the foul nests of the cormorants in danger' showing the primary (and secondary) actors of the Great Reform Act.

M. Dorothy George provides the following description in the 'Catalogue of Political and Personal Satires in the British Museum' (XI, 1954):

> Reformers (left) attack with axes a decayed tree, inscribed 'Rotten Borough System', which anti-Reformers (right) try to support, with arms or props. The tree has bare branches, on which are nests (rotten boroughs) containing cormorants. Nests and the branches near them are inscribed with the names of boroughs: 'Bossiney', 'Beeralston', 'Brackley' (twice], 'Heyden' (twice), (Higham) 'Ferrers', 'Newton', 'West Looe', 'Westbury', 'Bramber', 'Woodstock', 'East Looe', 'Seaford', 'Wendover', 'Old Sarum', 'Gatton', 'Blechingley', 'Bishops Castle', 'Wootem (Wootton) Basset', 'Bedwin', 'Petersfield', 'Boroughbridge' (large and central nest, cf. No. 16602, &c), 'Yarmouth', 'Dunwich', 'Aldborough', 'Appleby', 'Callington', 'Midhurst', 'Whitchurch', 'Orford', 'Saltash'. (A selection from the sixty doomed boroughs, but Westbury was to send one M.P.)
>
> At the base of the hollow trunk is a gaping hole from which serpents emerge, darting fangs at the Reformers. Toadstools, toad, and snake surround it. The foremost Reformers are Brougham, in wig and gown, and Grey: the former's axe-shaft is the mace, the blade is inscribed 'Reform Reform the Laws'. Between them are a boyish Lansdowne (his axe is inscribed 'Landsdowne') and Althorp whose axe is 'Bum Chopper'. Others are poorly characterized. Grey passively holds his axe, 'Grey's Family Chopper', against his shoulder, and hides behind his back a paper, 'Nepotism' (see BM Satires No. 16578,&c.). Burdett brandishes his axe. On the extreme left a man, probably Thomas Attwood, holds up a bludgeon with a blade inscribed 'Union Chopper'. Others are merely indicated.
>
> On the opposite side Peel sits with his back against the leaning trunk, while Wellington supports it with both hands; Scarlett, in wig and gown, hands on knees, pushes his posterior against that of Wellington (probably an allusion to the libel actions, see No. 16009, &c). Ellenborough also supports the tree with his arms, and with an elephant's trunk attached to his profile (see BM Satires No. 16038, &c). The dandified Marquis of 'Chandos' uses a prop inscribed with his name (see BM Satires No. 16768) as does Newcastle. Others cannot be identified. From this Tory band rise the words: 'You take our house when you do take the prop / That dost sustain our house / you take our lives / When you do take the means whereby we live' ('The Merchant of Venice', IV. i, adapted.)
>
> In the background (left), behind the Reformers, is a grassy hill, 'Constitution Hill' (cf. BM Satires No. 16634). On this, silhouetted against a huge rising sun, the King [William IV], in admiral's uniform, waving his hat, stands arm-in-arm with the Queen. Near them, also hat in hand, are Pat brandishing a shillelagh, John Bull in a smock, and Sandy in a kilt.

Bibliography

Abadie, A., Drukker, D., Herr, J. L. and Imbens, G. W. (2004), 'Implementing Matching Estimators for Average Treatment Effects in Stata', *The Stata Journal* **4**(3), 290–311.

Abadie, A. and Imbens, G. W. (2006), 'Large Sample Properties of Matching Estimators for Average Treatment Effects', *Econometrica* **74**(1), 235–267.

Acemoglu, D. (2009), *Introduction to Modern Economic Growth*, Princeton University Press, Princeton, NJ.

Acemoglu, D., Johnson, S., Robinson, J. A. and Yared, P. (2008), 'Income and Democracy', *American Economic Review* **98**(3), 808–842.

Acemoglu, D., Naidu, S., Restrepo, P. and Robinson, J. A. (2015), Democracy, Redistribution, and Inequality, *in* A. B. Atkinson and F. Bourguignon, eds, 'Handbook of Income Distribution', Vol. 2, Elsevier, Amsterdam, pp. 1885–1966.

Acemoglu, D. and Robinson, J. A. (2000a), 'Democratization or Repression?', *European Economic Review* **44**(4-6), 683–693.

Acemoglu, D. and Robinson, J. A. (2000b), 'Why Did the West Extend the Franchise? Democracy, Inequality, and Growth in Historical Perspective', *Quarterly Journal of Economics* **115**(4), 1167–1199.

Acemoglu, D. and Robinson, J. A. (2001), 'A Theory of Political Transitions', *American Economic Review* **91**(4), 938–963.

Acemoglu, D. and Robinson, J. A. (2006), *Economic Origins of Dictatorship and Democracy*, Cambridge University Press, Cambridge.

Adams, J. (2014), *Women and the Vote. A World History*, Oxford University Press, Oxford.

Aidt, T. S., Albornoz, F., and Hauk, E. (2021), 'Foreign Influence and Domestic Policy', *Journal of Economic Literature* **59**(2), 426–487.

Aidt, T. S. and Dallal, B. (2008), 'Female Voting Power: The Contribution of Women's Suffrage to the Growth of Social Spending in Western Europe (1869-1960)', *Public Choice* **134**(3-4), 391–417.

Aidt, T. S., Daunton, M. and Dutta, J. (2010), 'The Retrenchment Hypothesis and the Extension of the Franchise in England and Wales', *Economic Journal* **120**(547), 990–1020.

Aidt, T. S., Dutta, J. and Loukoianova, E. (2006), 'Democracy Comes to Europe: Franchise Extension and Fiscal Outcomes 1830-1938', *European Economic Review* **50**(2), 249–283.

Aidt, T. S. and Eterovic, D. (2011), 'Political Competition, Participation and Public Finance in 20th Century Latin America', *European Journal of Political Economy* **27**(1), 181–200.

Aidt, T. S. and Franck, R. (2013), 'How to Get the Snowball Rolling and Extend the Franchise: Voting on the Great Reform Act of 1832.', *Public Choice* **155**(3-4), 229–250.

Aidt, T. S., and Franck, R. (2015), 'Democratization under the Threat of Revolution: Evidence from the Great Reform Act of 1832', *Econometrica* **83**(2), 505–547.

Aidt, T. S. and Franck, R. (2019), 'What Motivates an Oligarchic Elite to Democratize? Evidence from the Roll Call Vote on the Great Reform Act of 1832', *Journal of Economic History* **79**(3), 773–825.

Aidt, T. S. and Franck, R. (2025), Democratization and the Threat of Revolution, *in* C. Bjørnskov and R. Jong-A-Pin, eds, 'Encyclopedia of Public Choice', Edward Elgar, Cheltenham, UK.

Aidt, T. S. and Jensen, P. S. (2009), 'The Taxman Tools Up: An Event History Study of the Introduction of the Personal Income Tax, 1815-1941', *Journal of Public Economics* **93**(1-2), 160–175.

Aidt, T. S., and Jensen, P. S. (2013), 'Democratization and the Size of Government: Evidence from the Long 19th Century', *Public Choice* **157**(3–4), 511–542.

Aidt, T. S. and Jensen, P. S. (2014), 'Workers of the World, Unite! Franchise Extensions and the Threat of Revolution in Europe 1820-1938', *European Economic Review* **72**, 52–75.

Aidt, T. S. and Jensen, P. S. (2017), 'From Open to Secret Ballot: Vote Buying and Modernization', *Comparative Political Studies* **50**(5), 555–593.

Aidt, T. S. and Leon-Ablan, G. (2016), 'The Democratic Window of Opportunity: Evidence from Riots in Sub-Saharan Africa', *Journal of Conflict Resolution* **60**(4), 694–717.

Aidt, T. S. and Leon-Ablan, G. (2022), 'The Interaction of Structural Factors and Diffusion in Social Unrest: Evidence from the Swing Riots', *British Journal of Political Science* **52**(2), 869–885.

Aidt, T. S. and Leon-Ablan, G. (2023), 'Does Political Representation Increase Activism? Evidence from the Great Reform Act of 1832', Working paper, Cambridge.

Aidt, T. S., Leon-Ablan, G. and Satchell, M. (2022), 'The Social Dynamics of Collective Action: Evidence from the Diffusion of the Swing Riots', *Journal of Politics* **84**(1), 209–225.

Aidt, T. S., Winer, S. and Zhang, P. (2022), 'Franchise Extension and Fiscal Structure in the United Kingdom 1820-1913: A New Test of the Redistribution Hypothesis', *Cliometrica* **16**(3), 547–574.

Albert, W. (1972), *The Turnpike Road System in England 1663-1840*, Cambridge University Press, Cambridge.

Allen, R. C. (2009), *The British Industrial Revolution in Global Perspective*, Cambridge University Press, Cambridge.

Allen, W. G. (1960), *William IV*, Cresset Press, London.

Altonji, J. G., Taber, C. R. and Elder, T. E. (2005), 'Selection on Observed and Unobserved Variables: Assessing the Effectiveness of Catholic Schools', *Journal of Political Economy* **113**(1), 151–184.

Angrist, J. D., Graddy, K. and Imbens, G. W. (2000), 'The Interpretation of Instrumental Variables Estimators in Simultaneous Equations Models with an Application to the Demand for Fish', *Review of Economic Studies* **67**(3), 499–527.

Ansell, B. and Samuels, D. (2010), 'Inequality and Democratization: A Contractarian Approach', *Comparative Political Studies* **43**(12), 1543–1574.

Ansell, B. and Samuels, D. (2014), *Inequality and Democratization: An Elite-competition Approach*, Cambridge University Press, Cambridge.

Archer, J. E. (2000), *Social Unrest and Popular Protest in England, 1780-1840*, Cambridge University Press, Cambridge.

Aspinall, A. (1952), *Three Early Nineteenth Century Diaries*, Williams & Norgate, London.

Aspinall, A. (1973), *Politics and the Press, 1780-1850*, The Harvester Press, Brighton.

Austen-Smith, D. (1994), 'Strategic Transmission of Costly Information', *Econometrica* **62**(4), 955–963.

Banks, J. (1970), *Marxist Sociology in Action: A Sociological Critique of the Marxist Approach to Industrial Relations*, Faber & Faber, London.

Barker, H. (2000), *Newspapers, Politics and English Society, 1695-1855*, Longman, New York.

Barker, H. and Vincent, D. (2001), *Language, Print and Electoral Politics, 1790-1832 - Newcastle-under-Lyme Broadsides*, Boydell Press, Woodbridge.

Barrell, C. (2021), *History and Historiography in Classical Utilitarianism, 1800-1865*, Cambridge University Press, Cambridge.

Barrios, T., Diamond, R., Imbens, G. W. and Kolesár, M. (2012), 'Clustering, Spatial Correlations, and Randomization Inference', *Journal of the American Statistical Association* **107**(498), 578–591.

Becker, S. O. and Ichino, A. (2002), 'Estimation of Average Treatment Effects Based on Propensity Scores', *The Stata Journal* **2**(4), 358–377.

Ben-Israel, H. (1968), *English Historians on the French Revolution*, Cambridge University Press, Cambridge.

Bentham, J. (1817), *Plan of Parliamentary Reform, in the Form of a Catechism, with Reasons for each Article: with an Introduction, Shewing the Necessity of Radical, and the Inadequacy of Moderate, Reform*, R. Hunter, St Paul Churchyard, UK.

Bentham, J. (1819), *Bentham's Radical Reform bill, with Extracts from the Reasons*, E. Wilson, London.

Berlinski, S. and Dewan, T. (2011), 'The Political Consequences of Franchise Extension: Evidence from the Second Reform Act', *Quarterly Journal of Political Science* **6**(34), 329–376.

Berlinski, S., Dewan, T. and Coppenolle, B. V. (2014), 'Franchise Extension and the British Aristocracy', *Legislative Studies Quarterly* **39**(4), 531–558.

Black, E. C. (1963), *The Association: British Extraparliamentary Political Organization, 1769-1793*, Harvard University Press, Cambridge, MA.

Black, J. (1993), *The Politics of Britain, 1688-1800*, Manchester University Press, Manchester.

Blaug, M. (1963), 'The Myth of the Old Poor Law and the Making of the New', *Journal of Economic History* **23**(2), 151–184.

Bohstedt, J. (2010), *The Politics of Provisions: Food Riots, Moral Economy, and Market Transition in England, c. 1550-1850*, Ashgate, London.

Boix, C. (2001), 'Democracy, Development, and the Public Sector', *American Journal of Political Science* **45**(1), 1–17.

Boix, C. (2003), *Democracy and Redistribution*, Cambridge University Press, Cambridge.

Boix, C. (2011), 'Democracy, Development, and the International System', *American Political Science Review* **105**(4), 809–828.

Bourguignon, F. and Verdier, T. (2000), 'Oligarchy, Democracy, Inequality and Growth', *Journal of Development Economics* **62**(2), 285–313.

Boyer, G. R. (1990), *An Economic History of the English Poor Law, 1750-1850*, Cambridge University Press, Cambridge.

Brash, J. (1974), *Papers on Scottish Electoral Politics, 1832-1854*, T. and A. Constable, Edinburgh.

Brewer, J. (1976), *Party Ideology and Popular Politics at the Accession of George III*, Cambridge University Press, Cambridge.

Brewer, J. (1989), *The Sinews of Power: War, Money, and the English State*, Alfred A. Knopf, New York.

Briggs, A. (1967), *William Cobbett*, Oxford University Press, Oxford.

Briggs, A. (2000), *The Age of Improvement 1783-1867*, 2nd edn, Longman, Harlow, UK.

Briggs, A., ed. (1959), *Chartist Studies*, Macmillan, London.

Brock, M. G. (1973), *The Great Reform Act*, Hutchinson University Library, London.

Brougham, H. (1871), *The Life and Times of Henry Lord Brougham: Written by Himself*, Blackwood and Sons, Edinburgh.

Brückner, M. and Ciccone, A. (2011), 'Rain and the Democratic Window of Opportunity', *Econometrica* **79**(3), 923–947.

Buchinsky, M. and Polak, B. (1993), 'The Emergence of a National Capital Market in England, 1710-1880', *Journal of Economic History* **53**(1), 1–24.

Bunce, V. J. and Wolchik, S. L. (2006), 'Favorable Conditions and Electoral Revolutions', *Journal of Democracy* **17**(4), 5–18.

Burke, E. (1790), *Reflections on the Revolution in France, Oxford World's Classics*, reissue ed., 2009 edn, Oxford University Press, Oxford.

Burke, P. J. and Leigh, A. (2010), 'Do Output Contractions Trigger Democratic Change?', *American Economic Journal: Macroeconomics* **2**(4), 124–157.

Butler, J. R. M. (1914), *The Passing of the Great Reform Bill*, Longmans & Green, London.

Butterfield, H. (1959), *George III and the Historians*, Macmillan, New York.

Cameron, A. C. and Miller, D. L. (2015), 'A Practitioner's Guide to Cluster-Robust Inference', *Journal of Human Resources* **50**(2), 317–372.

Cannon, J. A. (1973), *Parliamentary Reform, 1640-1832*, Cambridge University Press, Cambridge.

Caprettini, B. and Voth, H.-J. (2020), 'Rage Against the Machines: Labor-Saving Technology and Unrest in Industrializing England', *American Economic Review - Insights* **2**(3), 305–320.

Cary, J. (1793), *Cary's New and Correct English Atlas: Being a New Set of County Maps from Actual Surveys*, John Cary, London.

Castaneda-Dower, P., Finkel, E., Gehlbach, S. and Nafziger, S. (2018), 'Collective Action and Representation in Autocracies: Evidence from Russia's Great Reforms', *American Political Science Review* **112**(1), 125–147.

Chapman, J. (2018), 'Democratic Reform and Opposition to Government Expenditure: Evidence from Nineteenth-Century Britain', *Quarterly Journal of Political Science* **13**(4), 363–404.

Chapman, J. (2024), 'Gradual Franchise Extensions and Government Spending in Nineteenth-Century England', *The Journal of Politics* **86**(1), 369–374.

Charlesworth, A. (1979), *Social Protest in Rural Society*, Norwich University Press, Norwich.

Charlesworth, A. (1983), *An Atlas of Rural Protest in Britain 1548-1900*, University of Pennsylvania Press, Philadelphia.

Chase, M. (2007), *Chartism: A New History*, Manchester University Press, Manchester.

Chenoweth, E. and Stephan, M. J. (2011), *Why Civil Resistance Works: The Strategic Logic of Nonviolent Conflict*, Columbia University Press, New York.

Clapham, J. H. (1952), *An Economic History of Modern Britain: The Early Railway Age 1820-1850*, Vol. 1, Cambridge University Press, Cambridge.

Clark, J. (1986), *Revolution and Rebellion: State and Society in England in the Seventeenth and Eighteenth Centuries*, Cambridge University Press, Cambridge.

Clark, J. (2000), *English Society 1660-1832: Religion, Ideology and Politics during the Ancien Regime*, 2nd edn, Cambridge University Press, Cambridge.

Cobban, A. (1960), *The Debate on the French Revolution, 1789-1800*, 2nd edn, Barnes and Noble, New York.

Coll, S. (2008), 'The Origins and Evolution of Democracy: An Exercise in History from a Constitutional Economics Approach', *Constitutional Political Economy* **19**(4), 313–355.

Collier, R. B. (1999), *Paths toward Democracy. The Working Class and Elites in Western Europe and South America*, Cambridge University Press, Cambridge.

Cone, C. B. (1968), *The English Jacobins. Reformers in late 18th Century England*, Charles Scribner's Sons, New York.

Congleton, R. D. (2001), 'On the Durability of King and Council: The Continuum Between Dictatorship and Democracy', *Constitutional Political Economy* **12**, 193–215.

Congleton, R. D. (2004), 'Economic Development and Democracy: Does Industrialization Lead to Universal Suffrage?', *Homo Economicus* **21**, 283–311.

Congleton, R. D. (2007), 'From Royal to Parliamentary Rule without Revolution: The Economics of Constitutional Exchange within Divided Governments', *European Journal of Political Economy* **23**(2), 261–284.

Congleton, R. D. (2011), *Perfecting Parliament*, Cambridge University Press, Cambridge.

Conley, T. G. (1999), 'GMM Estimation with Cross Sectional Dependence', *Journal of Econometrics* **92**(1), 1–45.

Coppedge, M., Gerring, J., Knutsen, C. H., Lindberg, S. I., Teorell, J., Altman, D., Bernhard, M., Cornell, A., Fish, M. S., Gastaldi, L., Gjerloew, H., Glynn, A., God, A. G., Grahn, S., Hicken, A., Kinzelbach, K., Krusell, J., Marquardt, K. L., McMann, K., Mechkova, V., Medzihorsky, J., Natsika, N., Neundorf, A., Paxton, P., Pemstein, D., Pernes, J., Ryden, O., von Roemer, J., Seim, B., Sigman, R., Skaaning, S.-E., Staton, J., Sundstroem, A., Tzelgov, E., Wang, Y., Wig, T., Wilson, S. and Ziblatt, D. (2023), 'V-Dem [Country-Year/Country-Date] Dataset v13', Dataset, Varieties of Democracy (V-Dem) Project, University of Gothenburg, Sweden.

Cox, G., Dincecco, M. and Onorato, M. (2024), 'Window of Opportunity: War and the Origins of Parliament', *British Journal of Political Science* **54**(2), 405–421.

Cox, G., Fresh, A. and Saiegh, S. (2023), 'The Political Economy of Suffrage Reform: The Great Reform Act of 1832', *Journal of Historical Political Economy* **3**(1), 65–93.

Cox, G. and Saiegh, S. (2022), 'Suffrage Reform and Financial Volatility: Reconsidering the Great Reform Act', *Journal of Historical Political Economy* **2**(3), 415–447.

Cox, G. W. (1987), *The Efficiency Secret: The Cabinet and Development of Political Parties in Victorian England*, Cambridge University Press, Cambridge.

Crawford, V. P. and Sobel, J. (1982), 'Strategic Information Transmission', *Econometrica* **50**(6), 1431–1451.

Croker, J. W. (1884), *The Correspondence and Diaries of the Late John Wilson Croker*, Edited by Louis J. Jennings in Two Volumes, Charles Scribner's Sons, New York.

Dasgupta, A. and Ziblatt, D. (2015), 'How did Britain Democratize? Views from the Sovereign Bond Market', *Journal of Economic History* **75**(1), 1–29.

Daunton, M. J. (1995), *Progress and Poverty: An Economic and Social History of Britain, 1700-1850*, Oxford University Press, Oxford.

De Castro, J. P. (1926), *The Gordon Riots*, Oxford University Press, Oxford.

de Vries, J. (2008), *The Industrious Revolution: Consumer Behavior and the Household Economy, 1650 to the Present*, Cambridge University Press, Cambridge.

Dehejia, R. H. and Wahba, S. (2002), 'Propensity Score-Matching Methods for Non-Experimental Causal Studies', *Review of Economics and Statistics* **84**(1), 151–161.

Derry, J. W. (1990), *Politics in the Age of Fox, Pitt and Liverpool: Continuity and Transformation*, Palgrave, Houndmills Basingstoke, UK.

Dewan, T., Meriläinen, J. and Tukiainen, J. (2020), 'Victorian Voting: The Origins of Party Orientation and Class alignment', *American Journal of Political Science* **64**(4), 869–886.

Dickens, C. (1838), *Oliver Twist*, Penguin Classics [2003], London.

Dickson, P. G. M. (1967), *The Financial Revolution in England: A Study in the Development of Public Credit 1688-1756*, Macmillan, London.

Dieterle, S. G. and Snell, A. (2016), 'A Simple Diagnostic to Investigate Instrument Validity and Heterogeneous Effects when Using a Single Instrument', *Labour Economics* **42**, 76–86.

Dinwiddy, J. R. (1984), 'Early-Nineteenth-Century Reactions to Benthamism', *Transactions of the Royal Historical Society* **34**, 47–69.

Do, Q.-A. and Campante, F. R. (2009), 'Keeping Dictators Honest: The Role of Population Concentration, Governance', Working Papers 22076, East Asian Bureau of Economic Research, The Australian National University.

Dod, C. R. and Dod, R. P. (1832), *Dod's Parliamentary Companion*, Dod's Parliamentary Companion, Hailsham, UK.

Dorsch, M. T. and Maarek, P. (2015), 'Inefficient Predation and Political Transitions', *European Journal of Political Economy* **37**, 37–48.

Dorsch, M. T. and Maarek, P. (2020), 'Economic Downturns, Inequality, and Democratic Improvements', *European Journal of Political Economy* **62**, 101856.

Dozier, R. R. (1983), *For King, Constitution and Country: The English Loyalists and the French Revolution*, The University Press of Kentucky, Lexington.

Dyck, I. (1992), *William Cobbett and Rural Popular Culture*, Cambridge University Press, Cambridge.

Ehrman, J. (1986), *The Younger Pitt: The Reluctant Transition*, vol. 2, paperback ed., Constable and Co., London.

Eliot, G. (1871–1872), *Middlemarch. A Study of Provincial Life*, William Blackwood and Sons, Edinburgh.

Ellis, C. J. and Fender, J. (2008), 'The Economic Evolution of Democracy', *Economics of Governance* **10**, 119–145.

Ellis, C. J. and Fender, J. (2011), 'Information Cascades and Revolutionary Regime Transition', *Economic Journal* **121**(551), 763–792.

Falkinger, J. (1999), 'Social Instability and Redistribution of Income', *European Journal of Political Economy* **15**(1), 35–51.

Fisher, D., ed. (2009), *The History of Parliament: The House of Commons 1820-1832*, Cambridge University Press, Cambridge.

Fitzgerald, P., ed. (1884), *The Life and Times of William IV*, Tinsley Brothers, London.

Flora, P., Alber, J., Eichenberg, R., Kohl, J., Kraus, F., Pfenning, W. and Seebohm, K. (1983), *State, Economy and Society 1815-1975 (Vol. I)*, Campus Verlag, Frankfurt.

Foord, A. S. (1964), *His Majesty's Opposition*, Clarendon Press, Oxford.

Franck, R. (2016), 'The Political Consequences of Income Shocks: Explaining the Consolidation of Democracy in France', *Review of Economics of Statistics* **98**(1), 57–82.

Franck, R., Johnson, N. D. and Nye, J. V. C. (2014), 'From Internal Taxes to National Regulation: Evidence from a French Wine Tax Reform at the Turn of the Twentieth Century', *Explorations in Economic History* **51**, 77–93.

Franck, R. and Rainer, I. (2012), 'Does the Leader's Ethnicity Matter? Ethnic Favoritism, Education and Health in Sub-Saharan Africa', *American Political Science Review* **106**(2), 294–325.

Frohlich, N., Oppenheimer, J. A. and Young, O. R. (1971), *Political Leadership and Collective Goods*, Princeton University Press, Princeton.

Fry, M. (1992), *The Dundas Despotism*, Edinburgh University Press, Edinburgh.

Galor, O. (2005), From Stagnation to Growth: Unified Growth Theory, *in* P. Aghion and S. Durlauf, eds, 'Handbook of Economic Growth', Elsevier, Amsterdam, pp. 171–293.

Galor, O. (2011), *Unified Growth Theory*, Princeton University Press, Princeton, NJ.

Gash, N. (1953), *Politics in the Age of Peel: A Study in the Technique of Parliamentary Representation 1830-1850*, W.W. Norton [1971], New York.

Gash, N. (1956), English Reform and French Revolution in the General Election of 1830, *in* R. Pares and A. Taylor, eds, 'Essays Presented to Sir Lewis Namier', Macmillan & Co, London, pp. 258–288.

Gash, N. (1984), *Lord Liverpool: The Life and Political Career of Robert Banks Jenkinson, Second Earl of Liverpool, 1770-1828*, Weidenfeld, London.

Gelman, A. and Stern, H. (2006), 'The Difference between Significant and Not Significant Is Not Itself Statistically Significant', *American Statistician* **60**(4), 328–331.

Gilli, M. and Li, Y. (2015), 'Coups, Revolutions and Efficient Policies in Autocracies', *European Journal of Political Economy* **39**, 109–124.

Gonner, E. C. K. (1912), *Common Land and Enclosure*, Macmillan & Co, London.

Goodwin, A. (1979), *The Friends of Liberty: The English Democratic Movement in the Age of the French Revolution*, Routledge, London.

Gradstein, M. (2007), 'Inequality, Democracy and the Protection of Property Rights', *Economic Journal* **117**(516), 252–269.

Granovetter, M. (1978), 'Threshold Models of Collective Behavior', *American Journal of Sociology* **83**(6), 1420–1443.

Greenwood, J. and Greenwood, C. (1830), *Map of London; Made from an Actual Survey in the Years 1824, 1825, & 1826*, C. & J. Greenwood, London.

Greif, A. and Iyigun, M. (2013), 'Social Organizations, Violence, and Modern Growth', *American Economic Review* **103**(3), 534–538.

Grey, H., ed (1867), *The Reform Act, 1832; the Correspondence of the Late Earl Grey with His Majesty King William IV and with Sir Herbert Taylor, from Nov. 1830 to June 1832*, John Murray, London.

Grossman, G. M. and Helpman, E. (2001), *Special Interest Politics*, MIT Press, Cambridge, MA.

Gundlach, E. and Paldam, M. (2009), 'A Farewell to Critical Junctures', *European Journal of Political Economy* **3**, 340–354.

Guriev, S. and Papaioannou, E. (2022), 'The Political Economy of Populism', *Journal of Economic Literature* **60**(3), 753–832.

Gurr, T. R. (1970), *Why Men Rebel*, Princeton University Press, Princeton.

Halévy, E. (1923), *Histoire du Peuple Anglais au XIXe Siècle. De la Crise du Reform Bill à l'Avènement de Sir Robert Peel (1830-1841)*, Vol. 3, Librairie Hachette, Paris.

Halévy, E. (1935), English Public Opinion and the French Revolution of the Nineteenth Century, *in* A. Coville and H. Temperley, eds, 'Studies in Anglo-French History during the Eighteenth', Cambridge University Press, Cambridge, pp. 51–60.

Hamburger, J. (1963), *James Mill and the Art of Revolution*, Yale University Press, New Haven.

Hammond, J. L. and Hammond, B. (1911), *The Village Labourer*, Nonsuch Publishing Limited, Stroud, UK.

Hanlon, W. W. (2022), Suffrage in Historical Political Economy, *in* J. A. Jenkins and J. Rubin, eds, 'The Oxford Handbook of Historical Political Economy', Oxford University Press, Oxford, pp. C23.P1–C23.N8.

Harris, B. and Hinde, A. (2019), 'Sanitary Investment and the Decline of Urban Mortality in England and Wales, 1817-1914', *History of the Family* **24**, 339–376.

Hart, D. M. and Kenyon, R. (2014), *Tracts on Liberty by the Levellers and Their Critics (1638-1660)*, Liberty Fund, Indianapolis.

Healey, J. (2023), *The Blazing World: A New History of Revolutionary England, 1603-1689*, Alfred A. Knopf, New York.

Heckman, J. J., Urzua, S. and Vytlacil, E. (2006), 'Understanding Instrumental Variables in Models with Essential Heterogeneity', *Review of Economics and Statistics* **88**(3), 389–432.

Hibbert, C. (1987), *The Grand Tour*, Thames Methuen, London.

Hill, B. (1996), *The Early Parties and Politics in Britain, 1688-1832*, Macmillan Press, New York.

Hill, C. (1967), *Reformation to Industrial Revolution: A Social and Economic History of Britain, 1530-1780*, Weidenfeld and Nicolson, London.

Hilton, B. (2006), *A Mad, Bad and Dangerous People? England 1783-1846*, Clarendon Press, Oxford.

Himmelfarb, G. (1966), 'The Politics of Democracy: The English Reform Act of 1867', *The Journal of British Studies* **6**(1), 97–138.

Hobsbawm, E. J. and Rudé, G. (1973), *Captain Swing*, Penguin University Books, Harmondsworth, UK.

Hoffman, R. J. S. (1973), *The Marquis: A Study of Lord Rockingham, 1730-1782*, Fordham University Press, New York.

Holland, M. (2005), *Swing Unmasked: The Agricultural Riots of 1830 to 1832 and Their Wider Implications*, FACHRS Publications, Milton Keynes, UK.

Hoppen, K. T. (1984), *Elections, Politics and Society in Ireland, 1832-1885*, Clarendon Press, Oxford.

Hoppit, J. (2000), *A Land of Liberty? England 1689-1727*, Oxford University Press, Oxford.

Horn, N. and Tilly, C. (1988), 'Contentious Gatherings in Britain, 1758-1834', working paper 8872, Ann Arbor, MA: Inter-university Consortium for Political and Social Research ICPSR.

Horpedahl, J. (2011), 'Political Exchange and the Voting Franchise: Universal Democracy as an Emergent Process', *Constitutional Political Economy* **22**(3), 203–220.

Hume, D. (1752), Idea of a Perfect Commonwealth, *in* A. Coventry and A. Valls, eds, 'David Hume on Morals, Politics, and Society [2018]', Yale University Press, New Haven, pp. 227–238.

Huntington, S. P. (1977), *Political Order in Changing Societies*, 15th edn, Yale University Press, New Haven.

Huntington, S. P. (1991), *The Third Wave: Democratization in the Late Twentieth Century*, University of Oklahoma Press, Norman.

Jacob, M. C. (2014), *The First Knowledge Economy: Human Capital and the European Economy, 1750-1850*, Cambridge University Press, Cambridge.

Janowitz, M. (1976), 'Military Institutions and Citizenship in Western Societies', *Armed Forces and Society* **2**(2), 185–203.

Jones, C. (2012), *A Short History of Parliament: England, Great Britain, the United Kingdom, Ireland & Scotland*, Boydell, Woodbridge, UK.

Jones, E. (2017), *Edmund Burke and the Invention of Modern Conservatism, 1830-1914: An Intellectual History*, Oxford University Press, Oxford.

Jupp, P. (1967), 'Irish Parliamentary Elections and the Influence of the Catholic Vote, 1801-20', *The Historical Journal* **10**(2), 183–196.

Jupp, P. (1998), *British Politics on the Eve of Reform, the Duke of Wellington's Administration, 1828-30*, Macmillan, New York.

Jupp, P. (2006), *The Governing of Britain, 1688-1848: The Executive, Parliament and the People*, Routledge, London.

Justman, M. and Gradstein, M. (1999), 'The Industrial Revolution, Political Transition, and the Subsequent Decline in Inequality in 19th-Century Britain', *Explorations in Economic History* **36**(2), 109–127.

Kam, C. (2017), 'The Secret Ballot and the Market for Votes at 19th-Century British Elections', *Comparative Political Studies* **50**(5), 594–635.

Kam, C. and Newson, A. (2021), *The Economic Origin of Political Parties*, Cambridge University Press, Cambridge.

Kasara, K. and Mares, I. (2017), 'Unfinished Business: The Democratization of Electoral Practices in Britain and Germany', *Comparative Political Studies* **50**(5), 636–664.

Keith-Lucas, B. (1952), *The English Local Government Franchise*, Basil Blackwell, Oxford.

Knights, M. (2010), Participation and Representation before Democracy: Petitions and Addresses in Premodern Britain, *in* I. Shapiro, S. C. Stokes, E. J. Wood and A. S. Kirshner, eds, 'Political Representation', Cambridge University Press, Cambridge, pp. 35–58.

Kuran, T. (1989), 'Sparks and Prairie Fires: A Theory of Unanticipated Political Revolution', *Public Choice* **61**(1), 41–74.

Langford, P. (1973), *The First Rockingham Administration, 1765-1766*, Oxford University Press, Oxford.

Langford, P. (1976), *The Eighteenth Century 1688-1815*, Adam and Charles Black, London.

Langford, P. (1989), *A Polite and Commercial People: England 1727-1783*, Oxford University Press, Oxford.

Larcinese, V. (2024), 'Enfranchisement and Representation: Evidence from the Introduction of Quasi-Universal Suffrage in Italy', *The Journal of Politics* **86**(2), 565–581.

Laurent-Lucchetti, J., Rohner, D. and Thoenig, M. (2024), 'Ethnic Conflict and the Informational Dividend of Democracy', *Journal of the European Economic Association* **22**(1), 73–116.

Lehmann-Hasemeyer, S., Hauber, P. and Opitz, A. (2014), 'The Political Stock Market in the German Kaiserreich: Do Markets Punish the Extension of the Suffrage to the Benefit of the Working Class? Evidence from Saxony', *Journal of Economic History* **74**(4), 1140–1167.

Levitsky, S. and Ziblatt, D. (2018), *How Democracies Die*, Crown, New York.

Leys, C. (1955), 'Petitioning in the Nineteenth and Twentieth Century', *Political Studies* **3**(1), 45–64.

Lindert, P. (1994), 'The Rise of Social Spending, 1880-1930', *Explorations in Economic History* **31**(1), 1–37.

Lipset, S. M. (1960), *Political Man: The Social Basis of Modern Politics*, Doubleday, New York.

Lizzeri, A. and Persico, N. (2004), 'Why Did the Elites Extend the Suffrage? Democracy and the Scope of Government, with an Application to Britain's "Age of Reform"', *Quarterly Journal of Economics* **119**(2), 707–765.

Llavador, H. and Oxoby, R. J. (2005), 'Partisan Competition, Growth, and the Franchise', *Quarterly Journal of Economics* **120**(3), 1155–1192.

Locke, J. (1689), *Two Treatises of Government*, Cambridge Texts in the History of Political Thought, 1988 edn, Cambridge University Press, Cambridge.

Lodge, E. (1832), *The Peerage of the British Empire as at Present Existing*, Saunders and Otley, London.

Lohmann, S. (1993), 'A Signaling Model of Informative and Manipulative Political Action', *American Political Science Review* **87**(2), 319–333.

Lohmann, S. (1995), 'Information Access, and Contributions: A Signalling Model of Lobbying', *Public Choice* **85**(3), 267–84.

LoPatin, N. D. (1999), *Political Unions, Popular Politics and the Great Reform Act of 1832*, St. Martin's Press, New York.

Macaulay, A. (2016), *The Catholic Church and the Campaign for Catholic Emancipation in Ireland and England*, Four Courts Press, Dublin.

Macaulay, T. B. (1848), *The History of England*, reissue ed., 1979 edn, Penguin Classics, London.

Machin, G. (1964), *The Catholic Question in English Politics, 1820-1830*, Oxford University Press, Oxford.

Maehl, W. H. (1967), *The Reform Bill of 1832: Why Not Revolution?*, Holt, Rinehart & Winston, London.

Marino, M., Donni, P. L., Bavetta, S. and Cellini, M. (2020), 'The Democratization Process: An Empirical Appraisal of the Role of Political Protest', *European Journal of Political Economy* **63**, 101881.

Marshall, J. D. (1985), *The Old Poor Law, 1795-1834*, Macmillan, London.

Marshall, M. G. and Gurr, T. R. (2020), 'Polity IV Project, Political Regime Characteristics and Transitions, 1800-2018', Dataset, Center for Systemic Peace.

Martinez-Bravo, M., Padró i Miquel, G., Qian, N. and Yao, Y. (2022), 'The Rise and Fall of Local Elections in China', *American Economic Review* **112**(9), 2921–2958.

McCarthy, J. (1852), *The Epoch of Reform 1830-50*, Longmans, Green & Co, London.

McConnaughy, C. (2013), *The Women's Suffrage Movement in America: A Reassessment*, Cambridge University Press, Cambridge.

Meltzer, A. H. and Richard, S. F. (1981), 'A Rational Theory of the Size of Government', *Journal of Political Economy* **89**(5), 914–927.

Mill, J. S. (1931), *Utilitarianism, Liberty and Representative Government*, Dent, London.

Mitchell, A. (1967), *The Whigs in Opposition, 1815-1830*, Oxford University Press, Oxford.

Mitchell, L. G. (1992), *Charles James Fox*, Oxford University Press, Oxford.

Mitchell, L. G. (2005), *The Whig World*, Hambledon Continuum, London.

Mokyr, J. (2009), *The Enlightened Economy: An Economic History of Britain 1700-1850*, Yale University Press, New Haven, CT.

Morgan-Collins, M. (2021), 'The Electoral Impact of Newly Enfranchised Groups: The Case of Women's Suffrage in the United States', *Journal of Politics* **83**(1), 150–165.

Morrison, B. (2011), 'Channeling the "Restless Spirit of Innovation": Elite Concessions and Institutional Change in the British Reform Act of 1832', *World Politics* **63**(4), 678–710.

Moser, S. and Reeves, A. (2014), 'Taking the Leap: Voting, Rhetoric, and the Determinants of Electoral Reform', *Legislative Studies Quarterly* **39**(4), 467–502.

Mulligan, C. B., Gil, R. and Sala-i-Martin, X. (2004), 'Do Democracies Have Different Public Policies than Nondemocracies?', *Journal of Economic Perspectives* **18**(1), 51–74.

Munshi, S. (2011), 'Enfranchisement from a Political Perspective', *Constitutional Political Economy* **22**(1), 21–57.

Namier, L. (1957), *The Structure of Politics at the Accession of George III*, Macmillan, London.

Namier, L. B. and Brooke, J. (1964), *The House of Commons, 1754-1790*, Oxford University Press, Oxford.

Namier, L. and Brooke, J. (1985), *The History of Parliament: The House of Commons, 1754-1790*, The History of Parliamentary Trust, Secker and Warburg, London.

Nardinelli, C. (1990), *Child Labor and the Industrial Revolution*, Indiana University Press, Bloomington and Indianapolis.
Newbould, I. (1990), *Whiggery and Reform 1830-1841. The Politics of Government*, Stanford University Press, Stanford.
Nikolova, E. and Nikolova, M. (2017), 'Suffrage, Labour Markets and Coalitions in Colonial Virginia', *European Journal of Political Economy* **49**, 108–122.
North, D. C. and Weingast, B. R. (1989), 'Constitutions and Commitment: The Evolution of Institutions Governing Public Choice in Seventeenth-Century England', *Journal of Economic History* **49**(4), 803–832.
Ó Gráda, C. (2016), 'Did Science Cause the Industrial Revolution?', *Journal of Economic Literature* **54**(1), 224–239.
O'Gorman, F. (1986), 'The Unreformed Electorate of Hanoverian England: The Mid-Eighteenth Century to the Reform Act of 1832', *Social History* **11**(1), 33–52.
O'Gorman, F. (2016), *The Long Eighteenth Century: British Political and Social History 1688-1832*, 2nd edn, Bloomsbury Academic, London.
O'Leary, C. (1962), *The Elimination of Corrupt Practices in British Elections 1868-1911*, Clarendon Press, Oxford.
Olney, R. J. (1973), *Lincolnshire Politics 1832-1885*, Oxford University Press, Oxford.
Olson, M. (1965), *The Logic of Collective Action: Public Goods and the Theory of Groups*, Harvard University Press, Cambridge, MA.
Opitz, A. (2018), '"Comrades, Let's March!". The Revolution of 1905 and Its Impact on Financial Markets', *European Review of Economic History* **22**(1), 28–52.
Oster, E. (2019), 'Unobservable Selection and Coefficient Stability: Theory and Evidence', *Journal of Business and Economic Statistics* **37**(2), 187–204.
Ostrogorski, M. (1902), *Democracy and the Organization of Political Parties*, Macmillan and Company Limited, London.
Overland, J., Simons, K. L. and Spagat, M. (2005), 'Political Instability and Growth in Dictatorships', *Public Choice* **125**(3-4), 445–470.
Paine, T. (1791–1792), Rights of Man, *in* M. Philp, ed., ' *Rights of Man, Common Sense, and Other Political Writings [1998]*', Oxford University Press, Oxford, pp. 83–331.
Paldam, M. (2021), *The Grand Patterns of Development and the Transition of Institutions*, Cambridge University Press, Cambridge.
Papke, L. E. and Wooldridge, J. M. (1996), 'Econometric Methods for Fractional Response Variables with an Application to 401(k) Plan Participation Rates', *Journal of Applied Econometrics* **11**(6), 619–632.
Pares, R. (1953), *King George III and the Politicians*, Oxford University Press, Oxford.
Philbin, J. H. (1965), *Parliamentary Representation, 1832, England and Wales*, Yale University Press, New Haven, CT.
Pincus, S. C. and Robinson, J. A. (2014), What Really Happened during the Glorious Revolution?, *in* S. Galiani and I. Sened, eds, 'Institutions, Property Rights and Growth: The Legacy of Douglass North', Cambridge University Press, Cambridge, pp. 192–222.
Pittaluga, G. B., Cama, G. and Seghezza, E. (2015), 'Democracy, Extension of Suffrage, and Redistribution in Nineteenth-Century Europe', *European Review of Economic History* **19**(4), 317–334.
Plowright, J. (1996), *Regency England: The Age of Lord Liverpool*, Routledge, London.
Przeworski, A. (2009), 'Conquered or Granted? A History of Suffrage Extensions', *British Journal of Political Science* **39**(2), 291–321.
Przeworski, A., Alvarez, M. E., Cheibub, J. A. and Limongi, F. (2000), *Democracy and Development: Political Institutions and Well-Being in the World, 1950-1990*, Cambridge University Press, Cambridge.
Przeworski, A. and Limongi, F. (1997), 'Modernization: Theories and Facts', *World Politics* **49**(2), 155–183.

Randall, J. G. (1916), 'The frequency and duration of parliaments', *American Political Science Review* **10**(4), 654–682.

Robson, B. (2014), 'Maps and Mathematics: Ranking the English Boroughs for the 1832 Reform Act', *Journal of Historical Geography* **46**, 66–79.

Rosenbaum, P. R. (2002), *Observational Studies*, 2nd edn, Springer, New York.

Rosenbaum, P. R. (2010), *Design of Observational Studies*, Springer, New York.

Rosenbaum, P. R. and Rubin, D. P. (1983), 'The Central Role of the Propensity Score in Observational Studies for Causal Effects', *Biometrika* **70**(1), 41–55.

Rostow, W. W. (1948), Trade Cycles, Harvest and Politics, *in* ' British Economy of the Nineteenth Century', Oxford University Press, Oxford, pp. 108–125.

Royle, E. (2000), *Revolutionary Britannia? Reflection on the Threat of Revolution in Britain, 1789-1848.*, Manchester University Press, Manchester.

Rudé, G. (1962), *Wilkes and Liberty: A Social Study of 1763 to 1774*, Oxford University Press, Oxford.

Rueschemeyer, D., Stephens, E. H. and Stephens, J. D. (1992), *Capitalist Development and Democracy*, University of Chicago Press, Chicago.

Russell, J. (1875), *Recollections and Suggestions 1813-1873*, Longmans & Green, London.

Sack, J. J. (1980), 'The House of Lords and Parliamentary Patronage in Great Britain', *Historical Journal* **23**(4), 913–937.

Salmon, P. (2002), *Electoral Reform at Work: Local Politics and National Parties, 1832-1841*, Boydell and Brewer - Royal Historical Society, London.

Salmon, P. (2009), The English Reform Legislation, 1831-32, *in* D. R. Fisher, ed., ' The History of Parliament: The House of Commons, 1820-1832', Vol. I, Cambridge University Press, Cambridge.

Scheve, K. and Stasavage, D. (2016), *Taxing the Rich: A History of Fiscal Fairness in the United States and Europe*, Princeton University Press, Princeton, NJ.

Schonhardt-Bailey, C. (1991), 'Domestic Determinants of the Repeal of the Corn Laws', *World Politics* **43**(4), 545–569.

Schonhardt-Bailey, C. (1994), 'Linking Constituency Interests to Legislative Voting Behavior: The Role of District Economic and Electoral Composition in the Repeal of the Corn Laws', *Parliamentary History* **13**(1), 86–118.

Schonhardt-Bailey, C. (2006), *From the Corn Laws to Free Trade: Interests, Ideas, and Institutions in Historical Perspective*, MIT Press, Cambridge, MA.

Seghezza, E. and Morelli, P. (2019), 'Suffrage Extension, Social Identity, and Redistribution: The Case of the Second Reform Act', *European Review of Economic History* **23**(1), 30–49.

Seymour, C. (1915), *Electoral Reform in England and Wales*, Yale University Press, New Haven, CT.

Smith, E. (1992), *The House of Lords in British Politics and Society 1815-1911*, Longman, London.

Smith, H. L. (1998), *The British Women's Suffrage Campaign, 1866-1928*, Longman, London.

Somerset, A., ed. (1980), *The Life and Times of William IV*, Weidenfeld and Nicolson, London.

Stasavage, D. (2020), *The Decline and Rise of Democracy: A Global History from Antiquity to Today*, Princeton University Press, Princeton, NJ.

Stasavage, D. (2022), Democracy and Historical Political Economy, *in* J. A. Jenkins and J. Rubin, eds, 'The Oxford Handbook of Historical Political Economy', Oxford University Press, Oxford, pp. C8.P1–C8.N27.

Stevenson, J. (1992), *Popular Disturbances in England: 1700-1832*, Routledge, London.

Stokes, C. S., Dunning, T., Nazareno, M. and Brusco, V. (2013), *Brokers, Voters, and Clientelism: The Puzzle of Distributive Politics*, Cambridge University Press, Cambridge.

Stone, L. (1972), *The Causes of the English revolution, 1529-1642*, Routledge and Keegan Paul, London.

Stooks Smith, H. (1973), *The Parliaments of England*, Political Reference Publications, Chichester, UK.

Stubbs, W. (1873), *The Constitutional History of England*, Clarendon Press, Oxford, UK.
Szostak, R. (1991), *The Role of Transportation in the Industrial Revolution: A Comparison of England and France*, McGill-Queen's University Press, Montreal.
Tarrow, S. G. (2011), *Power in Movement: Social Movements and Contentious Politics*, 3rd edn, Cambridge University Press, Cambridge.
Teele, D. L. (2018a), *Forging the Franchise: The Political Origins of Women's Vote*, Princeton University Press, Princeton, NJ.
Teele, D. L. (2018b), 'How the West Was Won: Competition, Mobilization, and Women's Enfranchisement in the United States', *Journal of Politics* **80**(2), 442–461.
Thomas, P. D. (1996), *John Wilkes: A Friend to Liberty*, Oxford University Press, Oxford.
Thomas, P. D. (2002), *George III: King and Politicians 1760-1770*, Manchester University Press, Manchester.
Thompson, D. (1984), *The Chartists: Popular Politics in the Industrial Revolution*, 1st American edn, Pantheon Books, New York.
Thompson, E. P. (1963), *The Making of the English Working Class*, Vintage Books, New York.
Thorne, R. G. (1986), *The House of Commons, 1790-1820*, Oxford University Press, Oxford.
Ticchi, D. and Vindigni, A. (2008), 'War and Endogenous Democracy', IZA Discussion Paper 3397, Institute for Labor Economics, University of Bonn.
Tilly, C. (1988), *From Mobilization to Revolution*, Addison-Wesley, New York.
Tilly, C. (1995), *Popular Contention in Great Britain, 1758-1834*, Harvard University Press, Cambridge, MA.
Tilly, C. (2004), *Contention and Democracy in Europe, 1650-2000*, Cambridge University Press, Cambridge.
Tilly, C. (2007), *Democracy*, Cambridge University Press, Cambridge.
Trease, G. (1967), *The Grand Tour*, Holt, Rinehart and Winston, New York.
Trevelyan, G. M. (1920), *Lord Grey of the Reform Bill: Being the Life of Charles, Second Earl of Grey*, Greenwood Press, London.
Trevelyan, G. M. (1937), *History of England*, 2nd edn, Longmans, Green & Co, London.
Tridimas, G. (2021), 'Constitutional Monarchy as Power Sharing', *Constitutional Political Economy* **32**, 431–461.
Tullock, G. (1971), 'The Paradox of Revolution', *Public Choice* **11**, 89–99.
Tullock, G. (1987), *Autocracy*, Kluwer Academic Publishers, Dordrecht.
Turberville, A. (1958), *The House of Lords in the Age of Reform, 1784 - 1837: With an Epilogue on Aristocracy and the Advent of Democracy, 1837-1867*, Faber and Faber, London.
Turner, J. D. and Zhan, W. (2012), 'Property Rights and Competing for the Affections of Demos: The Impact of the 1867 Reform Act on Stock Prices', *Public Choice* **150**(3-4), 609–631.
Turner, M. J. (1999), *British Politics in an Age of Reform*, University of Manchester Press, Manchester.
Van de Ven, W. P. M. M. and Praag, B. M. S. V. (1981), 'The Demand for Deductibles in Private Health Insurance: A Probit Model with Sample Selection', *Journal of Econometrics* **17**(2), 229–252.
van Zanden, J. L. (2009), *The Long Road to the Industrial Revolution: The European Economy in a Global Perspective*, Brill, Leiden, Netherlands.
Vincent, J. and Stenton, M., eds (1971), *McCalmont's Parliamentary Poll Book of All Elections 1832-1918*, 8th edn, Harvester Press Limited, Brighton, UK.
Wade, J. (1834), *Appendix to the Black Book*, Effingham Wilson, London.
Wadsworth, A. (1955), 'Newspaper Circulations, 1800-1954', *Transactions of the Manchester Statistical Society* **20**, 1–41.
Walker, B. M. (1992), *Parliamentary Election Results in Ireland, 1918-92*, Royal Irish Academy, Dublin.
Walton, J. (1999), *Chartism*, Lancaster Pamphlets, Routledge, London.
Ward, J. (1973), *Chartism*, Barnes and Noble, New York.

Wedgwood, C. (1958), *The King's War: 1641-1647*, Fontana (1970), London.
Witmer, H. E. (1943), *The Property Qualifications of Members of Parliament*, Columbia University Press, New York.
Woodhouse, A. (1951), *Puritanism and Liberty, Being the Army Debates (1647-9) from the Clarke Manuscripts with Supplementary Documents*, University of Chicago Press, Chicago.
Woolley, S. (1938), 'The Personnel of the Parliament of 1833', *English Historical Review* **53**(210), 240–262.
Woolrych, A. (1987), *Soldiers and Statesmen: The General Council of the Army and its Debates, 1647-48*, Oxford University Press, Oxford.
Wright, D. (1970), *Democracy and Reform 1815-1885*, Longman, Harlow, UK.
Ziblatt, D. (2008), 'Does Landholding Inequality Block Democracy? A Test of the "Bread and Democracy" Thesis and the Case of Prussia', *World Politics* **60**(4), 610–41.
Ziblatt, D. (2017), *Conservative Parties and the Birth of Democracy*, Cambridge Studies in Comparative Politics, Cambridge University Press, Cambridge.
Ziegler, P. (1971), *King William IV*, Collins, London.

Index

Abadie, Alberto, 147, 155
Acemoglu, Daron, viii, ix, 3, 4, 11, 18–20, 30–33, 36, 40, 133
Acts of Union, *see* Ireland, Scotland
Agreement of the People, 40
agriculture
  production patterns, 149
  employment in, 108, 145
  interest of landed elite tied to, 24
  unskilled workers in, 25
Althorp, John Charles Spencer, third Earl Spencer, Viscount, 52, 207
Ansell, Ben, 32, 89
aristocracy
  landowning, 65, 73, *see also* landowners
aristocratic
  elite, 55, *see also* elite
  families, 44, 192, 193, 196
  government, 58
  influence, 63, 65–67, 89, 106, 145
  peers, 58, *see also* lord
  rule, 48
aristocrats, 43, 45, 65, 70, 75
Attwood, Thomas, 8, 54, 74, 175, 207
autocracy, 3, 32

Ballot Act (1872), 87, 203
Barker, Hannah, 63, 108
Barnsley, 100
Belgium, 141
Bentham, Jeremy, 51
Beresfod, Henry, third Marquess of Waterford, 178
Berlinski, Samuel, 31
Bethnal Green, 100
Birmingham, 84, 144
Birmingham Political Union, 8, 13, 54, 96, 100, 127, 171
Blackfriars Rotunda, 100, 171
Blandford, George Spencer-Churchill, sixth Duke of Marlborough, Marquess of, 54
Boix, Carles, 3, 11, 18, 20, 29, 30, 32
borough
  Abingdon, 60
  Amersham, 71
  Appleby, 46
  Banbury, 60
  Beverley, 67
  Bewdley, 60
  Boroughbridge, 50
  Boston, 67
  Camelford, 63
  Cardiff, 77
  Carlisle, 166
  Chatham, 87
  Colchester, 60, 61, 65, 98
  Cricklade, 47
  Durham, 42, 98
  East Retford, 53
  Gatton, 63, 132
  government, 9
  Grampound, 53, 55, 67
  Harwich, 60, 61
  Higham Ferrers, 60, 78
  Liverpool, 67, 137
  London (City of), 60, 99, 116, *see also* London
  Londonderry, 98
  Maidstone, 67
  Maldon, 60, 61, 82, 84
  Merthyr Tydfil, 77, 80
  Monmouth, 60, 168
  New Sarum, 66
  New Shoreham, 47
  Newark, 42
  Old Sarum, 63, 132
  Penryn, 53
  Preston, 127, 141
  rotten, 5, 9, 41, 44, 46, 47, 50, 52, 53, 55, 63, 70, 76, 106, 132, 145, 186, *see also* constituency, nomination borough
  Salisbury, 66
  Scarborough, 98
  Shaftesbury, 63
  Stockbridge, 65
  Swansea, 77
  Treasury, 65, 168
  Westminster, 50, 63, 68, 82, 84, 99, 116
  Weymouth and Melcombe Regis, 77
  Wootton Basset, 132

Boundary Commission, 71, 76, 79–82, 86
Brand, Thomas, 50, 129
Brewer, John, 39, 44
Briggs, Asa, 39, 91, 138
Bristol, 100, 173
Brougham, Henry, 7, 10, 69, 70, 127, 199, 207
Bulwer, William Henry Lytton Earle, 111, 121
Burdett, Francis, 50–52, 207
Burke, Edmund, 47, 48
Bute, John Stuart, third Earl of Bute (Lord), 39, 44

Caledon, Du Pré Alexander, second Earl of, 63
Canning, George, 50, 53, 54, 193
Caprettini, Bruno, ix, 13, 138
Captain Swing, *see* Swing riots
Carlile, Richard, 100, 138
Caroline of Brunswick, 52
Cartwright, Edmund, 40
Cartwright, John, 40, 46, 48, 51
Castlereagh, Robert Stewart, Viscount, 50, 53
Catholic
  emancipation, 53, 54, 69, 70, 168, 202
  king, 42, 43
  Relief Act, 8, 54, 90, 167
  church, 169
Catholicism, 58
Catholics, 39, 40, 53, 167, 169
Chandos, Richard Temple-Nugent-Brydges-Chandos-Grenville, first Duke of Buckingham and Chandos, Marquis of, 73, 207
Charles I, 40, 46
Charles II, 39–43
Charles X, 141
Charlesworth, Andrew, 14, 134, 139, 147, 161
Chartist, 8, 91, 138, 173
checks and balances, 17
Church, *see also* Catholic
  Anglican, 8, 39, 40, 42, 43, 48
  of England, 9, 59
  of Ireland, 9, 59
civic society, 13, 90–92, 96
Clark, J.C.D., 39, 42, 51, 141
Coase theorem, 19
Cobbett, William, 8, 51, 52, 138
collective action, 18, 20, 21
Congleton, Roger D., viii, ix, 3, 4, 11, 27–29, 39, 199
constituency, *see also* borough, county, constituency
  borough, 59, 63, 65, 66, 70, 73, 76, 77, 79, 82–86, 107, 137
  contested elections, 67, 84
  county, 59, 63, 65, 77, 107, 144
  economic characteristics, 108, 145
  governmental influence, 65, 87
  narrow franchise, 144
  single-member, 49, 77
  size of the electorate, 9, 79, 82
  university, 59, 80, 144
  Whig support in, 144, 146, 147, 165
constitutional bargaining, viii, 4, 27, 199, 202
  King-Parliament template, 199
Corn Laws, 35, 53, 91, 204
county
  Bedfordshire, 99
  Berkshire, 99
  Buckinghamshire, 71, 99
  Buteshire, 60
  Caithness, 60
  Cambridge, 99
  Cheshire, 99
  Clackmannshire, 60
  Clare, 54, 98
  Cornwall, 53, 63, 99, 139, 147
  Cromartyshire, 60
  Cumberland, 99
  Derbyshire, 51, 99
  Devon, 99, 139
  Dorset, 77, 99
  Durham, 99
  Essex, 60, 61, 65, 82, 99, 137, 165
  Glamorganshire, 77
  Gloucestershire, 99
  Hampshire, 65, 99, 138
  Herefordshire, 99
  Hertfordshire, 99
  Huntingdonshire, 99
  Kent, 14, 67, 87, 99, 134, 135, 138, 147–149, 157–159, 165
  Kinross-shire, 60
  Lancashire, 67, 99
  Leicestershire, 99
  Lincolnshire, 67, 99
  Middlesex, 63, 82, 99, 116
  Monmouthshire, 99, 168
  Nairnshire, 60, 98
  Norfolk, 99, 138
  Northamptonshire, 99
  Northumberland, 99
  Nottinghamshire, 53, 99
  Oxfordshire, 99
  Rutland, 99
  Salop, 99
  Somerset, 99

Staffordshire, 99
Suffolk, 84, 99, 138
Surrey, 99
Sussex, 47, 99, 138, 165
Warwickshire, 99, 105
Westmorland, 99
Wiltshire, 47, 63, 99, 138
Worcestershire, 99
Yorkshire, 46, 67, 77, 84, 99, 139
Coventry, 100
Cox, Gary W., 26, 30, 90, 91
Croker, John Wilson, 202
Cromwell, Oliver, 40–42
Cromwell, Richard, 41
Culloden, 42
Cumberland, Ernest Augustus, Duke of, 59

Darlington, William Harry Vane, third Earl of, 63
Days of May, 10, 15, 74, 172, 175, 187, 201
de Saxe-Meningen, Queen Adelaide, 75
decolonisation, 17
demagogues, 141
democracy
elements, 17
liberal, 3, 75
Pareto improvement, 23, 24, 27
partial extension of the voting franchise, 25, 27
root causes, 4, 7
taxpayer, 26
transition to, 19
democracy index, *see* Polity IV index, V-Dem Electoral Democracy index
democratic
change, 35
consolidation, 20, 32–34
institutions, viii, 3, 7, 47
reform, 3, 4, 10, 13, 15, 20, 32, 41, 96, 131, 133, 201, parliamentary reform, *see also* suffrage reform
reversals, 3
revolution, 141
democratisation
bottom-up, 3, 7, 11, 17, 18, 23, 32, 201
first wave of, 17, 19
historical process, 7
root causes, 201
top-down, 3, 7, 11, 17, 23, 24, 28, 202
Denman, Thomas, 125
Derby, 100
Derby, Edward Smith-Stanley, fourteenth Earl of (Lord), 39

Dewan, Torun, 31, 85
Dickens, Charles, 90
Diggers, 40
Disraeli, Benjamin, 162
dissenters, 43, 90, 167
distributional conflict, 4, 18
Dorsch, Michael, 20, 30
Drummond, Thomas, 76
Drummond-Burrell, Peter Robert, 192, 193

East Anglia, 138
Eldon, John Scott, Earl of, 50
elections
1768 election, 45
1774 election, 45
1802 election, 67, 161
1807 election, 129
1822 election, 129
1826 election, 66, 85, 86, 89, 134, 144, 161, 162
1830 election, 13, 66, 85, 86, 97, 105, 127, 128, 134, 135, 138, 139, 144, 148, 153–156, 158–161
1831 election, ix, 6, 10, 12–14, 16, 66, 67, 71, 73, 85, 86, 94, 127, 133–135, 138, 139, 141–145, 148, 150–156, 158, 159, 161, 162, 164, 168, 170–172, 201
1832 election, 85, 86, 162
1835 election, 85, 86, 161, 162
1837 election, 85, 86
1868 election, 31
after 1832, 77
before 1832, 9, 59, 62, 63, 65–67
uncontested, 9, 63, 67, 106, 129, 130
electoral corruption, 47
after 1832, 87
before 1832, 9, 63, 67, 144
electorate
size after 1832, 76, 79, 81, 82, 84, 204
size before 1832, 63, 204
Eliot, George, 6
elite
and peaceful agitation, 20–22, 28, 201
benefits from democratization, 23, 24, 26–28
commitment by the, 19
concessions from the, 18, 19, 21, 131
groups within, 23
industrial, 24, 25, 89
landed, 24, 25, 89
merchant and manufacturing, 70
repression by the, 20
revolution prevented by the, 19, 28
urban, 26, 27

Ellis, Charles Rose, 192, 193
Ellis, Christopher J., 18, 19
employment structure, 108, 114
equilibrium
  path, 20
  policy, 25
Europe, 26, 33, 141
  Central, 33
  Continental, 61
  Eastern, 33, 131
  Western, 24, 29, 30
Exclusion Crisis, 42
external validity, 5, 36

falsification test, 129, 130, 142, 160, 161, 171
Fender, John, 18, 19
Flood, Henry, 49
Fox, Charles James, 43, 48, 52
France
  1789 revolution, 39, 44, 47–49, 52, 141
  1830 revolution, 126, 141
  democratic consolidation, 33
  Grand Tour, 61
  octroi system, 148
  Old Regime, 48
  tricolor flags, 141
  Whigs' bond with, 61
franchise extension, *see also* democratic, democracy, democratisation
  £10 franchise, 71, 76, 79, 81, 85
  £20 franchise, 71
  and peaceful agitation, 20
  and policy outcomes, 24, 25
  and political competition, 24
  and political expedience, 34
  and public good provision, 24
  and social movements, 33
  Chandos clause, 73, 76
  competing theories, viii, 17, 29, 35
  during the 19th century, 17–19
  effect of inequality on, 19, 32
  endogenous, 26
  fiscal consequences, 29
  fiscal expansion, 27
  full, 25, 203
  household, *see* suffrage, household
  Pareto improvement, 23, 24, 27
  Pareto inferior, 25, 27
  partial, 25, 27, 171
  political consequences, 30
  political expedience, 23
  stock market consequences, 30
  under the threat of revolution, 19, 32, 33
franchise type
  in boroughs after 1832, 76
  in boroughs before 1832, 62–64
  in counties after 1832, 76
  in counties before 1832, 62
  in universities before 1832, 59
French Revolution, *see* France, 1789 revolution

Galor, Oded, ix, 40
Gash, Norman, 12, 50, 75, 87, 88, 141
Generalized Method of Moments (GMM), 157, 159, 164
geography of representation
  after 1832, 76, 77, 79, 84
  before 1832, 9, 60, 137
George I, 42–44
George II, 42, 44
George III, 42, 44, 196
George IV, 8, 44, 52, 69
Glorious Revolution of 1688, 39, 42
Gloucester, William Frederick, Duke of, 59
Goderich, Frederick John Robinson, first Earl of Ripon, Viscount, 50, 54
government
  cabinet, 39, 49, 56, 57, 71, 90, 173, 174, 199, 200
  First Lord of the Treasury, 39
  Prime Minister, 39, 44, 46, 47, 50, 56, 69, 70, 200
  Treasury, 45, 65, 106, 145, 167, 168
Gower, George Granville Leveson-Gower, 192, 193
Great Reform Act of 1832
  Chandos clause, 73, 76
  first draft, 71, 75
  main features of the final bill, 13, 75–77, 79, 96
  majority in the House of Lords, 10
  medium- and long-term consequences, 90–92, 202–204
  roadblock, 6, 9–15, 93, 94, 126, 131, 133, 135, 171, 172, 175, 201
  Schedule A, 76–78, 81, 88, 106, 114, 174
  Schedule B, 77, 81, 174
  Schedule C, 77, 81, 88
  Schedule D, 77, 78, 80, 81, 88
  second draft, 73
  short-term consequences, 79, 81, 82, 84, 87, 89
  third draft, 173
  votes in the House of Commons, 10, 71–73, 95, 201
  votes in the House of Lords, 10, 73, 74

Grey, Charles (Lord), 7, 8, 10, 12, 49, 52, 53, 68, 70, 71, 73–75, 87, 94, 95, 126, 133, 137, 171, 173–175, 193, 196, 199, 201, 202, 207
Grosvenor, Richard Grosvenor, second Marquess of Westminster, second Earl, 65

habeas corpus, 48
Halévy, Elie, 52, 137, 138, 141
Hanover
  Elector of, 43
  House of, 42
Harrowby, Dudley Ryder, first Earl of, 173
Harvey, Daniel W., 65
Heckman-probit, 111, 112, 114, 115, 186, 192
Himmelfarb, Gertrude, 25, 26, 29, 31
Hobsbawm, Eric J., 71, 100, 134, 139, 140, 142, 170
House of Commons, *see also* Great Reform Act of 1832, Members of Parliament, Parliament
  legislative process, 57
  relations with House of Lords, 56, 57
  unreformed, 8, 60, 62, 63
  voting procedure, 57
House of Lords, *see also* Great Reform Act of 1832, lord, Parliament
  legislative process, 57
  proxy voting, 58, 186
  relations with House of Commons, 56
  voting procedure, 57
Hume, David, 42
Hunt, Henry, 51, 127
Huntington, Samuel P., 17, 22

Imbens, Guido W., 147, 155
income
  and the right to vote, 17, 27
  distributions, 30
  growth, 19
  inequality, 32
  levels, 32
  shock, 32
  tax, 91, 204
  threshold, 25
industrial
  areas, 51
  artisans, 100
  centres, 53
  cities, 95, 96, 106, 137, 141
  north, 84
  revolution, 40, 44, 51
  sections of society, 91
  towns, 77, 84, 103
industrialists, 43, 44
industrious revolution, 44
industry, 60, 89, 145
inequality, 18–20, 30, 32
Instrument of Government, 41
instrumental variable estimator
  distance to Sevenoaks, 148, 157–160, 163–166
  GMM with spatial standard errors, 157, 159, 164
  local average treatment effect, 163, 165, 170
  weak instrument, 157, 159, 160, 164, 165
Ireland
  Acts of Union (1800), 47, 59
  consequences of reform, 85
  constituencies in House of Commons, 60
Ireton, Henry, 41
Italy, 61

Jacobin, 141
Jacobite, 42
James II, 39, 42, 43
Jews, 90
Jupp, Peter, 39, 43, 54, 69, 85

Kam, Christopher, 89, 91
King
  and the makeup of Parliament, 39, 45
  Civil List, 46, 70
Knatchbull, Edward, 54

Lambert, John, 41
Lambton, John George, 53
landowners, 45, 46, 60, 75, 77, 87, 89, 96, 135, 137, 138, 180, 187, *see also* aristocracy, elite
Langford, Paul, 39, 42, 45
Latin America, 29
Law, Edward, first Earl of Ellenborough, 207
Le Marchant, Sir Denis, 75
Leeds, 144
Levellers, 40
Lilburne, John, 40, 41
limited information maximum likelihood (LIML), 164
Liverpool, Robert Jenkinson, second Earl of (Lord), 49–54, 167
lobbying, 11, 20, 96, 116, 125, 201
  informational, 21
Locke, John, 42
Lohmann, Susanne, 20, 21

London, 12, 46, 52, 73, 95, 99–101, 103, 107, 108, 111, 115, 119, 125, 137, 138, 141, 149, 157–159, 162, 168, 171, 179, 186, 187
London Corresponding Society, 48
London Society for Mitigating and Gradually Abolishing the State of Slavery Throughout the British Dominions, 169
Lonsdale, William Lowther, first Earl of, 66
lord
  archbishop, 9, 59
  bishop, 9, 59, 69, 72, 73, 173, 175
  country home, 179–181, 186, 187, 189–191, 193
  hereditary peer, 9, 58
  Irish peer, 59
  London home, 179, 180, 182, 186, 187, 189, 190, 193, 196
  non-hereditary peer, 59
  party affiliation, 175, 179, 180, 183, 186, 187, 195
  political influence, 66, 70, 196, 200
  potential creation during the reform process, 73, 74, 174, 175, 196, 199, 200, 202
  Scottish peer, 59
Lovett, William, 91
Lumley, John Savile, 101
Lyndhurst, John Copley, first Baron, 174

Maarek, Paul, 20, 30
Macaulay, Thomas Babington Macaulay, first Baron, 75
Mahon, Philip Henry Stanhope, Viscount, 132
Manchester, 51, 84, 100, 103, 144
Mar, John Erskine, Earl of, 42
Mary II of England, 39
matching estimator
  average effect of the treatment on the treated (ATT), 147
  average treatment effect of the treated (ATT), 155
  covariate, 147, 154, 155
  matching, 156
  propensity score, 147, 154–156
Mayfair, 180
Melbourne, William Lamb, second Viscount, 39
Meltzer-Richard hypothesis, 27, 30, *see also* taxpayer democracy
Member of Parliament (MP)
  Grand Tour, 61
  occupation after 1832, 89
  occupation before 1832, 60
  party affiliation, 42, 43, 71, 96, 98, 107, 129, 135
Michalopoulos, Stelios, ix
micro-political
  approach, 4, 35
  data, viii, 4–6, 35
middle class, 26, 27, 89–91, 137, 138, 145
Midlands, 84, 103, 106, 138
Mill, John Stuart, 20, 45
Ministry of All the Talents, 49
Mitchell, Leslie, 48, 61, 141
mixed constitution, 43
modernisation theory, 32, 91, 145
monarchy, 40–43, 48, 75, 141

Namier, Lewis B., 39, 43–45, 47, 62, 68, 98, 167, 179, 198
Napoleon, 8, 50
National American Women's Suffrage Association, 34
National Association for the Protection of the Workers, 100
National Union of the Working Classes, 96, 171
Netherlands, 141
Newcastle, Thomas Pelham-Holles, Duke of, 44
newspaper, *see also* periodical, Swing riots
  articles, 21
  circulation, 103, 107, 108, 114, 149
  county, 103
  events reported in, 100, 173
  local, 100, 139
  London, 141, 187
  national, 100, 102
  regional, 102
  stamp duty, 51
  Tory-leaning, 141
nomination
  borough, 41, 46, 52, 70, 106, 132, 180, 186, 191, 196, 200, *see also* borough, rotten
  seat, 62, 63, 66, 69, 180, 198
North, Douglass, 42
North, Frederick (Lord), 44, 45

O'Connell, Daniel, 54
O'Gorman, Frank, 39, 43, 75, 81, 84, 89, 91, 92
Ordinary Least Squares (OLS), 128
  Conley spatial standard errors, 146, 153, 158, 159, 162, 168
  selection ratio, 152
outvoter, 65, 71, 76, 84
Overton, Richard, 40

Paine, Thomas, 48
Paldam, Martin, ix, 3, 32
Palmer, Robert, 125
Palmerston, Henry John Temple, third Viscount, 39
Pareto
improvement, 23, 24, 27, 202
inferior, 25, 27
Parliament
annual, 46, 48, 51, 75
legislative process, 56–58
Rump, 40
seven-year, 46, 50, 59, 71, 76
three-year, 50, 53
triennial act, 46
Unreformed, 11, 12, 39, 54, 56, 58, 60, 61, 63, 65, 66, 68, 70, 75, 76, 87, 106, 107, 133–135, 137, 144, 167, 169
Parnell, Sir Henry, 70
party, *see also* lord, Member of Parliament (MP), Radical, Tory, Whig
affiliation, 13, 42, 43, 68, 71, 96, 107, 124, 129, 135, 175, 179, 180, 183, 186, 187, 195
Court and Country, 43
discipline, 69, 91, 97
finance, 69
organisation after 1832, 91
patron, 9, 14, 46, 58, 63, 65–67, 69, 87, 88, 106, 107, 111, 114, 127, 129, 138, 145, 167, *see also* aristocratic influence,electorate size, franchise extension, outvoter, suffrage, Swing riots, threat of revolution
patronage, 44, 45, 65, 66, 69, 85, 88, 106, 129, 137, 144, 146, 150, *see also* electoral corruption
Peel, Robert, 8, 39, 54, 69, 70, 74, 91, 100, 174, 207
Pelham Fiennes Pelham-Clinton, Henry, fourth Duke of Newcastle-under-Lyne, 207
Perceval, Spencer, 50
periodical, 101, 102, *see also* newspaper
Peterloo, 51, 52
petition, 13, 21, 22, 33, 101, 110, 116, 119, 120, 125, 126
against Catholic relief, 168, 169
against slavery, 168, 169
election, 47, 87
for Catholic relief, 168, 169
reform-related, 71, 74, 91, 96, 101, 116, 119, 125, 127, 128, 131, 168, 169, 175
Petty-Fitzmaurice, Henry, third Marquess of Lansdowne, 207
Peyto-Verney, Henry, sixteenth Baron Willoughby de Broke and de jure twenty-fourth Baron Latimer, 192, 193
Pitt the Elder, William, 44, 46
Pitt the Younger, William, 46–50
Place, Francis, 8, 54, 74, 91, 173, 175
Plan of Parliamentary Reform, 51
political expedience
and democratisation, 7
disenfranchised borough, 114, 127
empirical test, 32, 34, 106, 110, 126, 131, 172, 180, 186
hypothesis, 11, 12, 17, 18, 23, 28–30, 34, 95, 96, 106
impact on the lords' vote, 191, 196, 199
impact on the MPs' vote, 13, 96, 107, 114, 121, 126, 131, 202
landed interest, 114, 121, 127
net seat gain, 114, 115, 119, 121, 127
nomination seat, 180
patron controlled, 114, 127
Polity IV index, 203, 204
Poor Law, 62, 90, 168–170, 204
Portland, William Cavendish-Bentinck, third Duke of, 50
Portugal, 19
private property, 48, 52, 137, 170, 202
probit, 110, 112, 115, 117, 119, 121, 124, 129, 130, 186–188, 190, 191, 194, *see also* Heckman-probit
process-focused approach, 5, 18, 35, 201, *see also* micro-political, roadblock
property rights, 24
protest
against the government of Lord Liverpool, 50
all, 114, 119, 179, 186, 187
gathering, 102, 103, 115, 119, 179, 199
geography, 5
impact on the lords' vote, 187
impact on the MPs' vote, 111, 114
in London, 103, 125, 179, 186, 187, 193
meeting, 21, 51, 74, 102, 103, 115, 119, 175, 179, 199
peaceful, 9, 34, 102, 103, 115, 119, 127, 131, 179, 182, 186, 187, 191, 193, 199
popular, 101
reform-related, 102, 103, 115, 116, 179, 187, 191
violent, 9, 34, 35, 103, 115, 127, 133, 179, 182, 186, 187, 191, 193, 199
violent rural, 102, 103, 115, 179, 187
violent urban, 102, 103, 115, 179, 187

Prussia, 34, 35
Przeworski, Adam, 26, 29, 32
public good, 21, 23–25, 202
Putney debates, 41

Queen Caroline, *see* Caroline of Brunswick

Radical
  ideology, 8, 68, 75, 79, 141, 171
  MPs in the House of Commons, 8, 12, 13, 50, 71, 97, 107, 114, 126
Radnor, William Pleydell-Bouverie, third Earl of, 126
Rainsborough, Thomas, 41
redistribution, 23, 29, 30, 32
  fiscal, 19
  maximum, 19
  spending on, 19, 30
  targeted, 23
Reflections on the Revolution in France, 47
reform, *see also* democratic reform
  institutional, 26, 90
  parliamentary, 11, 42–52, 54, 55, 68–70, 95, 96, 100, 101, 126, 127, 131, 134, 135, 137, 138, 142, 144, 168, 169, 171, 202
  suffrage, 12, 13, 21, 26–33, 35, 36, 42, 94, 96
reform act
  fifth (1928), 45, 203
  first (1832), *see* Great Reform Act of 1832
  fourth (1918), 45, 203, 204
  second (1867), 24, 26, 31, 45, 89, 161, 162, 203, 204
  third (1884-1885), 24, 31, 203, 204
religious
  congregations, 100
  minorities, 17, 167
  networks, 167, 169
  tolerance, 90
repression, 48, 51, 100, 139
retrenchment, 27
revolutionary fear, *see* threat of revolution
revolutionary threat, *see* threat of revolution
Rights of Man, 48
riots, 33, 51, 74, 133, 175
  1780 Gordon, 141
  agricultural, 165
  Bristol, 173
  food, 161
  rural labour, 161
  Spa Field, 51
Robinson, James A., viii, ix, 3, 4, 11, 18–20, 30–33, 36, 133
Rockingham, Charles Watson-Wentworth, second Marquess of, 45
Rosenbaum, Paul R., 147, 156
rotten borough, *see* borough, rotten
Rudé, George, 45, 71, 100, 134, 139, 140, 142, 170
Russell, John (Lord), 7, 52, 53, 70, 71, 73, 74, 90, 126, 129, 144, 173, 175
Russell, John, sixth Duke of Bedford, 53
Russia
  1905 revolution, 30
  local governments in Tsarist, 36

Saiegh, Sebastian, 26, 30, 90
Salmon, Philip, 12, 75, 76, 79–82, 84, 86, 87
Samuels, David, 32, 89
Sawbridge, John, 46
Scarlett, James, first Baron Abinger, 207
Schonhardt-Bailey, Cheryl, 35, 91
Scotland
  Acts of Union (1707), 42, 59
  consequences of reform, 85
  constituencies in House of Commons, 60
seat redistribution, 5, 13, 42, 46, 71, 76, 85, 96, 106, 107, 132, 171, 191, 196
secret ballot, 5, 9, 17, 48, 51, 63, 71, 75, 76, 87, 171, *see also* Ballot Act (1872)
selection bias, 111, 152, 158, 186, 192
selection on observables, 146, 147
selective incentives, 21
self-interest, *see* political expedience
Serbia, 19
Sevenoaks, 14, 135, 138, 148, 149, 157–160, 163–166
shocks
  region-specific, 148
  trade, 148
  weather, 35, 148, 149
Sidmouth, Henry Addington, first Viscount, 49
Six Acts of 1819, 51, 52
slavery
  abolition, 90, 136, 169
  anti-slavery advocates, 167
  in the West Indies, 53
  petitions against, *see* petition
social movement
  agitation, 13–15, 36, 97, 101, 107, 110, 111, 114, 119, 125, 127, 129, 131, 179, 183, 186, 191, 200, 201
  and democratisation, 7
  demand for reform, 11, 13, 35, 96, 100, 125
  empirical test, 32, 33, 110, 126, 172

hypothesis, 3, 11, 12, 18, 20–22, 28, 29, 33, 95, 96, 101, 115, 116, 125, 126, 179, 191, 193, 196, 199, 201
impact on the lords' vote, 187, 202
impact on the MPs' vote, 125, 126, 131, 201
Society for Constitutional Information, 48
Society for the Friends of the People, 48, 49
Society for the Supporters of the Bill of Rights, 45
South Asia, 33, 131
Spain, 19
Spitalfields, 100
St Peter's Field (Manchester), *see* Peterloo
Stasavage, David, 3, 17
Strode, William, 46
Stuart (House of), 42
Stuart, Charles Edward, 42
Stuart, James Francis Edward, 42
Sub-Saharan Africa, 33, 131
suffrage
extension, *see* franchise extension
household, 45, 49–51, 53, 71, 79
manhood, 40, 51, 70
reform, *see* reform, suffrage
secret, *see* secret ballot
universal, 5, 23, 68, 75, 141, 171
universal male, 31, 34, 46, 48
women, 17, 21, 26, 34, 45, 203
Sussex, Augustus Frederick, Duke of, 59
Sutton, Charles Manners, 74
Swing riots, *see also* threat of revolution
agricultural labourers, 13, 100, 105, 134, 137, 138
Captain Swing, 137, 141
diffusion pattern through newspapers, 147
diffusion through road network, 14, 134, 139, 147
geography, 9, 14, 134
heterogeneity and local average treatment effects, 163–165
impact on 1831 election, ix, 10, 14, 134, 135, 150, 152, 154, 156, 157, 160, 167–170
impact on voters and patrons, 14, 134, 135, 140, 141, 171
lack of relation with parliamentary reform, 138
letters, 138
local, 14, 142, 146, 147, 161, 163, 169–171
repression, 137, 140, 168, 170
rural, 16, 71, 95, 102, 116, 125
tenant farmers, *see* tenant
timing, 13, 100, 138, 144
travel-time distance, 135, 148
taxation, 26, 29, 41
Taylor, Sir Herbert, 199
Teele, Dawn Langan, 34, 45
tenant
at will, 73, 76
farmers, 65, 137, 138, 145
occupiers, 76
The Lancaster Gazette, 102
The Morning Chronicle, 100
The Morning Post, 141
The Political Register, 51, 138
The Royal Cornwall Gazette, 139
The Times, 100, 103, 108
Thomas, Peter D.G., 44, 45
threat of revolution
and change in reform support at the constituency level, 138
and democratisation, viii, 7, 13, 14, 30
economic conditions and shocks, 33
elite's perceptions of, 32, 133
empirical test, 32, 33, 110, 172
fear, 12–15, 21, 22, 28, 30, 96, 100, 114, 116, 135, 161
historiographical literature, 29
hypothesis, 3, 4, 11, 12, 18–20, 28, 30, 32, 36, 95, 102, 111, 115, 116, 125, 133–135, 142, 179, 180, 191, 193, 196, 199, 201
impact on the lords' vote, 187
in 1830, 126, 141
international diffusion of, 33
MPs' perceptions of, 102, 107, 119, 131
perceived, 12, 16, 95, 141
second reform act, 31
Swing riots as proxy for, 142
voters and patrons' information about, 142
voters and patrons' perceptions of, 14, 134, 142, 154, 165
Tilly, Charles, viii, 3, 13, 19, 20, 22, 29, 33, 91, 95–97, 99–102, 104, 105, 116, 127, 131, 134, 138, 141, 179, 181, 182
Tory
government under Lord Liverpool, 51, 54, 167
ideology, 8, 43, 48, 52, 68, 69, 136, 137, 173, 179, 191
liberal, 8, 54, 71
majority in the House of Lords, 9, 10, 14–16, 69, 74, 172, 199, 202
MPs in the House of Commons, 8, 12, 13, 68, 71, 95, 97, 107, 110, 114, 121, 127
name origin, 42, 43
party after Pitt the Younger, 50
party and Catholic emancipation, 53–55, 69

Tory (*Continued*)
party and the second reform act, 26, 31
ultra, 8, 54, 55, 70
waverer, 73
Townshend, Charles Vere Ferrars Compton, 121
trade
employment in, 108
free, 91
shocks, *see* shocks
unions, 138
Treasury, *see* borough, government
Trevelyan, George Macaulay, 18, 75
two stage least squares, *see* instrumental variable estimator

unions, *see* trade unions
university
Cambridge, 59
Dublin, 59
Oxford, 59
Unreformed Parliament, *see* Parliament
unrest, *see* protest, riots, Swing riots

V-Dem Electoral Democracy index, 203, 204
Victoria, 39, 53
Vincent, John, 63, 78, 80
Vivyan, Sir Richard, 54
voter, *see also* electorate size, franchise extension, outvoter, suffrage, Swing riots, threat of revolution
borough, 80, 81
county, 61, 65, 79
elite and non-voters, 23, 24
female, 34
median, 19, 25
middle-class, 31
newly enfranchised, 24, 25, 84, 87, 106
registered, 79–83, 86
working-class, 31
Voth, Hans-Joachim, ix, 13, 138

Walrond, Bethell, 121
Walwyn, William, 40
war
American independence, 39, 44, 46
civil, 17, 74
Cold, 17
Revolutionary and Napoleonic, 45, 47, 48, 50
second English civil, 11, 39, 40
Seven Years', 45
Waterloo, 8, 50, 51
Weingast, Barry R., 42
Wellington, Arthur Wellesley, first Duke of, 8, 10, 50, 54, 69, 70, 73, 74, 100, 173–175, 196, 199, 201, 202, 207
Whig
stance on the French Revolution, 48
bond with France, 61
government, 12, 15, 70, 134, 170, 172, 196
historians, 18, 75
ideology, 7, 43, 50, 52, 68, 69, 136, 137
landowners, 53
majority in the House of Commons, 10, 133, 135, 160, 171
MPs in the House of Commons, 7, 12, 13, 68, 71, 95, 97, 107, 114, 121, 126, 127
name origin, 42, 43
opposition politicians and the Society for the Friends of the People, 48
reform objectives, 70, 202
reforms after 1832, 90
social concerns, 90
support for Catholic emancipation, 54
Wildman, John, 40
Wilkes, John, 44, 45
William IV, 8, 10, 15, 56, 59, 70, 73–75, 172, 174, 196, 199, 201, 202, 207
William of Orange, 39
window of opportunity, 19, 22, 32, 33
workers, *see also* working-class
agricultural, 14, 25, 134, *see also* Swing riots, agricultural labourers
and revolution, 19
and the threat of revolution, 18–20
conflict of interest, 18, 21
in an urban economy, 26
industrial, 25
net transfer to, 19
potential joint uprising of the farm labourers and of, 141
share employed in trade and industry, 145
support for high taxes, 18
unskilled, 25
voting rights, 19, 20, 25, 27
working-class, *see also* workers
radicals, 91
unenfranchised, 27
Wyvill, Christopher, 46

Yorkshire Association, 46

Ziblatt, Daniel, 3, 30, 31, 34, 35, 131